EROS AND IRONY

SUNY Series in Systematic Philosophy
Robert C. Neville, Editor

Whether systematic philosophies are intended as true pictures of the world, as hypotheses, as the dialectic of history, or as heuristic devices for relating rationally to a multitude of things, they each constitute articulated ways by which experience can be ordered, and as such they are contributions to culture. One does not have to choose between Plato and Aristotle to appreciate that Western civilization is enriched by the Platonic as well as Aristotelian ways of seeing things.

The term "systematic philosophy" can be applied to any philosophical enterprise that functions with a perspective from which everything can be addressed. Sometimes this takes the form of an attempt to spell out the basic features of things in a system. Other times it means the examination of a limited subject from the many angles of a context formed by a systematic perspective. In either case systematic philosophy takes explicit or implicit responsibility for the assessment of its unifying perspective and for what is seen from it. The styles of philosophy according to which systematic philosophy can be practiced are as diverse as the achievements of the great philosophers in history, and doubtless new styles are needed for our time.

Yet systematic philosophy has not been a popular approach during this century of philosophical professionalism. It is the purpose of this series to stimulate and publish new systematic works employing the techniques and advances in philosophical reflection made during this century. The series is committed to no philosophical school or doctrine, nor to any limited style of systematic thinking. Whether the systematic achievements of previous centuries can be equalled in the twentieth depends on the emergence of forms of systematic philosophy appropriate to our times. The current resurgence of interest in the project deserves the cultivation it may receive from the SUNY Series in Systematic Philosophy.

EROS AND IRONY

A PRELUDE TO PHILOSOPHICAL ANARCHISM

David L. Hall

State University of New York Press
Albany

Published by
State University of New York Press, Albany

© 1982 State University of New York

For information, address State University of New York Press, State University Plaza, Albany, N. Y., 12246

Library of Congress Cataloging in Publication Data

Hall, David L.
　　Eros and irony.

　　(SUNY series in systematic philosophy)
　　Includes index.
　　1. Methodology.　2. Culture.　I. Title　II. Series.
BD241.H29　　149　　　81-16579
ISBN 0-87395-585-4　　AACR2
ISBN 0-87395-586-2 (pbk.)

10　9　8　7　6　5　4　3　2　1

For my mother, Julia

CONTENTS

ACKNOWLEDGMENTS

I have not always enjoyed the discipline of writing. The fact that I did so in the preparation of this work is largely because of the solicitation of a number of individuals who helped to sustain my enthusiasm and commitment. Robert Neville, editor of this series in systematic philosophy, has both explicitly and by example challenged me to re-think many of the issues central to this book. His own works in systematic philosophy have set the standard which all others who wish to perform that activity must strive to meet. I am grateful to Roger Ames and Wu Kuang-ming who, from their quite different perspectives, gave me some assurance that my understanding of philosophic Taoism is not altogether beside the mark. I am, of course, solely responsible for the manner in which I have employed that sensibility. Donald Crosby and Eliot Deutsch read the work in manuscript and provided forthright criticisms which enabled me to make some final improvements in the text. The University of Texas at El Paso Faculty Development Fund and University Research Institute gave material assistance in meeting the expenses associated with travel, research and manuscript preparation. I am especially pleased to express my gratitude to Diana Natalicio, Dean of the College of Liberal Arts at my institution, whose sensitive and imaginative administration helped to provide the sort of academic environment conducive to sustained intellectual endeavor. I am particularly indebted to students in my Plato seminar and Chinese Philosophy classes who helped me in the formulation and refinement of many of the ideas contained in this book. Finally, I must give special thanks to Debra Tischler. Without her I doubtless would have written a book, but certainly not this one. For it is from her that I learned of the profounder dimensions of eros. And of its many ironies as well.

David L. Hall
Honolulu, Hawaii
October, 1981

PRELUDE
WHAT ANARCHY ISN'T

The work which follows these prolusory remarks is itself a prelude. The justification for expending all my energies on foreplay lies in the fact that the subject of this essay is one that cannot be engaged directly until those biases and preconceptions which have so long precluded its sympathetic examination have been discarded. Attempting to consider the meaning and import of philosophic anarchism will necessarily involve me in advertising and celebrating forms of sensibility which are generally considered to undermine the foundations of responsible thought and action.

I insist that mine is not an attempt at philosophic reconstruction, if by that phrase we must mean the art of "rebuilding one's ship while at sea." Dismantling the leaky vessel transporting our cultural cargo and reconstituting it in more seaworthy form is, I believe, no longer a viable aim for the speculative philosopher. Nor (despite some common assumptions) is this work written in the *de*constructionist mode. I have sought to philosophize neither with Nietzsche's hammer nor Derrida's eraser. What I have primarily attempted is a reevalution of the cultural role of philosophy. This is an enterprise at once more radical and more conservative than the above named alternatives. More conservative in the sense that no more than a shift in current cultural priorities is called for. More radical because this alteration of priorities will dramatically transform the manner of understanding psychological, social, and cosmological contexts.

A primary assumption grounding this work is that experience in all of its modes constitutes not a cosmos but a *congeries*—rich, complex, and dissocial. Before they are synthesized for this or that practical or theoretical purpose, the elements of history and culture comprise a

perplexing laundry list of thoughts, actions and feelings; a graffitied wall
of unmatched sentiments. Therefore, in place of the dialectical strategy
of "either-or," I shall most often be employing the method of "both-
and." It is, clearly, self-defeating if the speculative philosopher narrows
the dimensions of his world by excluding that which does not fit his
idiosyncratic and, therefore, tendentious predispositions about the way
of things.

Some readers of this book may wish to charge me with false advertising because of the distinctive sense of the term "anarchism" I have pro-
posed. Though clearly not without social and political consequences of
the most profound sort, anarchism must initially be construed metaphysically. Anarchy involves the rejection of *archai*—that is, the denial
of principles as transcendent determining sources of order. A principle,
according to Aristotle, is that from which a thing can be known; that
from which a thing first comes to be, or that at whose will that which is
moved is moved or that which changes changes.[1] Principles both
establish and account for the order of the world. As principles of being
they are the source of origination per se. As principles of knowledge they
are origins of thought. Beginnings or principles in the social and political
sphere are due to *archai* or *princeps*—those who command. In any of its
senses a first principle functions as a determining source of order. And
standing behind the notion of principles as *archai* there is the intuition of
the challenge to order and harmony which our cosmogonic myths
celebrate as chaos.

Obviously the denial of principles should involve, a fortiori, the rejection of princes. The scorn for rulers is but the political consequence of
the metaphysical disdain for rules or norms. In the refusal to legitimate
authorities, one is merely claiming that is is philosophically unsound to
seek the authors of things outside the things themselves.

The apologetic task of philosophic anarchism is set by the fact that we
live in a world that is, for the most part, kindly disposed toward principles and princes, rules and rulers—a world which presumes order, in
both its cosmological and social senses, to result from *orders*. It is a
mistake, and a grave one, to believe that anarchism is primarily a social
or political doctrine. It is a perspective with the most radical of
metaphysical implications. To believe otherwise permits its easy refutation as a simplistic, philosophically unramified theory of insurrection, or
an overly idealistic vision of the gradual limitation of governmental
power, or of the development of syndicalist economies, or communal
societies.

The construction of the anarchist sensibility must proceed with caution in its critical and apologetic phases. The apologetic message of the anarchist always has at least the rhetorical appearance of negativity. Thus the critical anarchist who wishes to clear the way for the constructive anarchist to follow must not succumb to the naïve belief that one can productively tie the constructive efforts of anarchism to its critical and apologetic task. One of the clearest lessons to be learned from the history of our speculative endeavors is that the constructive character of a form of thought is seriously qualified by any associated apologetic and critical activity. A system of thought which begins with the dialectical refutation of another carries the stamp of that other as surely as the slave who, in rising up to slay his master, commits but the first of many violent acts to come. This is the essential reason for the separation of this prelude to anarchism from a more positive expression of the sensibility which I intend to produce in the near future. In a subsequent work the social and political dimensions of the anarchist sensibility will be positively developed in terms of the metaphysical and epistemological ideas adumbrated herein.

Having said this, however, I should hasten to add that even in this essay the dialectical and apologetic functions are subordinated to imaginative speculations which provide nondialectical alternatives to posited forms of thought and practice. It is a characteristic mistake of our tradition to assume that in the dialectical contrast of *sic et non* we create real alternatives and significant options. When Hegel—and Plato before him—demonstrated that all particulars could be understood as constituents of a more coherent whole which gave them both their identity and their relativity, the profoundest of our cultural tyrannies was celebrated. The insistent particularity of an object or event can by no means survive the sort of intellectual examination that presumes the reality of every existent to be nothing more than a consequence of its serving as an instance of a universal or a component of some harmonious pattern or matrix of relatedness.

Because of the distinctive method employed in the writing of this work it may not be immediately clear where one ought look to find the principal arguments. I must grant at the outset that many of the most significant aspects of the work are presented without the kind of dialectical arguments which seem to constitute the sine qua non of responsible reflection in our intellectual tradition. The sort of coherence for which I have striven could not survive continued engagement with this or that imagined critic. This is an essay in the philosophy of culture. As I conceive it such philosophy must presume that the richness of resource provided by any relatively complex cultural circumstance is such as to provide important alternatives to posited ideas and norms which, though alternatives, are not necessarily engaged with the current dominant principles and, therefore, need not bear the identifying marks of misshapen dialectical assumptions. Philosophic writing must not be permitted to degenerate into mere compendiums of sorites. The principal argument of this work is the work itself, considered not in terms of its isolated parts but as a (reasonably) coherent whole.

I should say a little about the relations between this work and my recently published book, *The Uncertain Phoenix*. In that work I attempted to trace the development of certain ideas and themes in Anglo-European culture which had come to fruition in advanced technological society. The claim of that book is that there is an intrinsic connection between the form of our present technological system and the kind of ideas which are culturally efficacious. I attempted to consider the manner in which alterations in the sphere of praxis associated with advancing technological society have rendered certain ideas relevant to a degree they heretofore had not been. Thus I was primarily interested in assessing the context of philosophic enquiry in its character as a sensibility matrix within which responsible reflections might take place. In this present work I am concerned with ideas per se.

In form this work also draws upon my first book, *The Civilization of Experience*. There I developed from Whitehead's philosophy a set of categories for the interpretation of intellectual culture. The discussion of the metaphysical grounding of the cultural interests of art, morality, science, religion, and philosophy derived from Whitehead's thought provided me with significant resources for the organization of this present work. Philosophy of culture, though not without profound normative consequences, begins as a sophisticated form of cultural commentary, and thus is grounded in descriptive, rather than normative, metaphysics. The cultural-interest theory considered in *The Civilization of Experience* serves initially merely as a means of assessing the character of certain cultural experiences. Only within the context of such an assessment can the question of norms and priorities be responsively addressed.

I should stress that though I have been primarily influenced by process philosophy, particularly Whitehead's version of it, I do not consider myself orthodox within that tradition. One of the implications of the remarks which follow is that we have passed the point in our theoretical development when philosophic schools and their epigoni are culturally relevant. I should therefore caution the reader familiar with Whitehead's philosophy not to assume automatically that when I use terms which seem to echo the tradition of process philosophy I have used them in the manner stipulated by Whitehead.

I do not mean to imply a rejection of the philosophic tradition. Even if that were possible it would be tendentious and absurd. In fact, this book clearly has a hero of sorts. It is Plato. That I should find in Platonic thought the richest of resources for the development of anarchist theory is but one of the many ironies I shall attempt to celebrate. There is a villain in this work, as well. Again, it is Plato. This is less paradoxical than it may seem, for the schizoid character of our culture is in large measure a consequence of the warring Platos—the mystical poet empowered by that eros which lures toward completeness of understanding, and the narrowly rational moralist who claims to have "gotten it right," at least in *theory*. In the extended footnote to Plato which follows, I have attempted to praise the former, hopefully at the expense of the latter.

PART ONE
THE ARCHAEOLOGY OF THEORY

CHAPTER ONE
THE CULTURAL SENSORIUM

One of the most inadequately treated of our strictly philosophic questions is that concerning the meaning of evidence. This is largely because the majority of philosophic discussions occur within a school, tradition, or movement the various members of which tacitly agree upon the source and character of legitimate evidence. Thus when disagreements occur, they more often concern the means of handling the evidence, or the precise conclusions to be drawn with respect to it. Raising the question of evidence in the most direct manner is extremely difficult since evidence does not permit of isolation from the contexts of discovery and of justification constituting most types of disciplined enquiry. Only on rare occasions are alternative systems of enquiry creatively engaged. Most often the evidential bedrock of one philosophy serves as a reef upon which other systems are shattered. The solution to this problem is obviously not to legislate uniformity of evidence in order to assure the success of a single family of theories, nor ought we be sanguine when we see the variety and incommensurability of evidences continually lead to the kind of sterile "refutations" that so often pattern intellectual culture. In approaching the fundamental issue of evidence there seems no safe course to follow. The Scyllan headland of narrow dogmatism extends to the very edge of the Charybdian vortex of extreme relativism.

If we ask, "What is evidence?," our initial reply must be that it is either that which is evident in itself, or that which makes something else evident, or both. Also, it is important to realize that some of our most evident forms of experiencing render little else evident whereas some of the de facto least understood of evidences have a great deal of efficacy in making alternative data evident. That the richness and power of evidence to render aught else evident bears no necessary relation to its own evidentness is an important, if often frustrating, insight into the nature of theoretical understanding.

Commonsensically, at least, the value of "truth" seems to occupy a preeminent place in our cultural consciousness. But truth is by no means the only value we wish to realize. We often seek evidence for the beauty of a work of art, or for the goodness of an ethical action, or for the holiness of a religious individual, or for the importance of a particular idea, event, or personage. In a more general sense we ask after the *meaningfulness* of a particular datum. Meaningfulness is then stipulated in terms of values such as truth, beauty, goodness, holiness, or importance. However, truth seems always to enter into the discussion, if only at the "meta-" level, for we seem implicitly to translate the proposition "x is beautiful" into "It is true that x is beautiful." We may forget that other values are equally implicit at this level. It is often worthwhile to determine whether it is *good* that x is beautiful or whether the goodness of x entails the quality of beauty as well. It is clear, however, that we are so seldom involved in explicitly and formally asking theoretical questions beyond the question of truth as to render our understanding of alternative values extremely vague.

There is a serious contender to the primacy of truth as a cultural value. For just as at the theoretical level we seek truth as the blunt conformation of appearance and reality or as the assured coherence of a judgment with its systematic context, and so on, so at the level of human praxis the efficacy of moral rightness is affirmed as primary. There are obvious reasons why this might be so simply in terms of the aim of achieving a certain social stability. Understanding the massive connectedness of our perceptions of the world with the world as it actually impinges upon us is of utmost value in serving the demands of praxis. And acting in accordance with that understanding is one of the principal ways of perpetuating a theoretical vision that promotes the conformance of appearance and reality. Ideally, the cultural interest of science, which above all seeks the truth about the nature of things, and of morality, which seeks to bring a significant type of harmony into the realm of social praxis, are intrinsically interdependent. *Science is the morality of understanding and morality is the science of praxis.*

Our culture has obviously not altogether ignored the alternative types of value. We do seek beauty; some of us seek to be holy. But the aesthetic and religious interests are acceptable in our culture almost precisely to the degree that they are disciplined by the rational and ethical impulses dominating our principal cultural expressions. Clearly an important theoretical issue centers in the answers to such questions as "What are the autonomous cultural values attainable in relatively complex societies such as our own?" "How may they be attained?" "What are the priorities among them?"

The primary processes in Anglo-European culture concerned with the formulation of facts and the appreciation of values are grounded in the cultural interests of art, morality, science, religion, and philosophy. Organized into a pattern of sense-making activities these interests constitute a *cultural sensorium* defining certain of the potentialities and limitations of individual and social existence within intellectual culture. The absence or derogation of a cultural sense is as threatening to our cultural well-being as is the failure of a physiological sense to our organic wholeness.

Ever since Plato's delineation of the functions of the psyche into reason, appetite, and "volition" and Aristotle's organization of the ways of knowing into the theoretical, practical, and productive sciences, there has been an important strain of speculative philosophy which has devoted itself to articulating this *speculum mentis* and to demonstrating its grounding in the World as experienced. Thus the most influential visions of culture in our tradition construe it as the mind "writ large." As will become clear as the argument of this essay unfolds, I do not hold to such a view of the relations of psyche and culture in the strong sense. However, I do believe that the analogical principle underlying such an understanding is broadly correct. That is, though there is no metaphysical rationale for the *speculum mentis* ideal, it *is* a contingent fact of our cultural experiencing that we have sorted our experiences out according to certain important interests and these interests have grown to characterize the very nature of our cultural rhetoric.

The model of a cultural sensorium is grounded in the understanding that experience itself, at the fundamental level of sensation and perception, is a cultural datum. According to John Dewey, "Experience is the result, the sign, and the reward of that interaction between organism and environment which, when it is carried to the full, is a transformation of interaction into participation and communication."[1]

As the "result" of interaction between organism and environment experience is any of a number of learned abilities to grasp the significance of one's environment or to exercise certain powers in relation to it. If we encounter an individual with such abilities we are provided a "sign" of his having experienced. The fact that experience is construable as a "reward" suggests the satisfying quality which attends the activity of experiencing and promises some basis for claiming that organisms are naturally motivated toward such activity. The fact that interaction may become "participation" and "communication" suggests that when the environment of a complex organism is dominated by other such organisms the result, the sign, and the reward will be particularly sophisticated.

Immediately following this characterization of experience, Dewey goes on to say, "Since sense-organs with their connected motor apparatus are the means of this participation, any derogation of them, whether practical or theoretical, is at once effect and cause of a narrowed and dulled life-experience."[2] A practical derogation could involve nothing more than closing one's eyes, or having the possibility of experiencing in complex visual, tactile, auditory, or olfactory ways negated through the manipulation of the physical environment. Theoretical derogations involve, on the other hand, biases, attitudes, or theories concerning the relative importance of certain types of sense experience which would dispose one to underrate the values of complex sensory experiences.

The analogy I wish to suggest between the physiological and the cultural sensorium extends, I believe, to this level of the characterization of experience as an interaction of organism and environment. Thus although there are doubtless continuities between fundamental forms of sensation and perception and the types of interpretations of experience provided by the notion of the cultural interests of art, morality, science, religion, and philosophy, it is wholly unnecessary for my argument that I develop a formal theory exploiting such continuities. My aim, rather, is to demonstrate some fruitful analogies between the evidences associated with primary sense-experience and the more sophisticated evidences associated with cultural life.

In every epoch human experience as culturally determined is a result, a sign, and a reward of the manner in which certain sophisticated interactions with the available environment are made possible. The health of a given cultural milieu is a function of the viability of a full range of these interactions. This is but to say that an optimal society is one which promotes the widest possible selection of evidences. A fortiori, a fully actualized individual is one who has the width of civilized experience to draw upon for his maturation and development.

The five principal sources of cultural experience listed above are contingent consequences of the perspectival limitations we have in fact placed upon our manner of being in the world. Data have been entertained as efficacious in the construction of an individual act of experiencing primarily in accordance with three distinct modes of perspective abstraction: as immediately felt, as a finite field of discriminated data the components of which are differentially relevant to the emergent efficacy of the individual experience, and, finally, as a putatively infinite, undiscriminated Totality. As immediate, the experienced data are referred to the private psychological field of the experiencing entity and felt solely in terms of their *suchness*, or just-so-ness. As proximate, the focus is upon the relevance of selected data to the individual in the act of self-constitution. The unlimited context of experiencing promotes the contrast of the individual as finite detail with the Totality of the experienceable world. These three perspectives provide the foundation of the cultural interests of art, morality, and religion, respectively.

We discover the grounding of the interests of science and philosophy at the more sophisticated level of conscious perception and knowledge. The scientific enterprise requires a contrast of the world as consciously perceived with that same world as causally efficacious in the constitution of an act of experiencing. Science extends beyond simply the causal interpretation of nature construed as the terminus of sense perception. It includes the logical and systematic interpretations of aesthetic, moral, and religious experience as well. The "scientific" interpretation of these interests is obedient to the criterion of truth as an expression of logical consistency and rational coherence. The intuitions and activities of the artist, the ethical agent, and the religious virtuoso, experienced in terms of the distinctive perspective limitation of each, constitute these interests in their most direct form. As traditionally understood, speculative philosophy functions as *scientia scientiarum*; it is primarily concerned with the organization into a coherent whole of the evidences of the four alternative cultural interests. Like science, it involves the formal interpretation of experience at the level of consciousness and concepts, but unlike the specialized sciences, it aspires to complete generality in its treatment of evidence.

Obviously these various modes of experiencing interpenetrate. The relative degree of distinctness involved in the differentiation of types of cultural interest is largely due to their articulation at the level of conscious praxis. A most significant consequence of this differentiation, however achieved, is that the various cultural activities grounded upon these modes of interest can lead to serious conflicts of value-orientation. It is, perhaps, not even possible to achieve a coordination of all of the principal cultural aims without relegating one or more of them to a decidedly ancillary role. Keats's roseate line, "Beauty is Truth, Truth Beauty . . . ," though possessed of poetic beauty, may, as a generalization, be untrue because of the existence of terribly blunt truths which seem to challenge all aesthetic feeling, not to mention the phantasmal beauty of certain products of an undisciplined imagination, having no apparent grounding beyond the flux of present circumstance. Nor may truth or beauty be always *good*. Value is the outcome of limitation, and that limitation, with respect to any given attainment, can lead to the exclusion of alternative values. Conflicts of beauty and goodness named by the phenomenon of censorship, or of truth and importance illustrated by the pendantic sense, or of holiness and goodness, evident in the morally questionable activities of some among our saints and mystics, speak all too clearly of the possible disharmonies resulting from the overly specialized production of value.

I hope it is clear that I am using the concept of a cultural sensorium by analogy with our physiological sensorium, not in order to construct an exhaustive typology of cultural experience and expression, but merely in order to raise the question of the sources of cultural evidence in a reasonably intelligent manner. Thus, when I consider the meanings of "art," "morality," and so on, presupposed by the broadest possible perspective upon intellectual culture, I am not attempting to determine what these various cultural interests *must* mean, or what, finally, the priorities among them ought to be. My argument assumes merely that it will be productive to characterize the sort of relations among cultural interests that has contingently arisen in our tradition and the manner in which this pattern of relatedness has promoted both the undue separation of our various modes of cultural expression and the extreme derogation of some of these modes at the expense of others.

In detailing the significance of the cultural sensorium as a means of understanding the character of our intellectual culture I shall by no means be engaged in the attempt to develop a normative epistemology permitting complete understanding of "what there is." Given the depressed state of contemporary philosophy, theories of culture are misconstrued if taken as normative in the strictest sense. For culture is always contingent. What persons have "thought and done" is contingent, of course, but more importantly, what they could have thought and done is equally so. The cultural sensorium is not to be reified as normative for all future developments in intellectual culture. It is the result of an inventory and assay which suggests what resources are available for the enrichment of our human experience and expression.[3]

Some may believe that the discipline of "history" ought to be included among the list of principal cultural interests; I should, therefore, account for its absence. On the abstractive criteria I have employed, history must clearly be considered ancillary. In the first place, I have construed the concept of culture in synchronic terms. Thus, from the distinctly cultural perspective, history is but the history of the distinct and autonomous interests already outlined. There is a history of art, or of science, and so on. A general history of culture is but one means of coordinating the various interests in terms of their changing contributions to the sphere of human praxis. Also, I hold that the ground of cultural interests is discoverable in the individual, private occasion of experiencing which, we must presume, is the foundation of the public, social world. If in some important senses the public is more dependent upon the private sphere for its particular character than the reverse, then to this extent history as a cultural category related to the articulation of public praxis is an ancillary interest.

I am certainly aware that such assumptions concerning the derivative character of the historical interest are debatable. In a real sense, much of what follows in this essay is a sustained argument in support of these controversial assumptions. By not insisting upon a parity of public and private praxis, and by not construing culture in diachronic terms, I have meant to promote the values of the intensity, and autonomy, of individual experiencing. Having said this, however, I am moved to repeat that I am by no means trying to develop a final statement as to the meaning of human culture. There are numerous ways of slicing a pie; I certainly have no objection to alternative visions of culture. The inclusion of the historical interest as a cultural enterprise would not be wholly inconsistent with the direction of this project, though it would hardly contribute to the most essential concern of this essay—namely, the assessment of the richest resources of cultural self-understanding available to us.[4]

In brief, I am not attempting to develop a theory of cultural interests as an end in itself but solely as a means of providing some interpretative concepts which may be seen as germane to the understanding of our cultural context. I fully recognize that concrete praxis is a mélange of distinct intentions and actions which, at best, will only approximate any normative scheme. And I have not the slightest interest in defending an abstract concept of culture apart from its efficacy in actual cultural interpretation.

In a fundamental sense the cultural interests I have been discussing have as their source more primitive modes of entertaining the world. In a derivative, but nonetheless important, sense these interests are also sources of what we presume to be these primitive modes of experiencing. This is but to say that the private, idiosyncratic, "inner" experiences of individuals as a complex of sensations, perceptions, imaginings, memories, and so on serve as sources of our reflective cultural experiencing. And the public, consensual realm of "outer" experience, once constituted, is fed back into our private psychological fields and becomes partially constitutive of our perceiving, imagining, and so on. After the development of complex cultural experiences this distinction between inner and outer experience is a metaphorical one which belies somewhat the manner in which idiosyncratic and consensual experiencings interpenetrate. Yet this distinction must be at least tentatively maintained if one is to lay claim to the importance of individual autonomy in the creation and elaboration of cultural significances.

Thus even though the question of the origins of consciousness is inseparable from the question of the origin of the world, without the contrast between the outer and the inner spheres, between, that is to say, This-Myself and That Other, no articulate consciousness could exist. Implicitly, then, self-consciousness and consciousness of a world are born together. However, this claim need not entail the doctrine that fully autonomous individuality must ground the emergence of self-consciousness. We can easily accede to the view that our modern sense of individuality is a later development, far removed from the cultural origins of consciousness. As a matter of fact, read in terms of materialist and atomistic assumptions undergirding modern forms of positivism and behaviorism, the sense we are likely to have of ourselves as individuals could have little to do with self-consciousness per se. Characteristic of these mechanistic approaches are the denial of the "inside" altogether, the reduction of experience wholly to behavior, and the claim that the only patterns available for the interpretation of behaviors are those forms of interaction characterized by extrinsic relations.

Self-consciousness as consciousness of world in the form of incipient otherness includes the possibility that self and world will have varying degrees of overlap. The relations of self and world have been characterized, philosophically, in terms of relative degrees of *idealism* and *realism*. Philosophic reflections, particularly in the form relevant to Anglo-European cultural self-understanding, are of relatively recent origin, however. And though it would be silly to pretend that we could successfully eschew our distinctly philosophic consciousness in the attempt to arrive at the naïve form of original conscious experience, we certainly ought to remain, *ab initio*, as untainted as possible by the more tendentious philosophic dogmas associated with schools of philosophy.

How are we to discover the origins of consciousness? Apparently, we have only two main routes of enquiry: the first leads us to the backward-looking quest for the original answers to the question of the beginnings of the World. But in addition to the question of cosmogenesis, we may ask the question of psychogensis. Each of these questions is addressed, of course, in the cosmogonic speculations which pattern the primordial past. And both questions receive an answer in the act of individual introspection, that is, through an inventory of our private psychological field.

From the perspective of cultural experience and articulation, mythopoetic expressions can be isolated and employed as etiologic stories indicating the origins of cosmos and psyche. Likewise, a regressive analysis of our private psychological field leading to our imaginative resources in their most (recognizably) pristine form leads us to confront primordial images capable of grounding our articulated expressions of the meaning of self and world. Granted, we can never completely experience with any clarity either a point in the cultural past, or a level in the presented immediacy of our psychological experience, at which we were (are) not culturally formed. This must be so for the obvious reason that the very "we" who search, along with the motivations for searching, are in part culturally determined. However, it is essential that we proceed as far along the path toward originality as possible if for no other reason than that the paradox of "nature versus culture" cannot be satisfactorily resolved by claiming that culture as context is inescapable. For equally inescapable is the recognition that culture as *artifice* suggests the necessity of makers and artificers whose creative activity cannot be construed totally as a function of cultural context.

Three principal accounts of the origin of things are to be found in the mythical resources of Anglo-European culture. In *Genesis*, influenced by the Babylonian *Enuma elish*, it is an act of Divine volition which provides the foundation of the rational and moral order. Depending upon one's interpretation, creation in *Genesis* is either *creatio ex nihilo* or it is the construal of order from the primal confusion of "the dark, formless void." In Plato's *Timaeus*, the order of the world is the result of *rationalization*—the conquest of blind Necessity by the rational persuasion of the Demiurge. In Hesiod's *Theogony*, it is neither volition nor reason, but the attractive power of Eros, which overcomes the "yawning gap," the "gaping void," of the Chaos originating with the separation of Earth and Sky.

Chaos is a dark emptiness that sets us to brooding or leads us to despair; it is a disordered confusion confounding our sensibilities; it is a separating chasm consuming us with yearning. As acting, thinking, and feeling creatures our fundamental cosmological problem is the maintenance of order in the face of Chaos. The assumption of the chaotic conditions of the primeval origins found in our principal cosmogonies has determined that our reasonings, volitional activities, and affective states are but instruments for the disciplining of Chaos. We are literally *agonal* creatures whose contest with Chaos is the primary defining characteristic of our natures.

Thus, even if there is no attempt to envision the cosmological context of one's speculations, that context is operative in the sense that it has defined the very nature of our thinking, acting, and feeling as ordering functions of the human psyche and as modes of the construal of social order. Any consideration of theoretical principles (*archai*) leads of necessity to this cosmological context in which *archai* function as determining sources of order. The etymological connection between "princes" and "principles," between "rules" and "rulers," is both direct and absolutely pertinent to our understanding of the means of establishing order.

Our cosmogonic myths are not simply quaint stories which bear little or no relations to our sophisticated visions of the nature of things. On the contrary, these initial speculations on the origins of the Cosmos actually determined the fundamental theoretical structure in terms of which we find ourselves able to think about "the world." In the beginning of Greek intellectual culture, there was no generally accepted notion of the Cosmos as a single-ordered, systematic whole. There were *kosmoi*, but there was no *Kosmos*. The transition in cultural consciousness from the conception of a relatively chaotic Pluriverse, in which supranatural gods intermittently intervened, to the notion of a single-ordered Cosmos, a Universe bound by rational and moral laws, occurred *pari passu* with the theoretical development of Greek intellectual culture. And this theoretical development is the story of a series of "cosmetic" activities designed to construe order from out of Chaos.

Cosmogonic myths, though they come in all possible varieties of mythopoetic form, are weighted quite clearly on the side of understandings of the origins of world and self which presuppose a condition of negative chaos. Whether this is because we have simply chosen to preserve these types of myths and discard others, or whether there is a more fundamental reason for this pattern, cannot be answered with any finality. The most plausible view seems to be that the character of our dominant myths as stories of the construal of order from out of a negative chaos understood as the emptiness of voidness, the emptiness of separation, or the emptiness of confusion and disorder, is a consequence of a perhaps inordinate emphasis upon the felt sense of causal determination experienced as an alienation from the creative process responsible for the harmonies of existence. In our Anglo-European tradition this has led to an understanding of the creative act as a single paradigm event which has a single, preeminent source.

At this point all I wish to consider is the apparent fact that understandings of the genesis of self and world in the form of our bifocal consciousness lead us to affirm the need for certain structural characteristics in our understandings of self and world, and that the source of these structural components is to be found in some paradigmatic act of construal. Such a claim is indifferent to the interpretation of creation as either *creatio ex nihilo* or as the rationalization of an antecedent, disordered matter.

For whatever reasons, our cultural development can be told in terms of the increasing organization, articulation, and ramification of certain posited structural components which allow us to make sense of our world. A consequence of this development has been that language as a complex of proposals for experience has gradually become the object of structural articulation which eschews the preeminence of metaphorical renderings in favor of literal descriptions and theoretical interpretations.

Originally, the strictly mythopoetic means of entertaining the world were expressed in language which functioned as both immediately efficacious and indefinitely allusive. This is but to say that the feeling component of language was, in the beginning, profoundly determinative of our understandings of self and world. Whatever else may be said concerning the meaning of the word "metaphor," a metaphor provides language with a means of evoking immediate aesthetic sense and of transcending immediacy at the same time through an allusiveness which suggests, but does not directly name, aspects of experience. The aesthetic component directs understanding toward an internal intensity which nonetheless remains inexhaustibly vague. The allusiveness of the metaphor suggests a source of experience in the world beyond the self. That beyond is not an alien beyond, however, but one in which there is direct participation through the entertainment of the metaphor.

Literal language attempts to describe in a fashion which is, ideally, univocal. At its literal extremes both the affectivity and allusiveness of language are completely lost. Of course, something is gained as well. That gain can be understood best in terms of the increased possibilities for control of the realm of praxis. To the extent that descriptive and naming functions of language are emphasized both self and world become drastically circumscribed. The participative function of language is lost and self is reduced to an entity among entities. The inside is poured into the outer world. Thus turned inside out the realm of praxis is the artifice, the self the artificer, and the relations of self and world are power relationships defined by concepts of organization and control.

The great irony concerning the mythopoetic origins of our culture is that it is the myths themselves which determined their own literalization. That is, the transition from *mythos* to *logos* is a consequence of the fact that the cosmogonic myths grounding our cultural psyche are myths of construal determining the organization of cosmos from out of Chaos. Given the cosmogonic grounding from out of which, willy-nilly, we came to be, there can certainly be no surprise that we opted for *logos* over *mythos*, and in place of the directness of aesthetic insight sought to promote *understanding* as a process of rationalization in accordance with principles.

Cultural experience and expression has as its *terminus ad quem* the cosmological structures born from out of our principal cosmogonic myths. We shall have occasion to examine these structures and their consequences with regard to our cultural self-understanding in a later chapter. In this present context, we shall be more concerned with the *terminus a quo* of cultural self-understanding: the idiosyncratic experiencing associated with the *imagination*.

The notion that imaginative capacities ought serve as the *terminus a quo* for the discussion of cultural experience in its most general sense and the "actual world" its *terminus ad quem* has much to be said for it since the polar contrast of private and public worlds, though ultimately indefensible in the strongest sense, has continually fascinated those philosophers who have endeavored to understand both the emergence of cultural significances from out of "the world of experience" and the emergence of the concept of "World" (in the capital "W" sense) from out of the internal experiencing of human beings.

The most dramatic illustrations of imaginative activity are to be found among our dream experiences, for it is in dreams that the spontaneity of imagination proceeds without the necessity of a grounding in a consensual world. "The waking have one world in common, whereas each sleeper turns away to a world of his own."[5] It is certainly not the case that the dreamer is necessarily less involved in the world than the waking individual, for it is conceivable that one may have an extremely mundane dream patterned solely by memory events which involve little or no spontaneity, while another, though at least minimally awake, is captured by the most bizarre and idiosyncratic of imaginings. The presumedly greater reality of the waking state over the dreaming state, or the state of intense imagining, is more a function of the importance of consensual understandings and activities as they serve to establish a public world than of any defensible claims concerning ontological priority.

Judged impartially in terms of the criteria normally employed to test reality in the waking state, some dreams are certainly more real than many waking experiences. The prejudice in favor of waking states is in large measure attributable to the fact that our dreams, however bizarre, can always be reflected upon, rehearsed, shared, and in other ways placed in context in our world of waking consciousness, patterned as it is by a consensual language and generalized value-commitments. However, our dreams are often refuges from a public, consensual, world. Our consensual world may not find expression in our dreams or imaginings to the degree that our dreams may be contextualized in our waking world. Thus idiosyncratic imaginings become problems in our waking world because, given the kind of social order we humans have in fact developed, only a part of each of us is ordered socially in the strictest sense. Individual human beings are each more complex than the society to which they belong.

This discussion hints at one of the ironies celebrated in the famous conundrum of Chuang-tzu who once, upon awakening, was puzzled as to whether he was in fact Chuang-tzu who had just dreamed of a butterfly, or was himself at that moment but the dream of a butterfly. Apparently some type of consensual world, replete with continuities and uniformities, must be asserted as dominating our experiences if a meaningful distinction is to be made between the waking and dreaming states. Ultimately the character of the consensual world must be cosmologically established in terms of a spatiotemporal matrix in which some type of lawfulness reigns. Cosmological notions of order guaranteed by this lawfulness must be stipulatable in terms of social and political orders which partly derive from, and partly serve to reinforce our belief in, the cosmological understanding of order.

The difficulty with the dreaming state, which can at times make such claims upon us by virtue of its vividness, intensity, and profundity, is that we suspect that the consensual world which guarantees the reality of the waking state over the (as least relatively unreal) character of our dreams is grounded in nothing more than convention. The vested interest in accepting such a consensual world is clear. We could not accede to the demands of dreams for as Plato, in his role as political theorist, recognized, "lawless" and "unnecessary" pleasures are aroused in sleep.[6] Thus the tyrant is one who is "in reality such as we said man was in his dreams."[7] That is to say, the tyrant is one who, in seeking to order the world after the fashion of his private pleasures, is in fact but attempting to pattern the political cosmos by reference to the chaos of sensibility constituted by the idiosyncrasies of a dream world.

It is not dreaming per se that presents the true danger to the massive dominance of the consensual world. It is the spontaneous and undisciplined imaginative activity manifest not only in dreams but in wakefulness as well. Rationality, as opposed to sheer imagination, is that part of our consensual understanding guaranteeing the existence and maintenance of an ordered cosmos. The extreme difficulty in discovering a means of characterizing reason and rationality in such a way as to prevent it from being challenged as to its precedence and transcendence relative to the world of consensus is one of the most serious facts concerning the character of our intellectual life. Ever since Plato's strictures against the full participation of the poet in the polis, there has been the tradition suggesting that the relation of the idiosyncratic musings of the artistic imagination to the dominant patterns of thought and action in a society ought be established de facto by political decisions.

The existence of an ordered, coherent understanding of the way of things seems best explicable in terms of factors of persuasion, intimidation, and coercion associated with a broadly political theory of consensus. The Protagorean principle asserting that "Man is the measure," especially when interpreted in accordance with the "might makes right" doctrine, provides the most defensible explanation of the emergence of an organized world of thought and action. Whether there is in fact a structure to our perception and consciousness that provides an antecedent *ratio* in accordance with which normative measures of the character of the real may be legitimately made remains, at the very least, an open question.

Though nothing I shall say in the following pages could possibly be construed as finally resolving the issue of objectivity of the consensual world, we can approach the center of our subject and begin to see the real issues involved in it if we proceed more directly to an analysis of the imaginative activity itself. For, to the extent our consensual world may be said to derive from the imaginative activity, our contemporary sense of the world has developed contingently in terms of an overweening stress upon certain cultural interests to the exclusion, or at least derogation, of other sensibilities which are more closely associated with the idiosyncrasies of the imagination. This development, furthermore, has truncated our vision of the nature of things by providing emphasis upon only some from among the possible sources for the enrichment of our cultural self-consciousness.

The phenomenological analysis of the private psychological field can only proceed via introspection which is experienced, naïvely, as both a turning away and a turning within. The process of turning away involves a selective abstraction from the welter of conscious experience in order to discover amid the complex of "seemings" that set of "seemings to me" which have as their primary referent the one who is the object of self-reflection. These "seemings to me" which form the background of all our experiences of the consensual realm can be made the focus of our experience through the activity of introspection. The introspective move occurs informally each time we feel the need to test the truth, interest, or importance of a proposal for experiencing offered to us from the "outside." In the course of listening to a lecture, for example, we may intermittently look within for evidence in relation to which we might accept or reject the propositions which we are entertaining. That evidence may constitute logical reasons for belief or disbelief; it may also be the somewhat vaguer sense of immediate trust or distrust which leads us to assess the authority of the source of these proposals offered for our experience.

Beyond this tacit form of introspection essential to any act of communication or learning there is the form of turning within which is predicated upon the wish for pure self-enjoyment. Vague sensations associated with inchoate desires, frustrations, or anxieties play about in the penumbra of our articulated consciousness forming a fertile source of ideas, beliefs, and visions of the way of things. Neither logic nor rationality can finally discipline the idiosyncrasies of our private psychological realm. Here we encounter the incidental and the accidental phenomena of the prefactual, prerational world of the inside. In a strange admixture of the threatening and the promising, bizarre and fleeting configurations of a World both assault and comfort us in the immediacy of passing circumstance. Here we find "effects" without causes, "causes" with no anticipated consequences, alternatives without a fixed ground of otherness, which, if they are to have any meaning at all at the level of consensual understandings, must be seen as *seeds* or *scraps* of knowledge in its more articulated forms.

It serves us ill to co-opt these internal resonances by defining them psychologically, either as sublimations of physiological impulse, or as representations of the archetypes of racial habit, and so on. Such theoretical construals, though relevant to the public consideration of these factors of the internal life, have no home amid the idiosyncrasies of individual experience as sheer self-enjoyment. For in this world eternity passes and time stands still, we are blinded by many-hued melodies and deafened by noisy trapezoids; sublimities and putrescences are united in a fleeting phantasmagoria which is the chaos of sensibility itself.

"Imagination," in the general sense in which I am using this term, includes this immanent chaos of unarticulated idiosyncratic experience, identifiable in its more familiar forms as the seeds and scraps of consensual understandings. As seeds of consensus imaginings are resources for creative activities leading to public understandings of the world in terms of those facts, hypotheses, ideologies, or theories which fix our relationship to the realm of praxis. As scraps, imaginings are the leftovers of that creative process which include unused or abandoned data relevant to our changing self-understandings.

There is, of course, a long history of speculation concerning the imaginative activity. Plato construed the relatively unarticulated realm of imaginings as the lowest form of knowing. As the vaguest, least coherent, and most transitory beginnings of thought, the constituents of the imagination were seen as *eikesia*, mere images or reflections, dimly witnessing to the truth of the realm of atemporal forms which alone were the objects of true knowledge. Aristotle thought imagination to be a prerequisite of thinking, since without images thought is impossible.[8] Aristotle's grounding of imagination in perception and memory, no less than Plato's interpretation of imagining as a vague grasp of forms, leads to the disciplining of imagination by scientific or theoretical understandings which constitute real knowledge. Hume continued Aristotle's empiricism by contrasting imagination with both memory and understanding in terms of its lesser claims to belief due to its insufficient "force and vivacity" as compared with our remembrances and understanding which are grounded more directly in perceptual experience. Kant adverted, somewhat waveringly, to both Plato and Aristotle in his claim that imagination is productive of a *via media* uniting sensibility and understanding.[9] For Kant, the sensuous intuition of, say, a triangle, is united with a priori categories of space and time through the activity of the productive imagination.

It was left to philosophers and critics interested primarily in aesthetic activity to develop the notion of imagination in such a way as to render it immediately relevant to artistic creativity. Schiller, in his *Letters on the Aesthetic Education of Man*,[10] found that the activity of the imagination in regard to the creation and appreciation of Beauty is a function of the play of the productive imagination. Coleridge's eclectic appropriation of Kant and his immediate successors in *Biographia Literaria* brings this line of philosophical development near culmination with the distinction between Fancy and Imagination.

"Fancy" serves to recall the narrowly empiricist understandings of imagination as a source of knowledge always subordinated to perception and memory. It is the mechanical, imitative, merely clever reconstruction of the aggregates of perception and understanding. Imagination, however, is aligned with symbolic and creative activities which promote a true grasp of that which is. In its primary sense, imagination is discernment associated with the original creative act of God or the Absolute. True perception is a function of this mode of imagination. Artistic, or poetic, imagination involves a secondary mode, however. In this mode the poet organizes, idealizes, and unifies experience in such a way as to attune himself and his creations with that which is vital in experience.[11]

Coleridge provided a rationale for the acceptance of the activities of the imagination as productive of real knowledge. It was left only to various philosophers in the twentieth century to draw the full implications of this conception of imagination as an autonomous activity. In the works of A. N. Whitehead, for example, there is an understanding of consciousness which at once frees the imagination from narrow empirical understandings and delineates the autonomous, creative functionings of this mode of knowing. For Whitehead, the world as being may be an object of consciousness only if conceived against the background of nonbeing constituting an ambience of alternative possibilities. Negative judgment, predicated upon an awareness of what is *not* the case, is the fundamental source of consciousness. In contrast to the world as a complex of perpetual objects whose being is present to acts of intuition, the objects of imagination are constituted by the world as it is not.[12] The crucial point of imagination per se is not to be found in the simple comparison of the real and imagined object, but in the immediate presence of the imagined objects to consciousness as lures for alternative experience. Since nonbeing is the precondition of negative judgment, which is itself the ground of our consciousness of the world, imagination is constitutive of all understanding, serving not only as its ground but its goal as well.

These remarks concerning Whitehead's theory of imagination could be applied without significant qualification to Jean-Paul Sartre's understanding as well. In complete independence of Whitehead, through critiques of Hegel and Heidegger, Sartre developed a theory of imagination which placed it at the very center of the creative enterprise. According to Sartre, "all apprehension of the real world implies a hidden surpassing toward the imaginary. All imaginative consciousness uses the world as the negated foundation of the imaginary."[13] For both Whitehead and Sartre, thinking itself is an aesthetic enterprise, and imagination is constitutive of thinking.

There is reason to believe that contemporary philosophers are beginning to recognize the terrible importance of the autonomous imagination
as a fundamental source of our understandings of the way of things.
That this reappraisal of the imaginative activity may be seen by many as
but a "return of the irrational" allied with the excesses of Romanticism
merely testifies to the consequences of taking seriously the chaos of imagination in its most undisciplined form. For this obviously involves us
in coming to grips with what is most essential in the cultural problematic
of our times. This reassessment of the value of the imagination flies in
the face of those trends in Anglo-European speculation which have
sought to ensure that the imaginative activity of individuals would remain subject to the disciplines of rational and ethical principles.

Just how the imaginative activities came to be disciplined by the moral
and scientific interests is a story perhaps too familiar to bear repeating.
Suffice it to say that Descartes and Bacon, as representatives of the
critics of imagination, established from the side of both scientific reasonings and technological practices that *system* and *method*, construed normatively in terms of the truest of systematic visions and the most fruitful
of practical techniques, are meant to discipline the excesses of the imagination. Ethical reasonings likewise determine strict limits for the imagination. Rational ethics require that imagination be limited to the
entertainment of alternative modes of decision and action which are
strictly germane to the needs of present practice. Imagination is the
source of alternative characterizations of norms from among which (in
accordance with the ethical principles established by the "best" theory)
the most excellent alternative is to be selected. Normative reasonings,
whether of a moral or a scientific sort, establish the alternatives
generated by imaginative activity as a hierarchy of values. Both classical
science and ethics are narrowed to the sphere of relevance established by
the interrelations of theory and practice. In addition to this narrowing effect, imagination is construed as culminating in a normative principle
which best serves the needs of enquiry and action.

The cultural interests of science and morality mutually ramify these
deleterious effects upon the imagination. Most generally expressed this
simply means that "the principle of plenitude"[14] is interpreted as meaning that even if somewhere and somewhen all possibilities must find instantiation in the concrete realm of circumstance, these instantiations are
to be viewed in terms of degrees of relevance, cosmologically construed.
Thus the relevance of theory in its most general sense is the characterization of this actual world in terms of fundamental laws and regularities.
The problematic for practices of a technological or moral sort, then, con-

sists in actions in conformity with these laws. The scientific mode of practice is stressed in accordance with prediction and control predicated upon an awareness of the strictures of nature construed as an objective system. Ethical actions of either a theological or naturalistic variety are associated directly (as in the case of theologically grounded ethics) or indirectly (in more humanistic and naturalistic ethical orientations) with the notion of a single ordered world contingent upon the authorship of an Absolute Agent.

The seeds-and-scraps theory of the imagination allows for the criticism of established modes of theory and practice, but only in terms of the desire to develop an alternative theoretical vision whose rational and moral implications are superior to those entailed by the object of critique. This is accomplished by recourse to the casting of unsown seeds, or by the reconstructions of reasonings and practice from the scraps of presumedly outworn visions. In either case the imagination is viewed as a repository of perhaps infinite novelties only a small selection of which are germane to the needs of rational experience. The "vasty deep" of the imaginative realm is viewed primarily as a source of mere play and fantasy, harmless enough if it does not influence overmuch the realm of public praxis.

Cultural creativity is always a function of the entertainment of alternative possibilities. But we must ask: How much novelty can we survive? And, equally important: How much germaneness can we afford? The tensions between novelty and germaneness provide one of the major dynamics associated with cultural activity. Absolute germaneness as a criterion of cultural activity is the impossible ideal of the uncompromising conservative. It would produce a world which is not, in any significant sense of the word, human at all. Its product would be a world patterned by the inertial repetitions of institutionalized social habit. Absolute novelty, on the other hand, just as unthinkable, is ipso facto undesirable. The transition from one vision of the world to another has always been patterned by those principles which establish the interplay of theory and practice. The sphere of praxis as a source of theoretical visions is itself a theoretical entity variously interpreted by the theories to which it supposedly gives rise. A theory is novel to the extent that it derives from novel elements in the sphere of praxis and to the extent to which it promotes novel modes or consequences of practice. This dialectic of theory and practice is itself called into question, however, by the recognition of the relativity, indeed the parity, of alternative modes of reasonings and practice. For such a dialectic argues too forcibly for germaneness as a criterion of imaginative activity. What is needed is not just a *play* of the imagination which promotes yet other theories grounded in and yielding new interpretations of the character of praxis, but a *leap* of the imagination rendering us capable of refusing the gambit offered by the overly structured interactions of theory and practice.

The accepted cultural problematic in our Anglo-European tradition is defined by the cultural interests of science and morality. Even the very general metatheoretical notion of the relations of theory and practice is dominated by these interests. Theoretical activity is construed paradigmatically in terms of internal consistency and systematic coherence. As source and consequence of theorizing, the realm of praxis is interpreted normatively in terms of ethical criteria. The romantic vision of the autonomy of the imagination, though a step toward the freeing of imaginative activity from the strictures of hierarchical germaneness to the exigencies of present circumstance, is finally a sham since it too merely perpetuates an alternative vision inviting systematic expression and practical applications which would instantiate an alternative set of moral values.

The moral interest is associated with the organization of cultural expression in such a fashion as to determine the efficacy of some selected components of experience. The intervention in natural circumstance armed with the desire to instantiate some values above others, promote some institutions above others, express loyalty to some projects among others, is of the essence of moral behavior. Not strangely, this conception of morality well suits the character of science as instrumentally construed. For that matter, it suits *any* instrumental action. Specialized sciences selectively abstract from the natural or social world, and then develop theories germane to those selected elements. The justification *in principle* for the development of specialized sciences is that they possess greater power in the task of controlling process so as to maximize a rather narrowly defined mode of efficacy.

I have been considering the manner in which the imagination, conceived as the *terminus a quo* of cultural experience, comes to be disciplined by rational and ethical criteria. Given the conception of the cultural sensorium presupposed throughout this discussion, such a development can only be construed as threatening the autonomy of the alternative cultural interests of art, religion, and philosophy. The remainder of this chapter will be devoted to an explicit consideration of the deleterious effects of the imposition of moral and scientific concerns upon the cultural interests of art and religion. In the following two chapters I will consider the depressed state of the philosophic enterprise resulting from that imposition.

Beginning with the most obvious illustration of the aesthetic interest—namely, fine art, particularly museum art—our case is easily made. For if, as Herbert Read has suggested, we look about us at our fellow-visitors to an art museum, what do we see? "Dim, bored figures, gingerly skating over waxed floors, drifting like chilled bees from one fading flower to the next."[15] Normal processes of education, claims Read, are sufficient to destroy aesthetic sensitivities by the age of twelve. Thereafter, with the exception of the most extraordinary of individuals, all that one may acquire through exposure to art is "the patter of appreciation, the accent of understanding."[16]

If this is so, it is at least partly because the "normal processes of education" which so exercise Read involve the distortion of the aesthetic sense through an overconcern with the moral and scientific sensibilities. For if we take a look at our traditional form of aesthetic education, we shall be hard put to say what is *aesthetic* about it. Our aesthetic sense is so distorted by the desire to understand our world and to dwell securely, if not responsibly, within it that we have a difficult time experiencing aesthetically.[17]

Primarily, we receive a thematic and technical education in art. That is, we are taught (and later teach ourselves) to resonate to the great moral themes of art and to analyze works of art in terms of the technical apparatus employed by the artist, and the attendant insights into physical, psychological, social, and divine natures expressed through the characterization of these thematic elements. Concentrating on these aspects of art objects tends to direct us away from the aesthetic enjoyment of the uniqueness, the just-so-ness of the artists' creations.

Consider the art of the Renaissance, still the dominant subject matter of formal education in the history of art and art appreciation. The preponderance of pedagogy associated with Renaissance art of northern Italy, for example, concentrates upon two of its primary characteristics: first, the visual expression of the ideals of humanism initially expressed in the literary movement from Petrarch onward. The "sensuous," "heroic," and "naturalistic" qualities of the works of Masaccio, Michelangelo, Leonardo, Raphael, and so on are associated with a "new optimism" regarding the potentialities of strictly human efficacy in meeting the problems of relating the individual to nature and society. The celebration of these broadly moral themes exhausts a great number of the discussions of Renaissance art history and criticism.

Second, art historians and critics concern themselves with the objectivist and scientific contributions of the artists in their appreciation of the natural world. In this regard we learn of the importance of the study of visual perspective in terms of the geometric theory of vision, the increased interest in anatomy and physiology, the wide applications of the mechanistic model to the understandings of nature, and so on. We learn that though Leonardo was not, in fact, a scientist in the manner of Galileo, he did have an objectivist and mechanistic imagination which led him to interrogate nature in much the same way as the scientists of the sixteenth and seventeenth centuries. Though it is obvious to anyone who bothers to look that the painter Leonardo employed his anatomic and mechanical genius in subordination to his aesthetic interests, most of us would be much more capable of appreciating certain technical innovations in his works than in noting precisely what of strictly aesthetic interest is to be found there.

Just as the art of the northern Italian Renaissance is more often than not seen to have as its primary significance its serving as a medium for the expression of heroic and naturalistic perspectives associated with the new humanism, the companion art of Germany is seen to foreshadow, and later to sustain, a vision of the world compatible with the religious Reformation. In Grünewald and Dürer, so we are told, there is a new "psychological intensity," a "moodiness," the use of "stark, near-mad facial textures," which undergird the pessimistic assessment of the individual associated with the theological anthropologies of Martin Luther and his ilk. Surely, from an aesthetic point of view, to compare Grünewald's *Isenheim Altarpiece* with the treatment of similar themes by Masaccio or Michelangelo, in terms of psychology or moral sense, would involve the most serious kind of category mistake. Yet the art historian seldom avoids this temptation. Likewise, to compare Dürer's portraiture to, for example, that of Raphael in terms of theory of proportionality or the use of visual space, is technically interesting but aesthetically irrelevant. The real excellence of each painter is indifferent to such questions.

Aesthetic excellence is found in the caves of Altimira and Lescaux expressed in paint and textured stone. Such excellence is likewise wrought from Greek terra-cotta, Florentine oils, German wood, Italian marble. But that excellence eludes us as long as we insist upon nonaesthetic criteria of greatness. We do seem to insist upon these criteria, however, if for no other reason than that they are easier to articulate and, therefore, more capable of direct communication. This concern with directness of communication is in large measure attributable to the fact that it is the moral and scientific interests which have dominated our conception of the meaning of civilized life, at least since the sixteenth century.

The strictly aesthetic appreciation of art would involve the discrimination of greater or lesser contexts serving to promote the enjoyment of intensities-in-contrast. One might move from the discrimination of a detail in a single work of art, such as the "veined hand" in Michelangelo's *David*, to the grasp of the *David* as a harmony of contrasting details. One might even enjoy the *David* itself as a detail within the epoch of Renaissance art, or Renaissance art in relation to art itself construed as a complex of human expressions. The aesthetic perspective is one which concentrates, no matter how extensive the context, upon the harmony of insistently particular details. Insofar as is possible, this experience selectively abstracts from moral or scientific questions in the interests of promoting the intensity of the aesthetic experience. That is to say, in a particular painting the harmonious unity is such as to require just those details of line, color, contrasts, and so on which are in fact present. The greatness of a painting lies in the greatness of its evocative intensity both in itself and as that intensity contributes to the recognition of a wider harmony of various aesthetic expressions.

Doubtless there is often a moral greatness expressed through art. A particular work may serve as a stimulus to alter behavior, reinforce norms, and, if only by its concreteness or the intensity of the interest it generates, to exclude alternative modes of efficacy potentially present in other works of art. Renaissance art has had the effect of celebrating the hero, the somewhat larger-than-life figure, as a model of human aspiration and adulation. Whatever may be said concerning the aesthetic intensities involved in the enjoyment of heroic art, it has affected radically the manner in which Anglo-European cultural self-understanding has served as a source for the energizing of activity in the public sphere. The so-called inspirational quality of Renaissance art has less to do with aesthetic appreciation and more with the manner in which certain experiences may inspire moral action, that is, actions aimed at the direction and coordination of experience so as to alter the future in such a way as to secure the world in relation to practical ends.

In addition to the approach to art through moral thematics, there is a second important nonaesthetic perspective—namely, the scientific. One of the principal lessons of Renaissance art, for example, concerns the intuition of space. The sacred triumvirate of length, width, and depth, patterned by geometric perspective, may be a doctrine of science, but it is a lesson learned through art. Scientific theories may discipline our reasonings and practice, but only art can educate our imaginations. Humanist naturalism and the use of perspectival presentations of space enforced the conception of a triad of spatial dimensions which determine so much of the character of our concrete intuitions.

The question whether intuitions are presented in perspectival or visually distorted space is ancillary to the presentation of the intuition expressed. The aesthetic value of the art object is not dependent upon accidental characteristics of space anymore than it is dependent upon a certain moral theme which constitutes its subject matter. The artist must employ *some* subject or theme, and he must have some intuition of space and the fixing of objects in that space. But what is novel concerning his art is not a function of these aspects. It is the insistent particularities of aesthetic expression which are essential to a given work of art.

Most of what we learn from art is essentially irrelevant from an aesthetic point of view. If we only gain moral inspiration, or practice in spatial visualization, we miss the point of art. The aesthetic experience is meant to turn us in the direction of the just-so-ness of things, to give us a sense of the uniqueness of details as constitutive of wider harmonies. This lesson is difficult to learn if our ostensibly aesthetic experiences are distorted by an appreciation of harmonies of a strictly logical or moral kind.

I do not wish to be understood as claiming that our various cultural senses are neatly isolatable one from the other. Each of our culturally grounded experiences is doubtless a mélange of the moral, the scientific, the religious, the aesthetic, the philosophic interests. By using the model of a cultural sensorium analogous to the physiological sensorium I merely wish to maintain that it is possible to consider the cultural senses in relative isolation one from the other as a means of discovering the relative contribution to a given cultural situation made by a particular sense.

I have used Renaissance art illustratively and in so doing may seem to have weighted my case for the dominance of the moral and scientific sense in the appreciation of art. Certainly it might occur to one to note that, say, the Romantic poets were obviously not concerned with teaching science. Granted. It is nonetheless true that the tensions between that moral and scientific interest determined the major expressions of that movement. Also, a significant part of our contemporary interest in the Romantics comes from the attempt to develop a broader scientific vision of nature.

Wordsworth's conception of poetry as having its origin in "emotion recollected in tranquillity" entails the view that the recollection of emotion is a means of educating the cultural sensorium since the expressions of the poet are to be judged in terms of the criterion of the widening of the sphere of human sensibility for "the delight, honor and benefit of human nature."[18] The poet of genius is a creator of taste precisely to the degree that he evokes and bestows power which leads to knowledge. The poet is a creative social agent insofar as he calls forth power to sustain and intensify feelings. These feelings are not ends in themselves but are intrinsically connected with the ideas which evoke and interpret them.

Wordsworth's strictures against "poetic diction" (the traditional and technically stylized language of the professional poet) stemmed from his feeling that such poetry perpetuates images and ideas in abstraction from novel and vivid emotions. But this is precisely the basis for the Romantic protest against the science of the eighteenth century. For classical science perpetuated a conception of lifeless nature bereft of secondary qualities, comprehensible only in terms of mechanistic determinism. In this sense, Wordsworth shares with Blake the animus against "single vision and Newton's sleep." The Romantic wishes not only to *delight*, but to *honor* and *benefit* as well. And this desire so to direct human sensibility is grounded in the moral sense. Doubtless, Whitehead was correct in noting that the Romantic reaction constituted "a protest on behalf of value."[19] The movement, however, was not a protest on behalf of *aesthetic* value, as Whitehead claimed, but *moral* value.

The chief limitation of the romantic vision of the imagination largely derives from the fact that the romantic reaction, as *reaction*, has maintained the character of dialectical critique of the narrow vision of the imagination grounded in rational science and ethics. Where the rational vision has stressed objectivity, the romantic opts for the value of the "subjective"; where scientific reason has attempted to get the human being (as observer and participant in nature) out of the way, the romantic vision has sought to place him again in the center of things. The seeds and scraps left over from the rationalist activity have been utilized to construct a dialectical alternative which serves as an inverted image of the classical form of received opinion, and is, thus, altogether too germane to serve as the most creative alternative vision.

The crucial point here with regard to the romantic vision of the autonomy of the creative imagination is that it is, in fact, a protest on behalf of the instrumental efficacy of an alternative vision of the world. As disinterestedly conceived that vision does not have to be interpreted solely in terms of its moral efficacy, but the activities of the Romantic reactionaries are best illustrated in their offering of an alternative theory of the way of things which has moral implications presumed superior to those perpetuated by "single vision."

The fourfold vision of Blake, in all its mandalic splendor, is expressed as a prophecy. It is a judgment upon the world which calls for *action*. The stipulations, clarifications, elaborations, and systematizations of the romanticist prophecies due to the subsequent thinkers, culminating in much of our contemporary existentialism and certain forms of phenomenology, have made a "science" of the new vision. In this manner the moral efficacy of the romantic vision has been increased by ensuring its greater power to control and redirect praxis.

Aesthetic purists, recognizing the tendentiousness of the romantic crusader, have attempted to detach art altogether from its world by developing aesthetic visions that stress autonomy and independence. Such views are seriously overdrawn. Though we must agree that at the most essential level *artis est celare artem*, art-for-art's-sake theories should rarely be taken with any seriousness since these doctrines are so seldom well thought-out. They usually celebrate the most bizarre and uncomfortable consequences of pure aestheticism. To believe with Oscar Wilde that "the fact that a man is a poisoner doesn't affect his prose" places us in a strange position vis-à-vis both poisoners and prose. And to accept without examination Wilde's claim that "the world is made by the singer for the dreamer" would likely lead us greatly to undervalue the ontological character of things. Most aestheticisms are simply not ramified in accordance with metaphysical and cosmological visions, and, as a consequence, are seen to be rootless and partial abstractions. Aestheticisms, as visions of the meaning of fine art and its relation to society, require some form of aesthetic ontology.

A second criticism of art-for-art's-sake visions is that they so often entail the rejection of context. Recognizing art on its own terms does not involve the belief that art has no context. The art object in its ontological character is appreciated aesthetically, but the individual who is capable of such appreciation need not thereby elide from his experience the ethical, rational, philosophic, or mystical interpretations of the object in its relations to its world. The work of art is not reducible to ethical or rational significances, but neither is it wholly independent of them. The aesthetic object exists in tension with its world. And although the richness of art simply as art is to be found in its just-so-ness, the richness of the world which serves as the context of aesthetic objects is a function of the mutual interrelations of the broadest possible selection of cultural evidences.

Understanding art on its own terms requires us to appreciate the distinction between types of harmony. Aesthetic, as opposed to logical or moral harmony, is limited only by the possibilities of intensity and contrast open to a particular terminus of experiencing. Rational or moral orders are specifiable within a more general aesthetic order. Logical consistency or contradiction are specific forms of aesthetic contrast. Likewise, moral orders characterized by the achievement of individual or social goods are established in accordance with principles which require, as do rational principles, selective abstraction from the fullness of the actualizable orders available through aesthetic experiencing. Education of an aesthetic, as opposed to a moral or scientific kind, involves sensitivity to the potentialities for the realization of harmonious experiencing conditioned solely by the criteria of intensity and contrast.

Artistic genius is a function of the ability to introduce novel patterns of aesthetic harmony into the wealth of expressions characterizing the complex of aesthetic activities of a particular cultural epoch. Often the artist may feel that certain concrete variations of detail have been exhausted within a set of possibilities for harmony. Thus, in ages of transition, the artist is faced by a double problem. On the one hand, he experiences the exhaustion of the principal variations within a given epochal style. On the other hand, he experiences the anxiety deriving from openness to unstructured novelty.

In times of transition, the artist's experience is qualified both by the excitement of eros and the stasis of oblivion. Between ecstasy and inebriation the artist wanders, exhausted by novelty or anesthetized by the threat of boredom. Transitions in art occur within that *epoché*, that break with tradition, in which the artist experiences, looking backward, the threat of sameness and repetition and, looking forward, the chaos of finite things in their wholly accidental, unfixed character. It is with regard to the disruptive character of the aesthetic enterprise, most obvious during periods of transition, that we discover the primary explanation for the disciplining of art by recourse to moral and scientific criteria. And though one can understand the motivations that lead to such discipline, and can appreciate that the securing functions of rational and moral principles are greatly to be appreciated, surely it is also clear just how much is lost if we allow the aesthetic interest to be glozed over by such a comforting veneer.

There is a great deal more to be said about the depressed state of the aesthetic enterprise in our culture as a consequence of the imposition of the demands of the moral and scientific interests. Enough has been said in this context, however, to support the plausibility of my thesis concerning the unbalanced recognition of the various cultural evidences. My case can be made even more plausible if we direct our attention to the manner in which the religious interest has been distorted and rendered nearly impotent by the impingements of rational and ethical motivations.

After we remove the strictly ethical injunctions thought to be entailed by our paradigmatic religious experiences, and after we have deleted all of the rational arguments and demonstrations informing our developed theological tradition, what remains? Apparently we have spent the greater part of our energies articulating the characteristics of the Primary Religious Object, constructing subtle arguments aimed at demonstrating Its existence, and affirming this Ultimate Being to be the authoritative source of those moral norms which stabilize our social existence. The *mysterium tremendum*, the holiness character of existence, the sense of mystical identity, the sacred aura surrounding certain places, events, and personages are celebrated by mystical poets, and more often than not, ignored by dogmatic theologians. Religion actually seems bizarre in our culture almost precisely to the extent that it is approached on its own terms, apart from the ethical and rational criteria which serve to organize and discipline our social and cultural activities.

The presumed warfare between science and religion has, on the whole, been greatly overemphasized. It is certainly not in terms of the open conflicts that from time to time break out between the religious and scientific sensibilities that the relations of the two interests are most dramatically to be assessed. On the contrary, such open conflict is evidence of the creative tensions that ought be maintained among all cultural interests. The ironic fact entailed by the interaction of science and religion is that, far from being at odds with one another, Athens has been altogether too appealing to Jerusalem. Indeed, whatever else may be said concerning the possible conflicts between science and religion, it is manifestly true that orthodox theology and classical science share a common apologetic structure. And that structure is fundamentally scientific in character.

In our tradition, religion is primarily a matter of belief. And belief is rendered plausible through *argument*. Granted there are many religious movements which do not seek rationally to defend beliefs, but the importance of the theistic arguments for the apologetic function of religion vis-à-vis the enterprise of science cannot be overstressed. For the prestige of religion in our culture is in large measure a function of its rational defensibility. Furthermore, the pietists and fideists who revel in their freedom from bondage to dialectic more often than not tacitly accede to the reduction of religious sensibility to the narrowest forms of ethical praxis. We shall soon have occasion to say more about this fact. But before we consider the domination of religious insight by the moral interest, we shall note the manner in which rational argument, a function primarily of the apologetic activity of Judeo-Christianity, has shaped the essential character of our culture's religious enterprise.

One of the most characteristic facts concerning the tradition of Christian orthodoxy is its dedication to the task of arguing for the existence of God. So much of the energy of theologians and philosophers of religion is expended on this enterprise that it is no exaggeration to say that arguments for the rationality of belief form the central focus of mainstream Christianity. It is hardly surprising, therefore, that the very concept of God has been shaped by the nature of the arguments employed.

There are three principal arguments for God's existence within the Judeo-Christian tradition: the ontological, cosmological, and teleological. The ontological argument is broadly Platonic and Neoplatonic; the cosmological arguments are best supported by the Aristotelian-Thomistic strain of philosophy. The teleological argument, the argument from design, has been expressed in both Platonic and Aristotelian forms. The Augustinian form of Neoplatonism provided the basis of the ontological argument perfected by Anselm. St. Thomas Aquinas's famous "Five Ways" constituted a somewhat loosely connected set of arguments predicated on cosmological presuppositions. Modern evolutionary theory gave renewed life to teleological forms of argumentation by permitting the reinterpretation of the notion of design so as to include the temporal dimension of nature.

We shall begin with perhaps the most intriguing of the arguments: the ontological proof. In its strongest form this argument purports to prove that necessary existence is a perfection predicable of a unique state of affairs. The Kantian criticism to the effect that an existing state of affairs, simply as existing, is not superior to that same state of affairs as nonexistent (since each is *essentially* the same) does not, of course, count against the ontological argument in this form. It is quite another question as to whether *necessary* existence is more perfect than contingent existence. Shifting the argument from the contrast between existence and nonexistence to that between two modalities of existence renders the argument more intuitively sound.

Structured in this way the argument depends upon no more than the following: (1) the assumption that "if perfection exists, it exists necessarily" ($\varrho \supset \Box \varrho$); (2) the postulates that "modal existence is always necessary" ($\Diamond \varrho \supset \Box \Diamond \varrho$ or $\Box \varrho \supset \Box \Box \varrho$)[20] and "necessary existence is not impossible" ($\sim \Box \sim \Box \varrho$).[21]

I am not concerned here with the complete form of the ontological argument, only with the nature of its assumptions, each of which depends upon the concept of necessity. Herein lies the apologetic brilliance of the argument. For presuming that each of these assumptions could be coherently denied, a consequence of that denial is that they could no longer be applied in rational arguments of any kind. That is to say, not only theologians but scientists as well would be denied the use of these assumptions. The thrust of the ontological argument as an apologetic device is that it highlights a set of assumptions which are not merely employed by the theologian attempting to argue for the existence of God, but are also the putative assumptions of other rational arguments insofar as those arguments depend upon the contrast of necessity and contingency. One cannot have it both ways, says the apologetic theologian. If theological arguments grounded on the assumption of necessary existence fail, so do all arguments thus grounded.

The ontological argument need not stand alone. It is normally employed in conjunction with the two other principal arguments. The cosmological argument assumes what we have come to call the principle of sufficient reason.[22] This argument depends upon the plausibility of distinguishing between dependent, or contingent, states of affairs and a self-caused, or necessary, State of Affairs and thus between those states of affairs explained by something outside themselves, and that state which has its explanation in itself. If every dependent state of affairs can be explained in terms of another state of affairs outside itself, what is it that explains the facticity of dependent states of affairs per se? Parenthetically, one can see why it has been maintained by Kant and others that the ontological argument undergirds the cosmological argument since the same distinction between necessity and contingency is at stake here.

Note that this argument does not involve the notion of infinite temporal regress; it does not even presuppose that the temporal question must be asked at all. The question does not assume that the totality of existing things has the same existential status as each individual thing. Instead it assumes the principle of sufficient reason and asks, "If every contingent fact can be accounted for in some rational terms, how are we to account for the fact that there are contingent facts?" Certainly not by appeal to this or that contingent fact. Though each dependent being may be explained by some other dependent being, to say that the fact of the existence of the entire collection of dependent beings may be explained by the dependent beings themselves leads to the commission of the part-whole fallacy. What seems to be required is an appeal to the notion of Self-Existent Being.

Apparently the only sound means of rejecting the cosmological argument is to deny the truth of the principle of sufficient reason. However, if we reject that principle in theology it may also be rejected in any other context of rational enquiry since there are simply no cogent means for denying a parity of argumentative norms as between theology and other enterprises which appeal to such reasonings for support.

The teleological argument employs analogical reasonings in two senses to establish the plausibility of the existence of God. In the first sense, the teleologist argues from the coherent order apparent in the natural world as it is experienced by human percipients to the character of an Orderer or Designer who has fashioned, or is in some other sense responsible for, the order of things. In the second sense, analogical reasonings are used to argue from the recognition of order in a local environment to the existence of an order of that or a compatible kind throughout the cosmos.

Expressed in terms of these types of analogical reasonings, the teleological argument may not appear excessively persuasive. But the fundamental assumption of this argument is in fact not so easily assailed. The teleological argument is grounded in the intuition that *the actual world is one*. That is to say, this proof depends only upon the assumption that there is a Cosmos, a single order of things. It is *this* order that requires an Orderer. Expressed in this fashion the argument is a variant of the cosmological proof expressed in final-cause language rather than the idiom of efficient causality. Taken in this form it is a challenging argument if for no other reason than that if we give up the notion of a single ordered world, we are hard put to defend the notion of rationality at any but the most finite and local levels. And if we appeal to chance and contingency to explain—via natural selection, for example—one area of order, we are forced to appeal to another mechanism to explain yet other illustrations of order. A single ordered cosmos thus becomes itself an irrationality (or at the very least, a mystery) since the rabid violation of Occam's razor involved in the continual resort to ad hoc principles means that we cannot construct a general theory with anything like cosmological relevance.

We certainly can give up the collection of assumptions that undergird the rationality of theistic arguments: we are free to deny the meaningfulness of necessary existence, the intuitive certainty of the principle of sufficient reason, and the notion that there is a single ordered world constituting our broadest ambience. Denying these assumptions frees us from the necessity to affirm the rationality of the arguments for God's existence. But what is left of rationality after the denial of these assumptions? Can we make our reasonings work without at least one of these assumptions? We can certainly speak and write. We can make claims and apply our understandings, albeit piecemeal, to the sphere of social praxis. What is called into question is theoretical integrity.

Behaviorists, instrumentalists, and "critical rationalists" among our contemporary scientists would not be overly affected by the theologian's apologetics. Among these scientists reason in the grand sense has certainly been abandoned. But the rhetoric of science remains disappointingly un-changed. Though Hume's criticisms of the theistic arguments are often thought by scientific thinkers to be devastating to the aims of theology, his equally viable criticisms of the rationality of the notion of cause have not been thought to undermine the nature of scientific rationality. Con-temporary scientific reasonings and practice are de facto irrational, even though they so often present themselves as rational in the extreme. The yawning gap between the public assertions of scientists concerning scien-tific methodology and their actual practices in their laboratories, at their desks, and in their conferences is but a reflection of that original chaos of irrationality against which Anglo-European culture has set its face from the beginnings of its intellectual activity. The hypocrisy of the scientist is a reincarnated hypocrisy once characteristic of the religious virtuoso.

I need not dwell on the irony of the inversion of the relations between science and theology in the twentieth century. The oft-repeated themes of the intrinsic interconnectedness of certain theological notions and the origins of modern science, and of the intimately theological grounding of the works of such thinkers as Newton, Descartes, Leibniz, and Einstein, have become cultural clichés. The irony, of course, is that the relatively recent scientific criticisms of classical theological understandings have promoted an argumentative context within which the rational defense of religion has resulted in laying bare assumptions fundamental not only to theological but to classically scientific reasonings as well. By attempting to establish the superiority of scientific principles of explanation over those of rational religion scientists have opened their discipline to the same criticisms leveled against religion. The fates of science and of ra-tional religion are intrinsically tied.

I began this discussion with the attempt to argue that the religious in-terest has been unduly affected by the rational impulse as expressed through the enterprise of classical science. I have not meant to claim that religion has been affected by science only since the advent of its modern form. Though the Renaissance is the watershed with respect to which we can measure the most profound effects of the ethical and rational in-terests upon our culture, we must presume that these effects were present from the beginning. The strange alliance of Athens and Jerusalem has contributed to the dialectical evisceration of the autonomous interest of religion. The price of defending the faith against the rational skeptic is that the Primary Religious Object has been conceived in accordance with the demands of theological apologetics. The God of Jerusalem came to be characterized by recourse to notions such as "necessary existence," "sufficient reason," and "cosmological unity." The question as to whether these concepts may in fact be made compatible with the experiential ground of the religious interest is one which continues to be debated.

The actual conflict between the orthodox theological notion of God and the subject of religious experiencing in its most profoundly mystical form is an important consequence of the tendency to permit rational apologetics to influence overmuch the constructive form of the religious vision. In orthodox Christianity, the explicitly theological form of the ultimate religious experience is the Beatific Vision. This theological doctrine is in terminal opposition to the mystical experience of Union expressed as the mutual immanence of God and the Soul. The Union of the Soul with God is theologically heterodox, of course, since such union threatens the aseity of God. Theologians and father confessors have not hesitated to reject the implications of the propositional description of a mystical experience in favor of the orthodox form of beatific vision in which the distinction of the soul and God is maintained.

Theological orthodoxy in Anglo-European culture depends upon the character and limitations of propositional utterance. One of the implications of this dependency is the belief that understanding derives from an assessment of the meaning of a datum of experience prior to the judgment as to its truth or falsity. At the very least an understanding of the language in which a knowledge claim is made is essential to the judgment of the truth or falsity of the claim. Unless the question of meaning is asked prior to the question of the truth we are apt to involve ourselves in ludicrous situations. Also, truth or falsity is traditionally held to be a characteristic of propositions, not of fundamental data of perceptual experience. Thus it is not perceptual objects but *claims about* these objects that have truth-value. Or so we normally believe.

It is otherwise with the majority of so-called mystics. Not only do the noetic claims of the mystic invert the relations between meaning and truth, in this mode of knowing it is the datum of experience that has immediately acknowledgeable truth-value. Thus if someone claims to have a vision of Jesus Christ, he may not immediately understand the meaning of the visitation. The mystic, however, does not allow the possibility that the vision is meaningless. The meaning is to be discovered subsequently, through arduous meditation and introspection. But the experience of the truth of the vision need not await the articulation of the meaning; it is a primary deliverance of the experience itself. Testing the truth of a mystical vision does not involve a simple comparison of the vision as Appearance with some ontic Reality known in other ways. The closest thing to truth-testing allowed by the mystic is what is termed in the Western tradition "the spiritual effects test." This test, however, has less to do with anything propositional and more to do with the existential correlates of the experience.

Traditional orthodoxy requires that God transcend the souls created by Him. The peculiar immanence asserted to obtain under the conditions of mystical union is such as to cancel that transcendence. The soul thus adds to the essence of an already complete Being. Orthodoxy requires that God be indeterminate with regard to His creatures. The preponderance of naïve phenomenological descriptions of the God-Soul Unity realized at the culmination of mystical experience requires that the soul in some very real sense be determinate of the Divine Being. An investigation of the classical mystical literature in the West will show that the mystic qua theologian is placed in conflict with the mystic qua mystic on this very point. To the degree that the naïve experience of the mystic is accepted as the basis for theological construction a rather heterodox form of theology is the result. The fate of Meister Eckhart, one of the few mystics who served as his own theologian, attests to the conflict of the empirical and rational tendencies within Judeo-Christianity.

I have attempted to offer cogent evidence that religion as a cultural interest is altogether too much constrained by the rational activity associated with the scientific interest. Theological arguments in support of God's existence advertise an apologetic relationship with scientific rationality, and doctrinal interpretations of the relations of the Soul and God give evidence of an important conflict between the experiential and rational interpretations of religious experience. We shall subsequently follow out some of the implications of this latter conflict (see Chapter 6). But enough has been said already to provide support for the presumption that a richer and more creative cultural experience can derive from reassessment of our cultural priorities in such fashion as to promote the autonomy as well as interdependence of each of our principal cultural interests. One of the things that principle entails with regard to the religious interest is that we attempt to see what remains of the religious sensibility after we detach it from the accretions of extraneous logic and apologetics.

It may, in fact, seem doubtful whether there is very much at all remaining after the extrusion of merely doctrinal propositions and the theological arguments supporting them. Moreover, the greater part of what remains is itself perhaps no more religious in the true sense than is the rational theoretical structure just rehearsed. For what is not "scientific" in the religion of Anglo-European culture is, for the most part, wholly *ethical*. The narrow character of Anglo-European culture is

demonstrated on its theoretical side by the importance of scientific rationalism; on its practical side, it is shown by the characterization of
religious interest in terms of ethical praxis. Our traditional understandings of religion are so closely tied to the ethical sensibility of our culture
that Matthew Arnold's ironic dictum claiming that religion is but
"morality tinged with emotion" is altogether too applicable to institutionalized religion.

Rationalistic interpretations of the sense of holiness, at both the
theoretical and practical levels, have greatly obscured the essence of
religious sensibility. The same rational impulse that requires us to envision God as a religious object serving as the subject of rational dogmas
and proofs, leads, at the level of ethical praxis, to the notion that the
primary function of God is to serve as the Ground of cosmic and social
law and order.

A consequence of this view of the Primary Religious Object is that the
religious sensibility is found to be expressed most notably in terms of
rules, laws, and doctrines rather than in terms of techniques of spiritual
transcendence or self-realization. Furthermore, the ethical and social
principles which organize the sphere of public praxis themselves find
legitimation in and through Divine sanctions provided by the orthodox
religious tradition. The paradoxical consequence of this tendency is that
religion is primarily a secular and secularizing activity. Those activities of
God which function within the predominantly secular component of
society are isolated as His primary functions.

Within our culture, those interpretations of religion that would render
it in the slightest independent of the interest of morality are highly
suspect. The shocked reaction to any claim that religion is "beyond good
and evil" ought to be an occasion for at least some curiosity. After all,
Brahmanic philosophies hold ethical systems to be mere relative systems
of value, of only penultimate significance in relation to the fundamental
religious insight. The Taoist sage claims that good and evil are born into
the world by virtue of the artifice of rational distinctions. And Jesus
himself urged against resisting evil. How does the ethical individual
reconcile his motivations with these troublesome aspects of religious sensibility?

The fact that we understand saintliness almost wholly in terms of
goodness, forgetting that our religious virtuosos are rarely characterized
primarily by their ethics, is revealing in this connection. On reflection, it
is hardly the moral severity of Jesus that most find disconcerting. We are
likely to be much more disturbed by his indifference to this or that moral
norm. Who of us could avoid moral indignation in the face of one who

said, "The poor you will always have with you"; "Let the dead bury the dead"; or "Resist not Evil." What is there, we may wonder, about the nature of the religious sensibility which permits it, in crucial instances, to run into severe conflict with the ethical sensibility?

Most of us will never know. For we have safely hidden ourselves from the discomforting encounters with the holiness that such understanding presupposes. The sense of the holy is, of course, allied with the aesthetic sense. Holiness involves the sense of the contrast between the finite particular and the totality of unassembled factors which comprise that which is. It is the sense of uniqueness against the background of the totality of things. The demands of religion are absolute demands and are thus of a qualitatively different sort than those which oblige one to act in relation to this or that discriminated context.

If we are to understand the autonomous value of religious experience and expression within our culture it is perhaps necessary for us to look to those mystical interpretations of religion wherein the sensibility resides in its purest form. The highest form of religious experience is the sense of unity with the Divine Presence. That experience enjoins no action; it requires no specific forms of behavior. Its locus is not in the world of praxis, and the translation of this experience into the mundane realm cannot be accomplished in doctrinal terms which spell out a specific plan of action. Religious actions are all symbolic in the sense that they have as their referent an infinite sphere of meaning and value which is incommensurate with the finite realm of praxis.

It is quite understandable that we should have some suspicion of the religious interest in its most radical forms. Undisciplined by moral concerns, religion may be a devastating factor within a society. The way is narrow and the gate is strait not only because of the intrinsic difficulty of maintaining religious allegiance; the fact is that, at our present level of social development, we cannot afford too many individuals who are "in the world but not of it." We ghettoize our religious virtuosos in much the same manner as we ghettoize our artists, for they are potentially disruptive to the realization of immanent social order.

Having said this we can recognize other societies than our own in which the religious sensibility has made perhaps a greater contribution than we are accustomed to. Our traditional criticisms of the Hindu social system, for example, are largely based upon the fact that we are much more sympathetic to a secularizing Calvinism than to a sacralizing vision which promotes a sense of the unreality of the realm of social praxis. The interesting balance achieved in Chinese society of the classical period between the dominant neo-Confucian social system and the Taoist forms of mystical anarchism is another case in point. This kind of accommodation is reflected in our own society in the manner in which dominant forms of theological orthodoxy have existed alongside a tiny but important strain of mystical religion which, though contradicting the vision of the mainstream in important particulars, has served to express the purest strain of religious sensibility.[23]

In this chapter I have tried to show that the scientific and moral interests, and the visions of the world attendant upon them, have dominated our cultural sensorium from very nearly the beginning of our intellectual culture. That is to say, the theoretical concern for truth guaranteeing a direct relation between Appearance and Reality, on the one hand, and a desire for the control of praxis so as to maximize its efficacy in the achieving of individual and social goods, on the other, have provided the fundamental principles for the organization of our cultural aims and interests. A consequence of this fact is that the remaining cultural interests, and the imaginative modes present within them, have been construed in terms of exigencies in what have been conceived to be the relations of persons and nature (the scientific relation) and persons and society (the moral relation).

The various interactions of these two dominant interests have significantly influenced the character of our cultural milieu. The scientific influence on the moral interest is evidenced in the development of ethical and political visions expressing the fundamental meanings of individual and social activities in terms of principles of conduct. The intuitive feelings which are the putative ground of ethical behavior are rendered ancillary and, more often than not, held suspect. Ethical and political behavior of a spontaneous sort is eschewed in favor of actions which either appeal to normative principles or are grounded in a prudent assessment of possible consequences. The moral interest impinges upon the scientific through its insistence that scientists concern themselves with the short-term achievement of specific personal and social goods. The instrumental rationality of science is stressed above its *theorial*, visionary character. The mutual disciplining of the scientific and moral interests is primarily responsible for the ubiquity of technological imperatives in contemporary society. As a complex of processes modern technology constitutes a wedding of the scientific and moral interests. Substantively considered our technological ambience is increasingly identified as both *physis* and *praxis* and, as such, may be seen to constitute both our "natural" and moral environs.

The intersection of the moral and scientific interests in contemporary society has seriously challenged the continued efficacy of art, religion, and philosophy. In our highly organized society the scientific concern leads to the intense specialization of cultural interests which, in turn, requires the relative detachment of these interests one from the other. The moral interest further ramifies this situation by influencing artists either to perform socially relevant activities or to accede to the relegation of their profession to the status of a ghettoized, albeit prestigious, superfluity. The moral interest combines with the scientific to influence theological enquiry away from the direct confrontation of mystical and sacred aspects of religious sensibility and toward the essentially apologetic function of legitimating specific forms of doctrinal and institutional commitments.

Under these conditions philosophy cannot but wither, detached as it is from the richness and complexity of its cultural resources. Philosophers must then have recourse to their traditional strategies of retreat: retreat into the analysis of isolated problems of language, logic, science, or the narrower forms of social praxis, or into the development of speculative visions which arise not from the concrete problematics of contemporary culture, but from the defects of other philosophic systems.

Just as is the case with our physiological senses, each of the specific interests comprising our cultural sensorium provides a distinct perspective on the world of experience. Thus the dominance of the scientific and moral sensibilities has determined that we see the world in terms of the stabilities and regularities required by moral norms and scientific laws. The ephemeral world of aesthetic experience, wherein the only norm or law is that celebrating the decay of realized perfections and the reemergence of novelty, is not one of our most fundamental concerns. Nor do we sufficiently appreciate the world of the mystic which, grounded in the experience of an interpenetrating unity, defies rational articulation. Interludes of irrational romanticism to the contrary notwithstanding, it remains a sad fact of our culture that neither the evidences of art nor of religion are given proper attention. Only through a disciplined attempt to free the aesthetic and religious impulses from the constricting influences of rational and ethical interests without thereby derogating the legitimate autonomy of these alternative interests may we begin to resort most creatively to an increased variety and richness of cultural evidences.

The problem one encounters in attempting to characterize the normative vision of culture is primarily one of evidence. One must know what evidences have in fact been used in the development of cultural self-understanding; one must also determine which evidences have been neglected. This latter determination leads to the consideration of sources of reflection and enquiry which have been insufficiently emphasized. It is essential that one not succumb to the fallacy of completeness in either of its guises—namely, either in the sense that one claims completeness with respect to evidences employed, or in the sense that one *requires* completeness in the use of evidence. Some degree of specialization is essential. The question is this, however: Has the specialized employment of evidences determined the omission of important areas of experience which may in fact be seasonally relevant in our period of cultural activity? To respond affirmatively to this question involves one in the criticism of the manner in which the inertial character of the past has overdetermined the nature of the cultural present.

The positivistic character of contemporary culture as a realm of posited, yet essentially unexamined, values expresses the failure of philosophy in its speculative mode. Philosophy is the critic of posited value, or it is nothing worthwhile. In his role as articulator of importances, the speculative philosopher confronts the condition of contemporary cultural existence and finds that some of the unexamined consequences of the dominance of the moral and scientific interests are deleterious in the extreme since they have led to the suppression of burgeoning interest in alternative modes of activity aimed at the realization of aesthetic and religious value.

Despite all of the signal achievements this specialization has permitted, the dominance of moral and scientific interests has occasioned a significantly narrowed and dulled complex of cultural experiences. The endeavor to release the aesthetic and religious sensibilities from the constraints of the scientific and moral impulses is an important cultural imperative. By performing this task contemporary philosophy can lay claim to its distinctive importance. Thus it is primarily the responsibility of the contemporary philosopher of culture to articulate the importance of aesthetic and religious interests, thus enriching our cultural expressions by enabling us to draw upon the width of civilized experience.

CHAPTER TWO
UTOPIA AND UTILITY

For both Plato and Aristotle, the ideal of human existence was contemplation (θεωρια). And the life of *theoria* is to be carefully distinguished from the *theoretical* enterprise. Though the strictly theoretical visions of Plato and Aristotle were clearly germane to the sphere of praxis, both the intuition of the Form of the Good and the activity of self-reflexive thinking are nonpraxial. Thinking, as a rational enterprise open to systematic articulation, and *theoria*, as the dialectical or self-referential consequence of thinking, are qualitatively distinct. By employing theoretical activity as a means of realizing the ends of *theoria*, the founders of rational activity in the West demonstrated the instrumental character of what has come to be known as theory.

We have accepted the instrumental character of reasoning at the theoretical level but, contrary to the genius of both Plato and Aristotle, have employed this instrument reductively rather than in a teleological fashion. That is, theoretical development has promoted the organization and control of contingencies in the sphere of praxis. The subsequent history of the relations of theoria and praxis is foreshadowed in the refusal to accept theorial contemplation as the end of theoretical activity. The intrinsic connections of theory and practice, whether construed in terms of the preeminence of theoretical activity aimed at practical application, or in terms of practical actions which give rise to theoretical articulations, have constituted a grand short-circuiting of the normative function of theoria. For theoria is, above all, obedient to that sense of eros which lures toward completeness of understanding.

The recognition of speculative wonder as the source of philosophic thinking is closely related to the claim that the highest form of self-realization is to be found in the life of contemplation. The fate of the activity of wonder as a beginning point of philosophic reflection is well-known. Historically, the dialectical tensions between speculation and dogmatism have provided the major dynamic for the development of theoretical understandings. Speculation has given rise to dogma and system which have eventually encountered skeptical doubt. After a brief period of skepticism a new quest for certainty has been launched via novel speculative adventures leading to yet other systems and dogmas which themselves subsequently serve as victims of skeptical doubt.

Greek philosophy, after the skepticism of the period following the collapse of the city-states, was held captive for the better part of a millenium by the dogmas of Christian and Muslim theologians. The slow erosion of the scholastic synthesis which culminated in the *quattrocento* return to humanistic values introduced a three-hundred-year transitional period. The so-called Renaissance constituted a cultural *bardo* in which the psyche of the Anglo-European wandered disincarnate until reborn in the body of emergent scientific orthodoxy.

Theological orthodoxies maintained at least a measure of the teleological emphasis of theory construed in terms of its theorial component. Though much of the theoretical energies of the theologians were spent in the apology for the authoritativeness of institutionalized religion and a great deal of the remainder was expended in the articulations of theological propositions as candidates for belief, the transcendent reference of theological reflections was explicitly maintained. Scientific orthodoxies tied the human imagination more closely to the realm of praxis through the development of physical and mechanistic models of the natural world which demanded extrapolations into the sphere of praxis. And though the direct relations of scientific theory and technological practice were not exploited for at least a century after the development of Newtonian orthodoxy, our current technological society is clear testimony to the fact that the transition from theoria to theory has as its immanent genius the substitution of technological management of our natural and social ambience for dispassionate contemplation as the desired route to self-actualization.

The growth of experience characterized in terms of increasing rationalization is at once a story of the greatness and the tragedy of our culture. The greater mastery of our world through increased mastery of systematic language should obviously not be looked upon with scorn. The difficulty is that the rationalizing trend has been unrestrained and has long ago overreached its ideal limits. These limits are set by the necessity to maintain the theorial dimension of experience which alone can serve as the means of preventing the reduction of cultural activity to the sphere of concrete praxis.

What is raised by this discussion is the general question of the varying functions of theory and theoria in terms of their efficacy for cultural self-understanding. The general answer is clear from the nature of the argument that has preceded this discussion: to wit, theory in its most recognizable guises is a special form of praxis hardly distinguishable from the practical and instrumental activities that are traditionally known as *practice*.

Materialistic and naturalistic visions of the origins of theory associated with such philosophers as Marx and Dewey seem perfectly correct if one accepts as normative the narrowest meanings of theory. Strictly systematic theory is more often than not an ideological epiphenomenon functioning apologetically with respect to current modes of practice. Thus theory is practical by definition if one means no more by theoretical endeavor than that systematic, principled form of thinking shaped by the desire for application.

It may seem somewhat paradoxical to claim that theories per se have a practical function when the history of theoretical reflection supports the generalization that cosmological theories are stipulations of mythical visions which deal only indirectly with the concrete pragmatics of practical existence. But the cosmogonic myths and the cosmological theories that developed from them were strategems for handling very practical problems associated with the experience of contingency and the sense of alienation from the natural world. The myths of cosmogenesis are myths of construal which provide models for the organization and control of our natural ambience. These myths, along with the symbolic behavior of formal rituals, provided a matrix for the spiritual securing of our natural ambience and its supernatural counterpart transcending the actual circumstances of the mythopoetic thinkers. The transition from the aims of theoria to those of theory was occasioned by the need for the immanent control of one's environs. As we have come to know it, the sphere of praxis is that realm which exists somewhere east of Eden, within which occurs the outworking of the alienated relationship of the human individual from the natural world which gave birth to him.

Because of the praxial grounding of mythical and theoretical activities among the ancestors of our Anglo-European heritage, we should not be surprised to find that all our forms of theorizing have been held captive to types of cosmological speculation motivated by the aims of rational control. If the cosmological models gained for mythical resources are to be seen in terms of the relationship between the necessary existence of a

Creator and the contingent existences of the created order, then the assumptions of the rational coherence of that order (i.e., the assumption that the world is an ordered cosmos) will form the basis of all theoretical reflections which qualify as scientific in any meaningful sense.

Moral reasonings and practice will be grounded upon the assumption of a common nature in accordance with which actions may be rationalized, or the existence of a source of formal or teleological principles which ground ethical activity, or at the very least upon the assumption of the efficacy of volitional activity as itself capable of bringing order into the sphere of social existence. These scientific and moral assumptions have their sources in the cosmogonic myths of construal of cosmos from chaos. Rational principles, then, are instances of the stipulation and ramification of aspects of these cosmogonies and the cosmological visions founded upon them.

The instrumental and utilitarian aspects of theory are of course derived from the moral and scientific impulses which theory best satisfies. The inclusion of aesthetic and religious sensibilities each on its own terms would provide a visionary aspect to thought which would again introduce the theorial component into the nature of thinking per se. The adjustment of the utility of thinking and its utopian impulses is the task of the philosopher of culture. This adjustment is nothing more or less than the attempt to provide a harmonious balance of the various interests which direct and discipline our cultural energies.

We can discover in the very beginnings of theory, both historically and in terms of any particular act of theoretical reflection, the contemplative and participative motivations of theoria. The initial motivation in theoretical acts seems to be determined by the desire to achieve a certain adequacy in the rendering of experience. But throughout the various stages of the history of theory, the motivation toward adequacy has been met with a challenge from another, equally significant, motivation: the concern for logical consistency. That the claims of adequacy and consistency are so often at odds with one another is perhaps most obvious in the history of speculative theory.

The fact that in order to mean some things we must avoid meaning some other things (namely, the contradictories of the first set of meanings) seems obvious. But the attempt to avoid contradictions leads inevitably to the exclusion of experiences or claims about experience which are consistent with alternative explanations of the way of things that, by virtue of their internal consistency and applicability to the world of experience, have an equal claim to be counted as theory. The suggestive, metaphorical, merely allusive aspects of our theorial or contemplative understandings lose adequacy when articulated in the form of a consistent theory. But the gain in consistency increases the relevance of the theory to the sphere of praxis. A scientific theory which promoted contradictory understandings of the world would not be as readily employable in the construction of technical devices instantiating the theory, nor could a theory which enjoined contradictory actions be said to serve the practical interests of a public morality.

Whatever the intrinsic satisfactions of paradox and mystery, they are not proper grounds for the application of theory to the interest of the control of praxis. Theorial contemplation cannot be stressed to the degree that theoretical systematization is if the dominant motivations of cultural expression are not grounded upon eros, the drive toward wholeness of understanding, but rather are impelled by the desire to overcome an alien world.

The interlude constituted by classical mechanistic science is to be seen not just as a way in which the mechanical model of nature developed from out of formalist and teleological understandings associated with the Greek origins of natural philosophy but equally as a revolution in the functions of theory. The theorial or contemplative component of theory was still dominant in the speculations of the Greeks. Scholastic philosophy introduced the conceptions of rationality and system as guarantors of the truth of theological propositions. But the reference of most of the theologians of the Middle Period was to a Transcendent Reality which precluded the exhaustive analysis of truth in terms of systematic rationality. That which is true, insofar as it is also important to the aim of human salvation, could be appropriated through faith grounded in revelation. Modern science was born when the stress of theoretical activity was placed upon the immanent character of the natural world perceived to be in some sense complete unto itself. The Cartesian separation of matter, soul and God grounded a purely rational and analytic approach to the natural world. Newton's deistic interpretation of God's relation to the world functioned in the same manner.

The revolution in understanding occurred in part because the mechanistic perspective allowed for the construction of models which were then immediately intuitable as having descriptive functions. It is not obviously true to ordinary consciousness how the world might in fact be actually made of numbers or mathematical relations—that is, patterns or structures not visible or palpable. A mathematical or formal model of the nature of things is obviously difficult to grasp as true of the actual state of nature. It is otherwise with a machine. At the level of sensation, the world may indeed be grossly experienced as a complex of externally

related parts causally related one to another. Thus, the dynamic interpretation of the geometrical insights of Descartes provided an extremely
efficacious metaphor in terms of which to understand the nature of the
physical world. That it was soon forgotten that this model was in fact but
a model is perhaps both a cause and a consequence of the fact that the
tendency to take visions of the world literally developed *pari passu* with
the growth of scientific orthodoxy.[1]

The conflict of Galileo and the church was not simply a conflict over
how one might best see the natural world from a theoretical point of
view. "It was not simply a new theory of the nature of the celestial
movements that was feared, but a new theory of the nature of theory;
namely, that, if a hypothesis saves all the appearances, it is identical with
truth."[2] However much Descartes, Galileo, and Newton might have been
guilty of forgetting the metaphorical character of their theoretical
models, and however much the conception of "literal truth" might have
captured the imaginations of subsequent thinkers, twentieth-century
science and philosophy have in many ways returned to the view that success in "saving the appearances" does not strictly guarantee the truth of
a theory. Conventionalisms, operationalisms, behaviorisms, instrumen-
talisms, all have abandoned this classical conception of truth as
guaranteed by an isomorphism of theoretical propositions and the facts
of the natural world. The increasing narrowness of the theoretical activities of scientists has led to a situation in which theory, as a systematic,
coherent, consistent articulation of the nature of things (already an extreme narrowing of the theoretical vision which found its satisfaction in
contemplation), has itself been placed under attack.

Behaviorism advertises itself as a "technology of behavior"
characterizable in terms of just a few fundamental propositions which
themselves do not require organization in terms of theory in any ordinary
sense. Behavioral techniques are like tools which function in the repair
and construction of machines without recourse to diagrams or models of
a "theoretical" sort. Conventionalist understandings maintain a
theoretical emphasis, but give up the hope for adequacy in the most
general sense. Conventionalists accede to incompatibility among distinctive theoretical formulations provided the alternative theories are fruitful
within their separate spheres of application.

Such challenges to the classical notion of theory have not occasioned a
return to the theorial attitude if for no other reason than that the element
of participation is missing in the contemporary attitude. True, the
observer has been put back into the scene in quantum and relativity
theory, but as yet he has only been mechanically reintroduced.[3] And the

mode of his interaction with phenomena is primarily construed as the constituting presence which defines the frame of reference within which phenomena are to be encountered. This anthropocentric construal of the mode of participation of the individual in his natural ambience is but a return to the Protagorean principle. This is, of course, the very opposite of what was meant by theoria as passive reception of the world.

If we are to find a sphere of intellectual activity within which the challenge to theory is such as to stimulate a return to the theorial function of thinking we shall likely have to look beyond the special sciences if for no other reason than that the more sophisticated of the arguments concerning the epistemology of psychology or physics are not apt to influence general cultural understandings overmuch. There is a broader kind of critique going on, of course, in the work of such individuals as Thomas Kuhn, P. K. Feyerabend, and N. R. Hanson who have argued for the understanding of theories as paradigms for research activity which have a limited life expectancy and which cannot, therefore, primarily serve to point us to the Truth. This kind of anaylsis, however, like the notion of the complementarity of theoretical formulations, merely serves to reinforce the interpretation of scientific theory as an instrument or tool of praxis rather than as a means of dispassionate understanding.

The development of our theoretical understandings in Anglo-European culture can perhaps best be seen as a parody of Plato's normative vision of the ideal progress of human knowledge provided in his "divided-line" model of the dimensions of knowing. If we are to grasp the true nature and import of this parody of Platonic thought, however, it is essential that we understand that Plato himself at times participated in it.

Presupposing the sense of eros which he saw driving individuals toward the attainment of wholeness of understanding, Plato critiqued the various ways of knowing evidenced at the level of human praxis. Some minimal knowledge must be claimed for those modes of entertaining the world associated with fanciful and imagistic activities. Vague understandings are adumbrated in ill-formed guesses, transitory impressions, and secondhand opinions. A certain degree of clarity and cogency is gained if we are able to exploit important regularities in our experience of the world, directing them toward the achievement of some practical end. Technical knowledge allows us to achieve specific goals even if we remain ignorant of the principles undergirding these regularities and these ends. Knowledge is attained, however, only when we are able to articulate principles of understanding.

This articulation begins with the proposal of hypotheses as principled explanations and interpretations of experience and activity. These hypotheses constitute *reasons* and are superior to techniques accepted simply because of their pragmatic value. General theories which permit the testing of hypothetical understandings provide the hope for the final claims to true knowledge. The culmination of the act of knowing requires the construction of a system of principles whose consistency, coherence, and efficacy in organizing and interpreting more limited understandings are functions of a single principle. This single principle, the Good, is the source and goal of that eros which grounds the search for completeness of understanding.

For Plato the fundamental philosophic problematic was to be understood in terms of the contrast between the manyness of the world at the level of concrete praxis and the unity of the realm of being and knowing whose source and ground was the Form of the Good. That no philosopher, returning to the sphere of praxis, has been able to demonstrate what the final systematic understanding would entail, and has not, therefore been able to make good the claim to systematic completeness of understanding, has not undermined the intuition of eros. Though we have in the main forgone the quest for certainty, the quest for completeness of understanding continues.

The flight from certainty which characterizes the greater part of our contemporary philosophic enterprise is complemented by a flight to the mystical sense of wholeness that lies beyond propositional conflict. Though "eros returned" must always be embarrassed by the partiality and contradictions of thinking at the level of praxis, there is yet the lure toward wholeness which is immediately expressed in the activity of the mystic and is implicit in the activity of thinking at any level. For the irreducible paradox of all responsible enquiry, whether explicitly acknowledged or not, is that it must proceed in accordance with the presupposition of wholeness or completeness of understanding. And though the testimony of that adventure in thinking we know as philosophy is that this assumption is at best heuristic, it nonetheless has served as the sine qua non of thought itself.

The sense of eros as the controlling dynamic of intellectual activities has often been ignored by those who would lay claim to knowledge. Each of the dimensions of knowledge has been employed as a means of establishing putative certainty. It is not only the systematic rationalist in the guise of scientist, theologian, or philosopher who has claimed certainty. Poets shouldering baskets of metaphor, sophistic politicians and religious fanatics armed with ideologies of true belief, have each mocked eros through their claims to dogmatic finality.

Putative claims to completeness of understanding, even those skeptical claims to the effect that no completeness is possible, are consequences of failed eros. But what are the consequences of eros which does not fail? The actualized philosopher, returning from the solitariness of cell or study, warmed by the ecstatic intuition of wisdom occasioned by the sense of eros, faces a world patterned by the failures of understanding. How ought he respond?

This question is difficult to answer because, though we are accustomed to rehearsing the ascent of the ladder of knowledge from perception to systematic completeness, we have little understanding of the proper mode of descent. The philosopher who returns to the world energized by the erotic sense, like the bodhisattva who returns from the place of his enlightenment to enlighten the world, "sees" differently. It is this difference we must try to understand. For if we do we shall be able to revision the philosophic task and to reassess the character of our cultural experience which is consequent upon alterations in the cultural sensorium.[4]

Plato seems to have two principal routes of descent from the intuition of unity which grounds his philosophic project. The first stresses the adequacy of his conceptual formulations and leads, if necessary, to the imposition of doctrinal orthodoxy upon those unwilling or unable to yield to rational suasion. The second, which has been largely ignored by Plato's expositors, requires that the transcendent reference of theoretical doctrines be maintained and that the aim of philosophic activity be a realization of the end of eros beyond the reach of doctrinal formulations. The first route of descent is strictly utilitarian in that it seeks to construe the realm of concrete praxis in accordance with the most general of philosophic principles. The second route is the utopian way which eschews the ultimacy of doctrinal formulations and affirms theoria as the *telos* of theoretical activity. The complex interweaving of these two strands of Platonic philosophy presents one of the most formidable difficulties in the interpretation of Plato's thinking and, indeed, of philosophic thinking per se.

These two strands of interpretation result from the ambiguous status of the Principle of the Good. The Good, which constitutes the apex of Plato's general philosophic vision, serves as both an abstract principle and a concrete intuition. As concept, the Form of the Good is the principle of normative measure permitting the philosopher to sort out the elements of theory and practice in accordance with a criterion which is both objective and axiological. As intuited, the Good grounds the experience of unity which lies "beyond being" and shares the ineffability of all such experiences.

The difficulty in claiming that the concept of the Good and its intuition are somehow connected lies in the fact that the forms of entertainment of the notion seem categorically distinct. The fact of the matter, however, is that the propositional form of the notion is meant to serve as the *occasion* for the experience of the unity and completeness of understanding and, as such, no specific conceptual form of it is essential. In other words, the philosopher's quest for wholeness of understanding, which proceeds initially by way of concepts and propositions, does not reach its fulfillment in any concept, or system of concepts, but in the intuition which the conceptual activity elicits. Thus a fundamental principle of Plato's philosophy is the presumption that the kind of experience associated with the mystic is connected to the philosopher's quest in a very real way.

Plato's *Seventh Letter* provides perhaps the best discussion of such an intrinsic connection. Philosophic understanding of the most significant sort cannot, for Plato, be contained within static verbal forms. No doctrine can express true wisdom. Philosophic understanding is a kind of insight which, "like a blaze kindled by a leaping spark . . . is generated in the soul and at once becomes self-sustaining."[5] This self-sustaining insight provides the ground for understanding the inadequacy of language enabling one to see through the propositional forms of expression to the essential character of what is real. Because of its inadequacy, "no intelligent man will ever put into language those things his reason has contemplated, especially not into a form that is unalterable."[6] The decidedly alterable forms of dialogue and mythopoetic language provide for that kind of participation of mind with mind through which a "leaping spark" may kindle the blaze of philosophic understanding.

We are presently examining the activity of the individual who, ablaze with philosophic understanding, confronts the realm of the unenlightened. It is important to recognize that Plato would not endorse any attempt to avoid the rigorous construction of philosophic doctrine. Understanding is consequent upon "practicing detailed comparisons of names and definitions and visual and other sense perceptions, . . . scrutinizing them in benevolent disputation by use of question and answer without jealousy."[7] Philosophic understanding is not the result of avoiding reason but of transcending it. The hard work of the philosopher is not expressed in a straining after truth through prayer and meditation, but in the difficult disciplines of analysis and dialectical disputation. But nowhere is it suggested by Plato that any verbal formula or systematic construction in propositional form constitutes the essence of philosophic wisdom. The aim toward clarity and systematic wholeness is essential to the discipline of the philosopher since these aims undergird the rigor of his pursuit. The goal, however, is not to be realized within, but beyond, system and science.

Most philosophers are perfectly willing to give lip service to the visionary character of Plato's thought but characteristically ignore the hermeneutical consequences of their concession when they approach his specific doctrines. Fundamentally, Plato's dialogues are exercises which prepare us for that "leaping spark" that will kindle understanding. If we accept the Platonic corpus as a congeries of doctrines with greater or lesser utility in the sphere of praxis we shall have directed our thinking in precisely the wrong direction. It is the utopian rather than utilitarian character of Plato's doctrines that is most relevant to true understanding. And the utopian character of Platonism does not lie in its ideal constructions of social and political institutions, but is principally to be found in the theorial ground presupposed by all philosophic activity.

The form of the philosopher's engagement with the world is that of *dialogue*. The art of the dialogue is, of course, quite distinct from that of the debate. Debate has as its aim the furtherance of one vision at the expense of the other. Dialogue (*dia-logos*) is a "talking through" aiming at that kind of clarity which permits the communication of truth. The philosopher is explicitly armed only with the tools of rational suasion. If he is not successful in making his case through the form of the dialogue, then he has no recourse but to remain open to further enquiry.

If we examine the return of the philosopher to the sphere of public praxis armed with the intuition of wholeness we find that this first step away from the immediate grasp of the real leads him into the world of conflicting theoretical understandings. From the purely conceptual perspective the explanation of such complexity is to be found in the abstract, partial, and overly specialized character of these conflicting points of view. Conflicts of scientific theories argue for a science of the sciences, a general theory which will locate the specialized theories as instances, or components, of the more general vision. Metaphysics is the science which aims to unite the various ways of knowing.

The embarrassment occasioned by the conflict of metaphysical views leads to the argument that alternative philosophic visions which make conflicting claims are products of differential abstractive emphases resulting from an acceptance of distinctive levels of insight. Plato's criticisms of his philosophical peers were based upon his notion of the levels of the clarity of knowledge. The atomists and materialists, for example, were condemned for theorizing from the perspective of physical sense impressions. Images suggestive of things or objects in the world formed the basis from which these philosophers theorized. The Sophists were but little better, establishing their philosophic claims to general understanding (to the extent that these critics of metaphysics made such claims) upon "belief." Theirs was a technical understanding which taught individuals how to win a case in court or how to win the admiration of their fellows. The mathematical speculations of the Pythagorean community exemplified understandings at the level of hypothetical and specialized knowledge. Any claims to general understanding from this perspective were inadequate since they were untested in accordance with the criterion of completeness.

Platonism confronts its most serious embarrassment when its rational arguments do not succeed in persuading others of the fundamental importance of the Platonic vision. There seems to be no way of making good the claim to completeness of understanding if it is impossible to convince one's philosophic rivals of the superiority of Platonic thought as the normative ground of speculative enquiry. The relativity of metaphysical systems, already emergent during the career of Plato, counts heavily against the ultimacy of systematic unity as characteristic of what is most real. There is no other means than the appeal to rational dialectic to realize agreement among philosophers. In the absence of that agreement the Platonist is left with the unavoidable relativity of knowledge claims.

Stepping to the level of knowledge grounded in ideological belief, the response must be to demonstrate a connection between propositional claims made with the subjective form of belief and theoretical statements which can appeal to rational principles for their defense. But the hope for the justification of belief is undermined by the Sophistic insight that irreconcilable theoretical conflicts which prevent the organization of the special sciences ensure that any ideological claim can receive theoretical justification. Conflicting theories justify conflicting ideologies. It seems quite legitimate to seek the unification of beliefs by appeal to theoretical contexts, but in fact the end result is a hardening of the conflicting positions. Each opinion, having found the respectability of rational justification, has increased apologetic force.

Viewing the chaos of images and impressions of the world of relatively private experience, the Platonist will demonstrate that there is some relationship between the world of these imaginations and fancies and the public consensual world of beliefs. But since the conflict of theories has undermined the unity of beliefs, there is nothing short of a political means of bringing the private world of images and vague biases into some coherent order. It is at this level that the poignance of the Platonic quest for unity of understanding is best seen. In the *Republic*, the educational program includes the strictest of censorships of poetry, myth, and the intuitions of the artists as a means of preventing some of the ideological conflicts which might otherwise occur.

One way of envisioning the return of the philosopher, then, is in terms of the failure of systematic philosophy to unite the spheres of theoria and praxis and the ultimate necessity for the philosopher to accede to political power as a means of attaining that systematic unity in the polis that could not be won through rational persuasion. This is, perhaps, the most fashionable reading of Plato. The trouble with such an understanding is that it forces one to ignore Plato's explicit demurrers concerning the adequacy of his doctrinal formulations. Moreover, it requires the omission of the spirit of the *Seventh Letter*, with its explicitly mystical overtones and its radical critique of the inadequacies of written philosophy.

Unquestionably, Plato himself is largely responsible for being so often understood as a dogmatic thinker. Moreover, the dogmatic strain in Plato's thought is not merely to be found at the level of this or that doctrine, but is discoverable at the most fundamental level of his philosophy. We recall that in the *Phaedo*, Plato has Socrates roundly criticize certain of the *physiologoi* because "they do not think anything is really bound and held together by goodness or moral obligation."[8] Again, in the *Philebus*, Socrates insists that one must oppose anyone who "asserts that the world is . . . devoid of order."[9] Plato's Cosmos was created by the Craftsman who ensured that "there is and ever will be one only-begotten and created heaven."[10] An infamous passage in Book X of the *Laws* provides severe penalties for impiety, which principally involves the denial that the cosmos is ordered according to "what is best." The purpose of these penalties (five years imprisonment for the first offense; death and burial outside the gates of the city for a subsequent impiety) was to render *practically unthinkable* the opinions of the *physiologoi*, first that whatever order the world has is wholly natural and immanent, and second that an infinite plurality of worlds (*kosmoi*) exists, either serially in time or contemporaneously in infinite space.[11] Clearly, one of the more important themes of Plato's philosophy involved the defense of the notion of a single-ordered cosmos against the view that there are many world-orders.

Here we encounter Plato unconsciously parodying himself. For the temptation to identify the wholeness promised by eros with the cosmological unity of a single-ordered world was too great even for Plato to withstand. The modesty and humility which at times led him to characterize his cosmological speculation as only "a likely story" and to assert that the Form of the Good lies "beyond Being" are forgotten whenever he insists that the actual world is one. And though we must postpone until a later chapter[12] a detailed discussion of the consequences of this claim, we may note at this point that all of the fashionable criticisms of Plato as a totalitarian thinker who opposes the promotion of a free and open society are grounded in the fact that his insistence upon eros as a drive toward wholeness of understanding is at times waveringly combined with an equally strong insistence upon a merely *cosmological* unity defining the end of eros. We shall have occasion to see, again later in this essay, that eros is simply not adequately characterizable in cosmological terms.

An alternative strain of interpretation is suggested by Plato when he appeals to the tentativeness of his doctrinal formulations and, as a consequence, resorts to the use of *irony* as the essential mode of philosophic communication. The proper response to the actual limitations qualifying every finite quest for ideal wisdom is neither skeptical surrender nor the dogmatic claim that finality has been reached. The only fruitful attitude is one of irony which promotes the sense that though one is on the road to a final destination the character of which makes the journey worthwhile, the failure actually to reach the goal does not cancel the desire to seek it.

It is difficult for some to accept the fact that there are some questions which cannot receive adequate answers, but which nonetheless function as essential possessions of every thinking being. Asking questions can thus be an end in itself. A question, that is to say, may be the "answer." And although the most important questions we can entertain probably have no ultimately satisfying answers, unless we *assume* such an ultimate answer we shall not be motivated to ask the question in the first place.

The fundamental anxieties occasioned by seeking but not finding, journeying but not arriving, can be allayed if we say to ourselves, "There is no answer, and those who believe that there is are fools." We can as easily avoid this anxiety by claiming, "I have the answer, and those who disagree with me are fools." But the response which leads one to say, "Asking the question is the answer, but only because there is an unrealized, perhaps unrealizable answer which makes my question a real question," is closest to the proper philosophic response. The mood in which one can experience the importance of this proposition is the mood of irony. For irony is but the recognition of that self-referential inconsistency which, beyond our powers to explain why, constitutes a primary fact about our world.

Understood ironically, then, philosophy in the most general sense aims at a reductio ad absurdum of any and all dogmatic claims to finality while nonetheless advertising the experience of eros which dignifies the aim at completeness of understanding. It is irony that humbles our claims to erotic success while the sense of eros prevents this irony from degenerating into cynicism and despair. Ideals serve to frustrate our need to decide. At times we are tempted by the quixotic decision to rush into battle because in our haste to resolve our doubts we experience, "They *could be* giants" as "They *are* giants." But the Hamlet in us could never suffer the embarrassment of mistaking windmills for giants. Hamlet's experience of the disquieting parity of alternatives for action precluded his making a timely decision.

Are we ever absolutely satisfied when we exclude alternatives and ground our actions on only one among a number of possible modes of endeavor? On the other hand, are we ever really justified in withholding actions, refusing to decide in order to give each possibility an equal claim upon us? The ambiguous ground separating Hamlet and Don Quixote provides the space where eros and irony interplay. Eros lures us toward the realm of theoria, toward the completeness of understanding; irony calls us back to the sphere of praxis where all claims to completeness are judged faulty.

He who is possessed by the sense of eros is oppressed by the finitude of actuality; but he is equally burdened by the insubstantiality of the realm of infinite possibility. Eros urges upon us the intuition of completeness and harmony and then mocks every attempt at the concrete actualization of this insight. Why should this be so? It is likely because we have misconstrued the goals of understanding as theory rather than theoria. If this is so it is because, first, we have not attuned ourselves sufficiently to the contribution of aesthetic and religious experiencing as media through which we come to grasp the end of eros, and, second, because even when we provide a place for the evidences of art and religion we seem to arrange those evidences in terms of a mistaken hierarchy of value.

He who is without the challenge and the comfort of religious and aesthetic sensibilities reduces the theorial sense of eros to the theoretical articulation of propositions and facts serving to organize the realm of praxis. Plato as systematic philosopher is the patron saint of all those who wish so to construe the world. But for those who see farther into the Platonic sensibility, far enough at least to see that aesthetic and religious harmonies are evoked as transcending experiences promoting the sense of a vision beyond systematization, whose articulation must always be recognized as but a "likely story," Plato must also be seen as the champion of something very like a *mystical* perspective.

It is precisely when Plato's philosophy is treated as a congeries of doctrines that it is most perniciously misunderstood. The permanent heritage of Plato's philosophy is to be found in the sophisticated interplay of eros and irony in his thought. The failure to recognize this interplay is both a fundamental cause and a primary consequence of that narrowness in the selection of cultural evidences against which I have been arguing from the beginning of this essay.

"Knowledge and virtue are one," claimed Socrates. And ignorance is the fundamental form of vice. To know the truth is to do the truth. But if true knowledge involves awareness of one's ignorance, are then the wise but more sensitive to their vices? The irony here is both direct and subtle. Claims to positive knowledge involve a kind of pretension which can only serve the ends of vice. But we cannot avoid such pretension if we wish to claim knowledge of anything. The rationale of knowing, therefore, can only be found in the seeking. "The road is better than the inn," stated the ironic Cervantes, a true spiritual in-law of Socrates. That we cannot travel continually, but must pause for refreshment along the way, is one of the essential ironies of the truly human life.

Even Socrates claimed to possess some positive knowledge. At several points in the dialogues we find him stating that he is an expert on the subject of love.[13] The juxtaposition of Socrates' claim that he knows only that he does not know, and his assertion that he is an expert on eros, illumines the very essence of Socratic irony. The desire for Beauty and for Wisdom are the two faces of that eros which drives toward completeness. Ignorance is the precondition of the desire for knowledge. The truly wise man has no need of eros. Only he who knows that he is ignorant can directly experience the meaning of eros both as love of wisdom and desire for beauty. Having attained both noetic and aesthetic ignorance, Socrates has moved beyond mere pretense to knowledge and realized the meaning of love.

One is here tempted to state that Socrates has the first and the last word on the subject of the relationship among ignorance, eros, and irony, the understanding of which is the sine qua non of the philosophic sensibility. Both true knowledge and true ignorance involve the recognition of limits. We can, perhaps, better understand the character of this recognition if we recall one of the main arguments of Plato's *Phaedrus*. In this work, an understanding of the nature of philosophic activity is presented in terms of a discussion of the meaning of love. The philosophic rationale for eros experienced at the sensual level is that whereas the form of Truth cannot be the object of sense experience, that of Beauty can. Love, as desire for beauty, is initially experienced toward the sensitivity to Form-Itself. Love as the desire for beauty occasioned by the beloved is a precondition for finally yielding to the eros character of existence which lures one toward the Form of Forms.

Knowledge is characterized in part by the recognition of the limits of embodied existence. At the mundane level of human praxis this recognition is expressed through the ironic sensibility. If we look more closely at the meaning of this sensibility we find that it is grounded in the experience of the tension occasioned by contradictions lying at the very heart of things. The antinomies of the finite and the infinite, of body and spirit, of time and eternity, of reason and experience, are simply not open to resolution as long as one recognizes the true limits of discursive knowledge. Irony is the acceptance of those limits. Eros, in its ultimate significance, drives us beyond these limits and beyond, therefore, discursive understanding. But even the discussion of the meaning and significance of eros must be undertaken in the ironic mood. For philosophic activity proceeds at the level of praxis.

At its most fundamental level irony does not involve pretense or dissimulation, it only appears to do so because the expression of real ironies involves the accession to contradiction. Thus the Socratic claim to ignorance was a claim to knowledge—the knowledge of limits. The Socratic claim to knowledge (the knowledge of love) was a claim to ignorance—the claim that he did not possess the object of his desire. Socrates does not pretend to be ignorant, he is so. His knowledge of love is the desire for completeness of understanding grounded in the absence of the object of that desire. What is knowledge if not the realization of limits? This is what we realize when we claim that the most important questions are important not by virtue of their having answers but by virtue of their guiding eros in its unending quest for wholeness. Irony involves no pretense. The contradictions are real. And such contradictions are the very stuff of which we and our worlds are made.

Part of the reason we are apt to interpret Socratic irony as mere pretense or understatement is that we are not clear about the relationship between Plato and his mentor. If we assume that Socrates's claims to knowledge are coextensive with those of Plato, even in the early dialogues, then Socratic humility must seem limited indeed. But Plato and Socrates are two different individuals, however intertwined they may be in the Platonic corpus. It hardly seems necessary to embark upon a quest for the historical Socrates to grasp the effect that Plato's role as student, disciple, and biographer of Socrates had upon his philosophic vision.

The heuristic assumption grounding the treatment of Plato and Socrates throughout this work is that the only views we may be reasonably sure belonged to Socrates are those which are consistent with the claims that ground his ironic stance—namely, that what he knows is that he does not know, that he is an expert in eros, and that knowledge and virtue are one. The rest is Plato. But what else is there? The cosmological doctrines of the *Timaeus* and the *Critias*, the logical and metaphysical analyses of the *Sophist* and the *Parmenides*, the utopian politics of the *Republic* and the (some would say) dystopian politics of the *Laws*, and so on, and so on. Quite a bit, actually. But one might ask, "What is the relation of Plato's constructive doctrines to the vision of Socrates?" This is an important question precisely because it allows us to learn something valuable concerning the meaning of philosophic irony.

We might begin to approach this issue by noting the obvious fact that Socrates plays a varied set of roles in the dialogues. In some he is the principal, in others a passive participant, or merely an auditor. His total absence is so conspicuous in the *Laws* as, in fact, to constitute a kind of brooding presence. Emerson's term, "double star," to refer to the Socrates-Plato binary system is quite apt.[14] The true sense of philosophic irony is that which is immanent in Platocratic philosophy. For the tensions that exist between the Socratic and Platonic sensibilities are paradigm illustrations of the fundamental tensions which have given rise to our cultural self-consciousness in its classical and contemporary forms.

If we understand irony as providing the basis for a both-and type of understanding, we shall have a means of interpreting the relations of Plato and Socrates that will illumine the ironic nature of philosophy itself. First we might see that the double star comprised by Plato and Socrates forms a combination which facilitates Plato's literary and philosophic task. For like the pseudonym which allows an author to say things for which he might not wish to be held accountable, Plato's use of the Socratic character allows him to maintain a critical perspective on his own philosophy which he could not otherwise have had. Plato seems to urge us to view his thought against the background of that of his teacher. There is never a break with his master, never a definite shift away from allegiance to him. Socrates seems always to serve as the standard against which we are to judge the efforts of Plato.

If we were to take the *Republic* literally, Plato would certainly have to receive censure for many of his pedagogical and political doctrines. And on the literalistic interpretation often given to that dialogue, Socrates' forced complicity makes Plato doubly reprehensible. But there is simply no compulsion to take the dialogue at its face value. We must not forget that Plato's ideal state was said to be realizable, if at all, only in some unknown foreign land or some distant time past or future.[15] Nor should we fail to remember that we are enjoined to read the dialogue first and foremost as a psychological rather than a political treatise.

Aside from all this, ought we not allow our vision of Socrates to temper our understanding of Plato's thought? It would not lead us astray were we to believe that Plato's explicit use of Socrates is consciously intended to provide a limiting context within which his doctrinal views are to be interpreted. Socrates' presence in the *Republic* signals us that it must not be taken simply as a straightforward political tract, but is to be understood ironically. Likewise, Socrates' absence altogether from the *Laws* suggests that this dialogue is not per se ironic. It is, of course, our option to take the dialogue *cum grano salis* by virtue of the purposeful exclusion from it of Plato's philosophic conscience.

Surely it is clear that if, as some have suggested, Plato had simply grown cranky and dogmatic in his old age and had produced the *Laws* as a repudiation of the utopian idealism of his early and middle years, he would have either sought to repress, or at least to criticize, his characterization of Socrates as free enquirer. But he did not. And the fact that Socrates would likely have met the same fate in a society patterned by the *Laws* as he met at the hands of the Athenian state does not, I take it, constitute a repudiation of the thought and values of Socrates. It seems more sensible to believe that Plato wishes his readers to keep the figure of Socrates in mind as they read the *Laws*. If they do, then the juxtaposition of the *Republic* as ideal and the *Laws* as "realistic" permits us to experience the poignance of the attempt to apply theory directly to the sphere of concrete praxis.

Plato has provided us with two alternatives. We can envision an ideal society which can only be realized through dialectical persuasion and, thus (given the irrational compulsions of brute circumstance), is impossible or we can construct a society of laws sanctioned by force through which the values and principles that lure us toward the truly human life find no expression. The message is clear. The tensions between the actual and the ideal, between praxis and theoria, cannot be resolved theoretically. It is this fact which determines that the sense of irony must accompany every yielding to the lure of eros.

Such a reading of Plato allows us to take his first- and second-best states in a sense perhaps intended by their author but which could not be so well expressed by rhetorical devices such as qualification and demurrer. In one sense it does not matter greatly whether Plato consciously intended such a reading (though I cannot avoid the belief that in fact he did). He is definitely open to this kind of interpretation if for no other reason than that he has done such a good job in providing a vision of the open, enquiring, ironic Socrates whom we can employ as a mitigating influence upon the more severe of the Platonic doctrines which we might otherwise be forced to take solely at face value.

What philosopher possessed of a finely tuned sensitivity to the complex tensions, incongruities, and contradictions of the realm of praxis might not wish to have a rhetorical device allowing him to say more than one thing at the same time? What philosopher in addition to the humility and modesty he might display in his prefaces and his footnotes would not like to have his own built-in critic, a kind of supplemental conscience allowing his work to be appreciated for the greatness of its errors as well as for the excellence of his constructive ideas?[16] Would the understanding of Plato be as deep and as broad were it not for his severe critics? Could his critics be as severe were it not for the example of Socrates? We can certainly enjoy the dramatic irony of the fact that the crusading anti-platonist Karl Popper holds Socrates in unparalleled esteem—the same Socrates who is Plato's literary gift to the world! Is it too much to believe that Plato, somewhere amongst the shades (or perhaps fixed in a peculiarly immanent relation to the vision of Beauty and the Good), is most pleased with the mixed reception his thought has received? Surely this philosopher, whom Western thinkers have annotated ad infinitum, would enjoy the fact that not all of the commentaries have been encomiums.

What makes Karl Popper's *The Open Society and Its Enemies* most unconvincing is that he has read Plato from the narrowest of perspectives, isolating the doctrinal consequences of the Platonic dialectic and ignoring Plato's broader vision. It is not just that Popper has treated Plato's concepts and theories out of context, he misconstrues both the relations of Plato's theoretical activity to the theorial vision which transcends systematic expression, and the effect which Plato's systematic philosophy (and here I must repeat that I mean by this term not merely the production of systems, but, more importantly, thinking that has as its immanent goal the realization of systematic coherence, but which accepts the limitations of one's own efforts insofar as a wholly adequate system has not been realized) has had upon the realization of cultural self-understanding.

Popper's inability to discern the interplay of eros and irony in Plato's thought leads him to miss the subjective form of feeling with which Plato's philosophy was produced. The interplay of these two notions in Plato and in subsequent philosophic thought provides not only a viable understanding of the intent of philosophers of Plato's ilk, but provides, as well, the proper understanding of the aesthetic attitude in terms of which philosophic speculations are to be properly understood. The claims of eros involve one in the unstinting search for the truth of the way of things. This truth, moreover, is the object of an experience transcending propositional language altogether. Irony is a necessary consequence of the ineffability of that experience at the theoretical and practical levels.

What so many critics of Plato miss is the fact that his systematic intent was continually held subject to the ironic principle that truth transcends dialectical constructions. Truth is a mystical experience which lies beyond discursive knowledge and transcends, therefore, the possibility of its actualization in the form of linguistic propositions or social institutions. The most serious charge that may be made against Plato is that he may have believed that the propositional form in which he expressed his thought could serve as the proper *way* of progressing to that point at which the experience of the Form of the Good might be possible. But to say this of Plato is to make of him merely a methodologist and to divorce his explicit concerns from any substantive intuitions of the sort which serve to render his thinking suspicious.

It is a mistake to interpret Plato as a dogmatic methodologist. Platonic irony is evidenced by the fact that though Plato was extremely suspicious of the aesthetic approach to knowledge, and voiced this suspicion in any number of ways, nonetheless he acted as an artist in his production of his principal philosophic doctrines. Popper sees the aesthetic basis of Plato's social theory very clearly, but because of his refusal to understand Plato's ironic distancing from that aesthetic mode of presentation, fails to recognize the tentative, open-ended aspect of Platonic thought. According to Popper,

> [the] extreme radicalism of the Platonic approach . . . is, I believe, connected with its aestheticism, i.e., with the desire to build a world which is not only a little better and more rational than ours, but which is free from all its ugliness; not a crazy quilt, an old garment badly patched, but an entirely new gown, a really beautiful new world . . . . But this aesthetic enthusiasm becomes valuable only if it is bridled by reason, by a feeling of responsibility, and by a humanitarian urge to help. Otherwise it is a dangerous enthusiasm, liable to develop into a form of neurosis or hysteria.[17]

This paragraph is characteristic of Popper's rather one-sided perceptiveness. He has seen what very few commentators on Plato have seen with such clarity—namely, the intrinsic connection of the aesthetic and the rational aspects of the Platonic vision. But largely because of his lack of stress upon the ironic disposition in Plato's works, this incisive perception leads to a conclusion at variance with the immanent rationale of the Platonic vision. One cannot begin to understand the subtlety of Plato's thought unless one possesses that type of humor associated with the sense of irony. This is the chief failing of Popper's critique of Plato. In defense of Popper it may be said that his criticisms, unfortunately, do not badly miss the mark if directed against Platon*ism* as opposed to Plato. For many of those who have sought to read Plato sympathetically have done so in such a way as to misunderstand, or to ignore, the ironic genius of his dialogues.

It is patently untrue that Plato lacked a sense of responsibility, or was without a humanitarian urge. It is closer to the truth to say that it was precisely because of the profound sense of responsibility that Plato introduced the element of discipline suggested by the interrelations of eros and irony into his thought. For Plato, aestheticism does not energize the moral impulse, turning it into potential hysteria; rather, art disciplines the moral sense, suggesting the tentative and allusive character of thought. The moral aims associated with the definition of justice and with the construction of a social context within which justice may be realized are transcended by the aesthetic intuitions of an order and a harmony of a kind unrealizable through the instrumental applications of reason. Together the tensions of the aesthetic and moral impulses qualifying Plato's social thought require for their appreciation the ironic sense which, as I have suggested, must be the presupposition of any responsible thinker attempting to articulate the meanings of reasoning and practice at the level of social existence.

This interpretation of Plato's thought will seem highly questionable to any who lack an ironic sense, for it is just this lack of irony which prevents one from withstanding the extreme ambiguity embodied in all theorizing. Ideal theory of the expressly utopian variety remains detached altogether from the demands of concrete praxis. However noble its ends, it is clear that one cannot "get there from here." Theories which thrive upon the blunt conformation of principles and circumstances are little more than rationalizations of current modes of practice serving only ideological and apologetic ends. The demand for "realistic" theories is based upon the judgment that the adequacy of a theory is to be assessed in accordance with its proximity to present forms of praxis. But it is dangerous to credit theories with an efficacy they do not in fact possess simply because they illustrate congruence with concrete circumstances. If it is a realistic and nonutopian vision of society we seek, on what grounds do we stop short of determinist theory?

Kurt Vonnegut has grasped the essence of determinist forms of theory in a single axiom which grounds his vision of ethics and politics:

We do, doodily do,
What we must, muddily must.

That is realism. For compared with the "muddily-do" principle, all normative theories share with "the light that never was, on sea or land" an essentially ideal character. Indeed, next to this form of realism, theories which characterize human freedom in terms of choices among significant alternatives, which seek to establish values as the basis for decisions and actions, which strive for a free rational consensus among individuals in a society, and so on are so radically utopian as to count for nothing but fanciful and harebrained schemes. The poetic and imaginary origins of that which is truly excellent in our theoretical visions are not really in dispute once we move beyond the muddily-do style of ethics and politics. Thus, from the perspective of the "realists," most philosophers are fools. Disputes among theorists, then, are disputes concerning degrees of foolishness.

The modern belief that a theory is viable only if it is germane to concrete modes of praxis is not a view shared by the Greeks, particularly not by Plato. If knowledge and virtue are one, and knowing what is right is a prerequisite to performing right actions, and knowledge is the consequence of dialectical enquiry, then Plato's theories are not to be implemented except through rational appeal. This means that the theory contains its own means of implementation by virtue of its degree of rational persuasiveness. If we read Plato in such manner as to suggest that we should rearrange the sphere of praxis through violent interference in order to bring about a better world then, rather than believe that he has given up those fundamental principles concerning the relations of theoria and practice which give his dialogues their theoretical coherence, we should seek a way of reconciling the apparent contradiction.

Such a reconciliation is achieved, at least in part, if we recognize that the utopian and utilitarian impulses in Platonic thought are necessarily in tension, but that each impulse must be recognized if we are properly to understand the world in which we exist. A suitable sense of irony, as the experience of the contradictoriness of existence, is the only means of experiencing the intrinsic connectedness of the claims of the actual and the ideal.

Although, finally, the criticisms of the type Karl Popper levels against Plato are beside the point, Popper does perform a real service by warning us implicitly (and by example) of our tendency to misconstrue the subtle nuances of philosophic thought by virtue of our narrow forms of rational and moralistic attitudes which do not permit the appreciation of the theorial background of all theoretical endeavor. It is this attitude which leads us to suspect all forms of aesthetic visioning since, having already construed art as irrelevant to the public sphere, we must believe that the sole function of the aesthetic impulse is to energize the moral aims in such manner as to exclude them from rational criticism.

I insist that I am not trying so much to defend Plato in this context as to use Plato's thought as a means of illustrating the importance of the aesthetic and mystical senses to the theoretical enterprise. If Plato were sometimes guilty of forgetting that his theories were but extended metaphors, and forgetting that system must not take precedence over reflection and enquiry, we should certainly condemn him. The ironic fact, of course, is that if we do, then we at the same time praise him, for Plato himself provides us the criteria in terms of which we may judge the failures of his thought. We are much closer to grasping Plato's vision, however, if we understand that most of the failures we attribute to him likely derive from our inability to recognize the interplay of eros and irony in his philosophy.

It is not only Popper and the Popperians, but all of the positivists, substantive and methodological alike, which comprise the most influential elements among our intellectual elites, who subject speculative philosophy to critique of this variety we have been considering. Our philosophic elite is positivist to the extent to which its representatives posit the givens of present social and ideological praxis as the foundation upon which to ground all significant reasonings and actions. Such positivism is born of the uncritical acceptance of the cultural interests of morality and science as the primary criteria for the development of socially relevant theory. It is this form of positivism which is the subject of my present critique.

The most general aim of this critique is to promote an understanding of a broadened conception of rational enquiry, and to suggest that criticisms from both empiricists and the narrower types of rationalists may be beside the mark. If we are truly to have an open society we must open it not only to the complaints of the critical rationalist; it must be open to the broadest possible selection of critical perspectives. Only in this way can we have a *wide* open society. The narrower kind of openness called for by scientific rationalists is based upon an arrogance born of the ignorance of the width of civilized experience.

Thus far I have concentrated upon the contributions of the aesthetic sense of Platonic thought. I must now consider the religious elements in Plato's philosophy. For the positivist, mysticism, like aestheticism, is a form of irrational thought. As the artist ought to remain in his specific area of competence and not wander into the field of philosophic expression which requires him to express his intuitions in a medium inappropriate to the functions of theory, so the mystical philosopher is guilty of translating his experience into a field of expression utterly inappropriate to it.

> . . . since the day of Plato, it has been characteristic of all mysticism that it transfers [the] feeling of irrationality of the unique individual, and our unique relations to individuals, to a different field, namely, to the field of abstract universals, a field which properly belongs to the province of science.[18]

Nothing could be clearer than the fact that Popper construes science in a way that is absolutely at variance with the understanding of Plato. Plato saw a continuity between rational and nonrational (Popper's use of the term "irrational" in this context effectively begs the question at issue), between, that is to say, the grasp of those principles which are open to verification and the grasp of that Principle (the Principle of the Good) which, because it lies "beyond Being," is not open to systematic justification.

Plato and Popper do not seem to be as distinct as Popper wishes to believe, however. For Popper acknowledges that a minimal concession to irrationalism in the form of the affirmation of a "faith in reason" is necessary to ground what he terms critical rationalism.[19] The question is whether or not Plato's claim regarding the mystical character of the intuition of the Form of the Good leads him into an uncritically rationalistic position any more than does Popper's "moral decision" which requires him to accept the necessity of faith in reason involving the presumption of a truth which is immune to rational demonstration. I cannot see that it does. Plato's strictures against written philosophy, his claim that the writing of philosophy is a kind of "play,"[20] the imposing force of the Socratic personality as expressive of the tentative nature of all enquiry, and the saving irony which pervades Platonic dialogues from the beginning to the end of his nearly half a century of philosophic creativity, all serve to qualify any dogmatic claims which might be made regarding the mystical basis of Plato's philosophic vision. The difference between Plato and Popper on this issue seems to lie in the richness of the thought of the former as opposed to the relative narrowness of the claims of the latter. Plato has simply thought through the implications of "faith in reason" to a degree that Popper has not.

The fact of the matter is that Plato has not attempted to translate the mystical experience into the "province of science" which deals with abstract universals. Plato's strategy is expressed in the return of eros to the world. This return allows for the intrinsic appreciation of the world of individuals by virtue of their "participation" in the Form of Forms which provides them their place in the totality of experienceable fact. In short, Plato is not first and foremost a mystic; he is, rather, a philosopher who has allowed the mystical vision to make its proper contribution to the development of his understanding of the world.

Popper's mistake is to isolate the mystical aspect of Plato's thought and to interpret it in terms of a Neoplatonic, basically Christian, form of the *philosophia perennis*. We should, of course, grant that fundamentally religious types of mysticism are at variance with the kind of approach to philosophy that Popper wishes to defend, but Popper has not appreciated the limitations Plato has placed upon the mystical aspects of his thought.

We can distinguish at least one fundamental element, among many, which distinguishes Plato's thought from mystical philosophy as we have subsequently come to understand it. This is the notion of the continuity between science and mystical intuition. For Plato, contrary to the fideistic element in certain forms of mysticism, it is precisely through dialectic, and its final transcendence, that salvation is achieved. There is no conflict between the rational sciences and the mystical vision. Plato does not—at least not heuristically—begin with the mystical intuition; he brings his philosophy to a close with it. The mystical insight does not render, as it reputedly did for Saint Thomas, all other reflection and enquiry "as straw," it is the completion and culmination of enquiry.

Whatever may be said of the intrinsic joys of the mystical vision of the Good, it cannot, given Plato's specific philosophic commitments, serve as an end in itself in the sense that no further activity on the part of the philosopher is called for. Plato's mysticism is a socially conditioned, politically oriented mysticism. The return of eros is required. Plato's vision is related to other forms of mysticism in a way analogous to that of the contrast between Mahayana and Theravada Buddhisms. The philosopher-king is the bodhisattva, the "erosopher" returned.[21]

To say this, of course, is to raise the question which troubles Popper so much—namely, "Will not such a philosopher be a real danger to the realm of social praxis?" That is, will he not feel justified in enacting the most pernicious forms of tyranny since he now "has the truth"? But this is precisely the doubt that a proper understanding of Plato allays. For if we take Socrates as the model for the philosopher returned, we should see in the irony and tentativeness, coupled with the unyielding demand to recognize a Truth above truth, a rejection of any form of dogma. Thus, properly understood, we shall see in Plato's thought an example of a philosophy which includes the mystical sensibility in such a way as to allow irony to discipline eros in every case.

What is truly at issue here is the place of art and mysticism in theory of culture. The narrower forms of scientism and moralism which have sought rigorous systematic control of the sphere of praxis find in art and religion mere archaisms left over from a mythopoetic sensibility. The aesthetic and mystical sensibilities are deemed largely irrelevant as resources for the determination of the proper ends of human existence. But even those forms of religious thought which employ the Platonic vision generally support art only insofar as it is a means to religious insight. In rationalistic understandings, speculative philosophy is the handmaiden of systematic construals of the sphere of praxis. Philosophic visions of the sort illustrated most grandly by Hegel range religion above art, employing speculative philosophy as the means of articulating in a direct fashion the transcendent unity of experienced reality. In neither case is the aesthetic or religious dimension given its proper due.

A balanced assessment of the aesthetic and the religious impulses in cultural experience depends upon the recognition that the intuition of the inexhaustibly allusive character of the insistent particularities constituting what is real is inexorably tied to the sense of mystical unity which serves as the putative source of religious experiencing. The One as an object of experience continually resolves itself into a Many in the act of communication. The Many continually realize concretion in the union which serves as the background of aesthetic experience. The shifting gestalt of religious and aesthetic experiencing provides us with dual foci—the one and the many, order and disorder, cosmos and chaos.

It is the dual character of the shifting gestalt which provides the fundamental context of aesthetic and religious experience calling for the mutual autonomy of the two experiential modes. Speculative philosophy, in its role of assessing the contributions of art and religion to our primary forms of cultural experience and activity, is not (pace Hegel) a unification of the "pictorial representations" (*vorstellungen*) of art and religion, but is precisely that which celebrates the tension that exists between the sense of manyness in oneness which is the aesthetic intuition and the sense of oneness in manyness which is the religious insight. Strict monisms and strict pluralisms alike are consequences of failures of nerve which attempt to overcome the embarrassment of understanding first by acknowledging a dualism of the one and the many and then by resolving that dualism through a sleight of hand which miraculously reduces one of the two aspects to the other.

The fault lies in our preeminently rational understandings which lead us to deplore paradox. For the rationalist, a paradox is but a vague contradiction, and a contradiction is the illustration of the failure of reason. The inconsistencies, paradoxes, inelegances of experience are the very stuff which wonder, *theoria*, finds most interesting about the world of praxis. We have not accepted these paradoxes as final facts about the nature of things because we believe that, though philosophy begins in wonder, responsible thinking must conform to those limitations set by systematic or methodological principles. We can discover the reason for the merely instrumental employment of the evidences of religion and art in the overriding importance of motivations toward organization and control which characterize the essentials of our intellectual heritage.

If we seek to realize the aim of balancing the various experiential modes illustrated by the aesthetic, moral, religious, scientific, and philosophic sensibilities, we shall find it impossible to do so in a strictly *theoretical* fashion. For theory per se tends to stress the primarily moral and scientific modes of interest. And the principal solution offered heretofore to this limitation of theoretical activity is that, from time to time, we have allowed our theories to be turned away from the sphere of mundane praxis toward a World beyond this world of human affairs, giving at least lip service to the religious sense of unity as a complement to the systematic unity realized in the sphere of praxis. As a consequence, the balanced tension of art and religion is ignored and religious insight is construed merely as an experiential reflection of the systematic unity already realized through the scientific and moral sensibilities.

I have been rehearsing the romance of Platonic thought as a means of raising the question of the role of theory in its most general sense. Theoretical reflection, as the studied attempt to envision the cosmos in a humanly relevant manner seems to point in two directions: outward, *horizontally* if you will, to the sphere of human praxis from which in fact it largely derives, and *vertically*, to the ontological sphere which grounds, and serves as context for, the cosmological speculation of systematic thought. The most general characterization of the world as Cosmos requires resort to consistency and adequacy in the development of logical systems of concepts which chart the world in terms of the mutual determinations of the items comprising it. This theoretical activity has, we presume, pertinent applications to the sphere of praxis. But, in addition to the practical function of theory, there is a theorial function as well. Here concepts become metaphors whose mute appeal is to the ontological sphere transcending propositional characterization.

What I am dealing with under the rubric of Platonism is, of course, much broader than the thought of Plato per se; it is the thematic recognition of the nature of thinking itself which leads us to accede to Polanyi's poignant phrase, "We know more than we can say." Because of their delimiting function, concepts and theories enclose a world. The most general philosophic systems purport to enclose *the* World. But the act of enclosing which presumes the possibility of disclosing the nature of the enclosed contents is one which inevitably leads to the question of what lies beyond. Plato's "likely stories," with no little risk, may be accepted as applicable to the world of praxis; they are only tenuously "applicable" to the sphere of contemplation.

The utopian function of theory is not to be separated from its utilitarian function. Philosophic wisdom, which permits the refined adjustment of utopia and utility, is the presupposition of all adequate thought. The failure to recognize the ambidextarity of theory is, at the most fundamental level, the failure of philosophy itself. The expression of this failure involves first the capitulation to theoretical relativity as an irrevocable fact of intellectual culture which can be successfully confronted only at the level of praxis, and second the rejection of all normative visions on the ground that such visions are politically dangerous since they seem to require the kind of consensus which can only be achieved through totalitarian methods.

The skeptical response to the relativity of theories is futile at best. The celebration of conflicting theories merely as incommensurable mappings which do not admit of sufficient engagement for mutual adjustment and refutation is a de facto capitulation to the dominant patterns of thought which, willy-nilly, characterize a cultural present. The sterilizing humility of the philosophic skeptic only makes the arrogance of the scientist, the politician, or the moral crusader, all too easy to bear.

The vision of philosophic activity as primarily therapeutic is only slightly more responsible. Here the philosopher, as one who, in Wittgenstein's sadly abused metaphor, "scratches where it itches," remains essentially unconcerned about itch prevention. Such restricted *therapeia* trivializes the character of thinking, rendering it ad hoc by definition. But the principal difficulty with this therapeutic approach is that there are simply some itches that this modest incarnation of the philosopher cannot get at. The itch of eros is beyond the reach of such simple therapy.

The kind of failed philosophy which ignores the theorial dimension of thought and insists too literally upon "not speaking of what cannot be said" seems eminently reasonable until we recognize that we continually include what cannot be said in every act of speaking. The enclosing act of conceptual definition is a disclosing act as well; and the disclosure is of what lies beyond, as well as what lies within, the concept.

The confusion resulting from the panicky response to theoretical relativity is a consequence of failing to acknowledge that the presupposition of wholeness which every act of understanding entails does not require that the wholeness be realized at the level of human praxis. The wholeness promised by eros is not to be found in the theory itself or in the relative adequacy of its applications to the sphere of praxis. Such wholeness is only realized through a mystical act which takes place "on the other side" of theory, where concept becomes *meta-phora*—metaphor.

CHAPTER THREE
THE MYTH OF CONSENSUS

Our subject here, as in the previous two chapters, is philosophic theory. In discussing "the cultural sensorium" I attempted to illustrate the consequences for theoretical activity of narrowness in the selection of evidence. I continued that theme in Chapter 2 by highlighting the contrasting functions of theory, theoria, and praxis. The failure to recognize that theoretical reflection and construction is to be distinguished from both contemplation and action has had serious consequences for cultural self-understanding. Theory per se has the characteristic of bifocality which permits it to function in both utopian and utilitarian manners. Sorting out the various distinctions among the notions of theory, theoria, and praxis is one of the most important prerequisites of responsible enquiry.

The dominance of narrowly rational and moral considerations in the development of our cultural traditions is primarily responsible for the shift from theoria to theory as the primary form of intellectual activity. For it is reason in its scientific mode, directed toward specifically practical ends, which eschews the evidences of aesthetic and religious sensibility. And without such evidences thinking per se is but an instrumental reflection or anticipation of action. Moreover, the rational and moral interests require of theoretical reflection something that the aesthetic and religious sensibilities obviously cannot demand: consensus.

It may not be initially obvious that the need for theoretical consensus is an eminently practical necessity. But consensus is the ground and goal of efficient action. Thus it is for the sake of praxis that something like consensual understanding is sought. The divergences that so enliven the realm of intellectual discourse cannot be translated into the realm of praxis without disastrous consequences. However pluralistic complex societies may be, some very strong consensus at the level of cultural values and ideology seems essential to the ongoing vitality of a social or political complex. Consensus is normally grounded in a common language and tradition, a common set of problems to which the effective majority of a people must respond, a common allegiance to symbols of authority, political office, or charismatic presence, and so on. However characterized, consensus is a distinctly political, not a philosophic necessity.

By claiming that the problem of consensus is primarily a political one, I am suggesting that the question of how to attain consensus or how to understand the character of a given consensus involves the fundamental political category of *authority*. It is the authoritativeness of one's beliefs or of the source of one's beliefs that renders consensus possible. Classically, we have sought the fundamental source of authority and its justification in the foundational myths which have grounded our cultural self-understandings. These cosmogonic myths, whether read in the Hebraic and Babylonian voluntarist forms, the Hesiodic and Orphic visions of a uniting Eros, or the Platonic vision of a demiurgic victory of persuasion over Necessity, have found the source of authority in primal acts of construal which author the cosmological order of things.

A principal implication of this discovery of authority in the cosmogonic myths is that the sphere of praxis is apparently meant to be characterized in terms of the conception of nature as a cosmic order or orders. The celebrated *physis-nomos* controversy in early Greek philosophy specifies the problematic suggested by the early cosmological understandings of the social realm. Plato's ideal society is to be construed in terms of formal structures which comprise what is truly real; Aristotle understands the conventional and artificial character of social activity as a form of *technē* which is merely the extension of *physis* per se through the activities of the *physis* of human nature; Democritus and the atomists conceive the conventional status of society to be ultimately reducible to the determinations of material necessity.

These visions are not first and foremost ethical or political understandings, but *cosmologies*. Thus the strictly human sphere is an instantiation of principles which find their most general application beyond the human sphere. In these visions, the sphere of social praxis is reducible to the cosmos. But the cosmos itself seems to be but an invention or construction associated with human needs, desires, and actions. It is a commonplace among scholars of Greek philosophy and culture that the

Greek word for cosmos (κοσμος) is associated with two other forms, neither of which has current usage in the languages of Anglo-European culture. In English, for example, there is no true equivalent of the verb *kosmeo* (κοσμεω), or the plural *kosmoi* (κοσμοι), though I suppose we have something of the verb form remaining in "cosmetize." One of the epithets of Zeus—*Kosmetas*, "orderer"—preserves the explicitly dynamic meaning of *kosmos*.

The interesting thing about the word "cosmos" as employed by the Greeks is that it was used, initially, in terms of artificial or humanly construed order and ordering processes, only subsequently being employed to apply to the general nature of things. Until, perhaps, Heracleitus, there was no conception of Cosmos as a single-ordered, systematic whole characterizing the principal meaning of the natural world. The movement away from the notion of a relatively haphazard Universe in which the supernatural realm of the gods subjected the natural realm to unpredictable intervention led to the development of the conception of a rational universe. It is easy to see how the Sophistic response to the conflicting claims of the *physiologoi* should have been to interpret them as the consequence of cosmetic actions resulting in a set of conventional construals of order ensuring the existence of a rational world by the insistence of ordering actions.

Cosmos, the single-ordered world, was an *invention*. The Latin term *invenire* means "to come upon, to discover." The term also connotes endeavor, effort. When by effort we come upon something, we have no assurance that the effort has not resulted in the construal of that which we seek. Invention is an active kind of dis-covering. The history of thought as an increasing ramification of the *kosmoi* invented by the early philosophers leads ultimately to the reintroduction of irrationality as a primary characteristic of "the" cosmos. That irrationality was originally a consequence of the mysterious or theistically interpreted arbitrariness and unpredictability of natural phenomena. Our contemporary experience of irrationality tends to be more closely associated with the relativity of cosmological speculations which require the recognition of competing *kosmoi*, overlapping without harmony. Apparently, the only way out of this difficulty is the way suggested by the Sophists—namely, a return to "practical philosophy" which abandons both cosmological speculations per se and the tendentious endeavors to construe the sphere of praxis in terms of variant cosmological theories. The history of the search for consensus by appeal to accepted authority shows the insight of the Sophists to be perfectly on target. For the search for consensus has not only shown itself to be eminently nonrational, ridden as it is with the motivations of power and domination, but it has become increasingly recognized as a fruitless endeavor.

We do not feel hopeful about the possibility of grounding authority in the Mind or the Will of God. The overly sanguine rationality of medieval theologians argues as forcefully against the former as the excesses of the reforming prophets of the sixteenth century militate against the latter. And appeals to the authority of tradition are more often than not either narrow provincialisms easily countered by equally narrow appeals to alternative "sacred pasts" or, if they are broad enough to be accepted transculturally, constitute no more than an appeal to the inertial character of history, or the compulsion of brute circumstance.

The implausibility of mythical, theological, or traditional sources of authority undermines any attempt to establish authority in relation to the demigod, hero, or charismatic individual. It was not Friedrich Nietzsche, but Pope Gregory the Great in the sixth century who first articulated the doctrine of the superman. Gregory claimed that the ruler of a Christian empire was a *supra-homines* who possessed his power and authority by virtue of a *coelestis conversatio* which made him a direct representative of God.[1] The fact that Gregory was called upon to write polemics against the notion of superhumanity implicit in the claims of those august Caesars who served to focus the energies that spawned the Roman Empire suggests the limitations of that view. For such claims as those of Gregory, supported in advance by the Augustinian account of the founding of the City of God, have received no more substantive or widespread legitimation than the claims of Augustus, supported by Virgil's appeal to the figure of Aeneas, by which he sought to defend the founding of the Roman City of Man on the ashes of Greek glory.

Judged in relation to these conservative appeals to various sources of authority, radical theories of revolution fare no better. To derive norms for the justification of authority by appeals to revolutionary praxis raises the question of just how massive and widespread that praxis should be, as well as in what specific manner, and by whom, such norms may be legitimately derived. Proletarian praxis does not (pace Marx) directly give rise to articulated revolutionary theory. It is doubtful if any social grouping spontaneously ideologizes its aspirations. Formal ideologies are the products of intellectuals who, more often than not, seek to articulate the inchoate aspirations of others. In the case of Marxian theory, the articulation of revolutionary praxis was performed by one whose authority for such theorizing was derived from an alternative social grouping.

In modern times, particularly in so-called democratic societies, the principal source of authority is often thought to be "free, rational consensus." Individual freedom and reason arc thought to be factors sufficient to allow for the achievement of a spontaneous agreement as to social values and their priority. But without an appeal to the authority of tradition, or the sanctity of cosmogonic myths, or the absoluteness of God, or the belief in some *supra-homines*, the appeal to rational consensus seems to lack any substantial foundation. But with such support, the belief that consensus is rational is clearly contradictory. Without the character of rationality consensus is often suspected, if not actually abhorred. And, more importantly, without the notion of consensus as a regulative principle we cannot truly judge the rationality of a conviction or proposition. The question of greatest importance for the understanding of the notion of theoretical consensus is, "May we responsibly hope for the achievement of a free, rational consensus as the ultimate legitimation of common norms and values?"

I cannot see how. We cannot even agree on the meanings of the terms "freedom" and "reason." And if we lack a consensus at the level of semantics, it is hardly likely that we could recognize a meaningful consensus were it somehow to be achieved. Freedom, as a socially relevant term, has been variously characterized as the possibility of making significant choices or decisions, limited only by objective circumstances informed by natural and conventional laws or rules; as the power to actualize one's individuality within the public sphere; as the right to know and the capacity to act in accordance with that knowledge; as the epiphenomenal consequence of determinations associated with genetic, economic, social, or political influences, and so on. Reason is held to be a grasp of eternal patterns defining the possibilities of thinking itself and of the objective world; the understanding of the laws of organic nature and of society as a modeling of that nature; the power of persuasion functioning within the social or political sphere; or as the rationalization of more primitive desires, drives, or impulses.

Theorists, faced with this wealth of ambiguous resources, may discuss the question of free, rational consensus in any number of ways. One might emphasize material necessity and the forms of economic relations capable of best meeting these needs. Or one could stress the need for consensus concerning the rules or laws that promote the organic functioning of society. Consensus may be thought to emerge from the spontaneous acts of charismatic individuals. Finally, consensus might be constituted by recourse to the norms, principles, or ideals originating in the reason of the best among a society's intellectuals but capable of becoming common coin through rigorous attention to pedagogical technique. And so it goes.

In contemporary societies, the appeal to the Diety, Consensus, is an appeal to a legion of spirits.

Consensus has recently become such an issue largely because of increased cultural self-consciousness. The most powerful source of consensual actions and understandings is that of tradition. Sharing a common past which is simply given and from out of which one decides and acts guarantees, at the very least, that the problems and questions one confronts, as well as the solutions one promotes, will be broadly held in common. The enemy of such consensus is reflection and self-consciousness. Once the given is no longer merely taken for granted, but is contrasted with alternative givens or is subjected to criticisms based on the novelties of present circumstance, or the idiosyncrasies of individual needs or aspirations, consensus dissolves. But it is precisely with the emergence of cultural self-consciousness that the recognition of the source of the motivations toward consensus is born. Consensus is a narrowly rational and moral problem. It is for the sake of common action that consensus is sought. And it is in the support of such action that a common vision is entertained.

Theoretical differences result from differential emphases placed upon the conceptual elements derived from the experienced world. The fact that we have no instance of a successful scheme which unites the principles arising from this differential emphasis presents the cosmological problem of our time. We can see this rather well in terms of classical as well as modern theories. It is easy enough to see how Platonic theory skews the data in favor of the principle of "knowledge," or how the Aristotelian theory leads to an understanding of society by recourse to the ends or aims of organic relations in a society expressed as the norms or laws which promote and protect these interactions, or how Sophistic theories urge upon us the principle of "power" as self-actualization in accordance with the Protagorean principle.

Hedonist and Epicurean visions, grounded in materialist or atomist cosmologies, employ the principles of pleasure and pain in the construction of ethical and social theories. Modern forms of social and political idealism, or social philosophies grounded in natural law, or theories which rationalize the rights of power either in terms of charismatic influence or in terms of positivist forms of the "might makes right" doctrine undergirding the conception of *realpolitik*, have made but little progress beyond their antecedents in Greek and Roman philosophy. Moreover, that progress has not been in the articulation of new principles, or in the construction of coherent schemes which related the old principles (the only kind of progress which would be welcomed), but merely in the ramification, elaboration, and sophistication of the classical principles.

Whatever might be said about the possibilities of progress in philosophic understanding, it is clear that there has, at least, been a progressive change in the manner in which philosophy has been conceived. Thus, at the metaphilosophic level, two kinds of progress might be noted: first, there has been an increasing awareness of the apparent incommensurability of philosophic theories which compete for allegiance. That is to say, the problem of theoretical relativity has become more subtly understood, and its consequences more sensitively appreciated. But this alteration in our understanding of the philosophic enterprise is in large measure a function of a second change in the philosophic activity. In a manner that was not the case in the beginnings of philosophic speculation, philosophy has come to be defined by the aim of achieving consensus.

One may easily concede that our first philosophers, including Plato and Aristotle, were not altogether concerned with achieving consensus based upon doctrinal orthodoxy. The vast majority of philosophers from the medieval period to the beginning of the twentieth century claimed to have discovered *the* path to *the* Truth. One could conceivably excuse the medieval thinkers on the ground that they were captive to theological assumptions which were ultimately alien to the philosophic enterprise. But what of Descartes's claim to have achieved "clear and certain" principles and a rigorous method from which philosophic truths could be finally and irrevocably established? Along with his fellow rationalists—Leibniz and Spinoza—Descartes attempted to construct a rational system meant to withstand the withering effects of time and circumstance.

A primary motivation of the modern philosopher was to construct a system, and to "get it right," so that the less general activities of thought and action could proceed in accordance with a common set of rules. This is the view of philosophy as *scientia scientiarum*, that way of knowing which serves to coordinate ways of knowing. On this view philosophy is meant to serve as the foundation for consensual discourse and activity.

Recalling the argument of the last chapter it is important that we qualify this understanding of philosophy, at least with regard to the Greeks. Partly because of the fact that the systematic activity of Greek thought as exemplified in the systems of Plato and Aristotle occurred at the stage of Greek civilization that it did, and partly because of the conception of the role of the philosopher that imbued Greek culture, it would be tendentious to claim that philosophy was then envisioned as the ground of consensus. The owl of Minerva took its flight at the twilight of Athenian culture, of course, leaving Platonic and Aristotelian speculations without the political and cultural context for which they could most appropriately serve as ground. More importantly, the aims of philosophic speculation for both Plato and Aristotle were so connected with elitest notions derived from the character of Athenian culture that the notion of consensus was alien indeed. The rational activity which defined the character of the philosopher was open to but a few.

The historical phases in which philosophy has been claimed to serve as the ground of consensus have been those of the Middle Period culminating in the high Scholasticism of the thirteenth and fourteenth centuries, and the so-called Modern Period which begins with Descartes and, for all practical purposes, ends with the Hegelian system. The first of these epochs was one in which philosophy was the handmaiden of strictly theological and ecclesiastical imperatives which served to define the character of theoretical activity as the ground of consensus. It was the strictly moral concern which provided the interest in consensus with regard to doctrinal and institutional commitments. Not only in terms of the institutional church, but equally in terms of the university structure which took its modern form during this period, philosophy was thought to be the architect of consensus.

However dominant were the strictly moral directives guiding the aim at consensus, the rationalistic interest was certainly strong. The desire for systematic philosophic constructions as determining the validity of philosophy as a science was a powerful motivation of the later Scholastics. It was this type of motivation that helped to prepare for the development of the scientific sensibility of the sixteenth and seventeenth centuries. Descartes's self-conscious search for a method undertaken in the wake of the collapse of Scholasticism was hardly a repudiation of the aims of the later Scholastics. He sought certainty, clarity, and systematic coherence in a manner not wholly unlike his immediate predecessors. It was the power of the mathematical and formal modes of thinking in combination with an emergent naturalism that suggested the revision of method in accordance with a novel set of metaphors. In one way or the other, the Cartesian, Leibnizian, and Spinozistic systems were developed in terms of mathematical models. And each thinker had the concern for living up to the putative burden of the philosopher as a builder of consensus.

By the time of Immanuel Kant's *Critique of Pure Reason*, something like a consensus was in fact emerging in terms of Newtonian natural philosophy. Reflecting upon the physical model of the universe contained in Newtonian thought led Kant to offer his philosophy as the ground of a consensus in both cosmological and ethical matters. The starry heavens above and the moral law within would be understood in a manner conducive to common understanding and action. As many philosophers before him, Kant cast a "cursory glance" back over the history of philosophic speculation and saw "many stately structures, but in ruins only."[2] Nonetheless, Kant was undismayed by the tawdry character of the history of philosophy. Indeed, he thought, by virtue of his intellectual efforts, that

> it may now be possible to achieve before the end of the present century what many centuries have not been able to accomplish; namely to secure for human reason complete satisfaction in regard to that with which it has all along so eagerly occupied itself, though hitherto in vain.[3]

From Descartes to Kant, systematic motivations of the philosophers did seem to aim at something like dogmatic certainty. Kant's profound attempt to render philosophy *scientific* is, apparently, the farthest cry from Plato's acknowledgment that philosophy is primarily an activity, not a set of doctrines, and that wisdom is sparked by benevolent disputation rather than by consensual agreement. But, in fact, the difference is less than one might think, for Kant's vision of philosophy is, *mutatis mutandis*, eminently Platonic:

> *Philosophy* is the system of all philosophical knowledge. . . . Thus regarded, philosophy is a mere idea of a possible science which nowhere exists *in concreto*, but to which, by many different paths, we endeavour to approximate, until the one true path, overgrown by the products of sensibility has at least been discovered, and the image, hitherto so abortive, has achieved likeness to the archetype, so far as this is granted to (mortal) man. Til then we cannot learn philosophy . . . we can only learn to philosophise.[4]

Accepting this vision of philosophy, Kant held that it would be "vainglorious to entitle oneself a philosopher and to pretend to have equalled the pattern which exists in the idea alone."[5] We encounter again the strange paradox that so characterizes the rationalistic philosopher: the need for certainty which, as a motivating factor, grounds the search for rational system, coupled with the acknowledgment that his reach may exceed his grasp. Here we see awesome ambition coupled with a sensitivity to the dimensions of one's failure; a disconcerting arrogance mixed with disarming humility. This is the very stuff of philosophic irony.

The real effect of philosophic theory as regards the desire for consensus has been felt only indirectly at the level of concrete doctrines. Consensus as to general vision is the primary product of philosophic investigation. Plato and Aristotle provided distinctive visions of philosophic enquiry. When Coleridge claimed that every man is born either a Platonist or an Aristotelian he was but noting that the broad approaches to enquiry evidenced in the synthetic vision of Plato and the analytic and problematic orientation of Aristotle provide an elaboration of basic human possibilities regarding the nature of thought as a cultural product. The much-maligned Cartesian dualism which established the grounds for the modern search for the realization of philosophy as *strenge Wissenschaft* culminating in the Kantian endeavor doubtless provided a consensual basis upon which philosophic problems and questions were to be understood. And there is a sense in which Kant and Hegel suggested the grounds for a real praxial consensus in their respective cultures, as John Dewey has served American society. But the closer one gets to the notion of doctrinal rather than visionary consensus, the less pervasive is the cultural influence of a philosophy. And, of course, the enterprise of science itself has come to be known by its self-conscious recognition of the corrigibility of its facts and explanations.

The argument of the last chapter attempted to establish the view that theory per se is ambidextrous. On the one hand, it arises from, or is directed toward, praxis and thus serves to organize, rationalize, or guide actions in the social realm. On the other hand, theory points to the non-praxial realm of contemplation which is characterized by the aim at completeness of understanding. Though only broad commonalities are essential if one wishes to engage in theoretical interchange aiming at theoria, the sphere of praxis, insofar as it represents a realm of potentially common action, depends to a much larger degree on some sort of consensual understandings and beliefs. Thus the importance of consensus as a broadly *political* problem takes precedence over the notion of purely speculative interests in consensuality.

The construal of consensus as fundamentally a problem to be engaged at the level of concrete praxis does not require the view that theory is in every case the product of public praxis. The existentialist, Marxian, and pragmatic conceptions of the origins of theory are, I believe, tendentious and overdrawn. In addition to important practical sources of theory, there are purely contemplative, nonpraxial sources. Finally, theory may have its origin in another theory or theories via critique and reconstruction. In this latter case theoretical structures are indirectly related either to contemplative and/or praxial sources from which they ultimately derive. Although the development of theories calls upon both contemplative and praxial resources, the desire for theoretical consensus is primarily motivated by necessities in the realm of concrete praxis.

It is important to take into account that the traditional distinction between theory and practice does not conform to the essential requirements of the Greek vision of the superiority of contemplative knowledge. One must recognize a dichotomy between theoria as contemplation and theory in its instrumental character paralleling the disjunction between theory and practice. The latter disjunction obtains primarily within the sphere of praxis.

Rehearsing the many noble attempts to achieve rational certainty as a ground for consensual belief could be an extremely embarrassing enterprise for the philosopher if he were not instinctively aware that the fundamental value of philosophy is to be found in its continual assault upon the infinite complexity of the way of things and not the least in the various ways of rendering the infinite in finite terms. Whatever Descartes or Kant or Hegel might have thought about the certainty and adequacy of their respective philosophic theories, the primary value of these philosophers' work has not been in the establishment of consensus. The supreme value of passionate theoretical activity lies in the engagement with alternative understandings and the enthusiasm and excitement thus engendered. The by-product of the collision of alternative claims to certainty is that mutual engagement in the enterprise of thinking which needs no apology or vindication.

Confusion concerning the relevance or viability of the philosophic enterprise have been largely caused by the fact that for the greater part of its history Anglo-European philosophy has not been sufficiently free of the taints of extraneous purpose. Kant's philosophy is perhaps a watershed in our tradition because it instantiated in a most explicit manner the problematic associated with the narrowed understanding of the relations of theory and practice. Theory, as the ideal system of principles in accordance with which understanding could be achieved, and practice as defined by specifically ethical ends, provided the polar notions which ensured the overweening importance of the scientific and moral interests as modes of cultural activity and sources of cultural evidence.

Kantian thought was a watershed in yet another way. In *The Critique of Judgment* and *Religion Within the Limits of Reason Alone*, Kant provided systematic construals of the aesthetic and religious sensibilities which, though slanted toward the principled mode of scientific enquiry, nonetheless were extremely influential in ensuring these modalities of experience and expression the status of cultural interests alongside the ethical, scientific, and philosophic.

The twentieth-century revolt against systematic philosophy is best understood in terms of Hegel's awesome attempt to construct a complete philosophic system. Systematic thinkers from the sixteenth century on were enamored of mathematical and physical models. The mathematical insights of Descartes and Leibniz and the geometrical method of Spinoza, along with the employment of the structure and aims of Newtonian physics by Kant grounded the hope that consensual understanding could be closely identified with the goals of rational science. Hegel's philosophy rejected the mathematical and scientific ground and returned to the original sources of Greek philosophy. Hegelian thought is a philosophy of culture in the broadest sense. It is reflective of the history of cultural consciousness and is an attempt to maintain an essentially nonreductive stance as regards the various cultural interests. And though philosophy as *scientia scientiarum* is provided esoteric status as the capstone of the Hegelian system, at least *The Phenomenology of Spirit* ensures some autonomy for the variety of cultural forms.

Not only did each of the principal cultural interests find a place in the Hegelian system, dominant philosophic schools and traditions were each "sublated" by Hegel's program. The often-heard claim that contemporary philosophy may be understood in terms of a variety of reactions against Hegel is perfectly apt. For the complex of theoretical visions woven into the Hegelian tapestry was easily unraveled by those subsequent thinkers less enamored of theoretical system and coherence. But without the framework provided by systematic coherence the elements of Hegel's thought are shown to constitute an embarrassing pastiche of philosophic methods, principles, and interpretations.

The dissolution of the Hegelian synthesis in the nineteenth century and the emergence of competing philosophic visions such as Marxism, existentialism, pragmatism, phenomenology and linguistic philosophy, and so on affected not only the substance of philosophic activity but the direction of that activity as well. Not unlike their Sophistic ancestors, those philosophers born of a reaction against the Hegelian project parodied the notion that philosophy should aim at theoretical *system*. They sought to call philosophy down from its Olympian heights and render it germane to the sphere of human praxis.

The most dramatic instance of this type of reaction was, of course, that associated with Marxism. For all the dogmatism inherent in the Hegelian perspective, at least Hegel was *broadly* dogmatic. Marxian dogmatism was greatly narrowed with the reversal of the polarities of Hegel's philosophy, rendering praxis the ground and goal of philosophy. And all vestiges of philosophic irony were lost when the almost humorless Hegel was parodied by the absolutely humorless Marx.

The nineteenth century saw a transvaluation of theoretical activity in the minds of many eminent thinkers. Marx and Freud, and to a lesser extent Charles Darwin, are associated with the development of programs which deny the traditional functions of theory as a ground of consensual *understandings* and direct attention to an involuntary consensus at the level of praxis. Common to the disciples of these three individuals, not to mention the contemporary behaviorists, is the attempt to discover the ground of consensus in the determinations of a common "nature."

In physiology the term "consensual" can refer to an involuntary action associated with a voluntary one. If, for example, one chooses to open one's eyes, the involuntary action associated with the choosing includes the response of the iris to the light experienced. If one chooses to consume food, that voluntary action has a consensual counterpart in the provoking of digestive behaviors in the stomach and intestines. Freudian and Marxian theories, along with sociobiological and behavioral methodologies, may be understood in terms of this conception of the relations of the voluntary and the involuntary modes of behavior, with the polarities reversed. Consequent upon involuntary stimuli (libidinal impulses, economic needs, etc.), "voluntary" actions of a specific nature may be expected.

Part of the difficulty in appreciating the functions of theory in the classical sense seems to result from the understanding of all theoretical activity after the pattern of these modern distortions of that mode of thinking. If the theorial dimension is missing from one's understanding of theory then it can only be the case that the efficacy of theory will be judged solely in terms of its intimate connections with the sphere of praxis. Theories which purport to establish what is inevitably the case by virtue of appeals to the determinations to which human activity is bound will always have a profounder air of cogency. Such theories can become self-fulfilling prophecies if those in power in a society so act as to arrange the social environment in such a way as to exclude "unrealistic" alternatives.

Skepticism directed toward theory leads us into an attempt to demonstrate its relevance, not as a description of the way of things, but as so many instruments or tools which permit us to realize an increase in satisfactions at the social level. Marxian strictures against theory as so much ideology unless provoked by ideal forms of praxis, are matched by behavioralists who eschew theoretical schemes in favor of the development of mere techniques for the organization of the contingencies of reinforcement in terms of which the sphere of praxis may be understood.

Theories which lose their transcendent relationship to the sphere of praxis cease to be theories in the fullest sense because they lose the theorial dimension which all theoretical reflection must maintain if it is to serve as more than a political tool. The bifocality of theory for which I have been arguing throughout these pages is an essential consequence of the fact that at the level of cultural praxis there are aesthetic and religious claims upon experience which serve to balance the purely rational and ethical demands.

The recognition of aesthetic and mystical resources for philosophic construction has significantly influenced speculative approaches to the crisis of relativism in contemporary culture. Figures in twentieth-century philosophy as diverse as Wittgenstein, Heidegger, Dewey, and Whitehead have found mystical and aesthetic evidences crucial in their formulation of philosophic questions and the construction of suggested solutions. It will be most enlightening to consider each of these philosophers in turn beginning with the one to whom the generalization I have just made seems least to apply.

It may certainly seem strange to some to characterize Wittgenstein's philosophy as in any positive sense mystical, such has been the successful public relations campaign by those of his disciples who wish to expurgate his more troublesome intonations. But one need only recall the dramatic comment Wittgenstein made concerning Heidegger's notions of Being and Dread in order to understand how significant he thought *das Mystische* to be.

> I can readily think what Heidegger means by Being and Dread. Man has the impulse to run up against the limits of language. Think for example of the astonishment that anything exists. This astonishment cannot be expressed in the form of a question and there is no answer to it. Everything which we feel like saying can, a priori, only be nonsense. Nevertheless we do run up against the limits of language.[6]

And this running against the limits of language is something which concerns "what is really important."[7]

For both Wittgenstein and Heidegger the appeal to the category of *das Mystische* is a response to a running up against the limits of language. And though the bulk of Wittgenstein's professional activity went on within the sphere set by the limits of language, whereas Heidegger sought to remain open to the possibility of transcending present forms of rational discourse in order to discover the appropriate language of Being, the problematic in each thinker is the same. Each seeks to deny the gambit that heretofore had led philosophy into the demand for consensus.

One of the more interesting connections between the apparently dissociate projects of Wittgenstein and Heidegger concerns the manner in which each was forced, against the Heracleitian advice, to enter twice into the stream of philosophic speculation. Wittgenstein's retirement from philosophy for nearly nine years was a result of "having gotten it right" in the *Tractatus Logico-Philosophicus*. Even though this treatise established limits to the nature of philosophic enquiry in a way that contrasted significantly with dogmatic philosophers of the classical tradition, the *Tractatus* clearly lies within the tradition of dogmatic philosophy. The metaphysical and mystical elements of experience lie outside of philosophic activity, since "it is not how things are in the world that is mystical, but *that* it exists,"[8] and philosophy can only deal with how things are in the world.

The method of dealing with how things are in the world outlined in the *Tractatus* involved an analysis of propositions which demonstrated that the process of naming establishes a correspondence between the basic units of language and fundamental physical entities. When Wittgenstein abandoned this logical atomism in his *Philosophical Investigations*, the consequences for the very meaning of philosophic activity were vast. By giving up the ontological foundation of propositions, and by claiming that the usefulness of a proposition did not depend upon its truth-value or the truth-value of a proposition or set of propositions upon which it may be said to logically depend,[9] he rejected the notion of absolute simplicity. Philosophic analysis becomes a description of the rules of languages. No single language can be adequate to characterize our senses of the world. "The World" cannot, therefore, be said to have an ontological ground.

Philosophy is no longer a system of doctrines nor yet the *Idea* of such a system; it is a vision, an activity, a manner of achieving (limited) clarity—that is, clarity about a limited number of things. But as Garth Hallett has astutely noted, the great commonality between the *Tractatus* and the *Investigations* lies in "the large area of their common silence."[10] Contrary to the positivists and other tough-minded thinkers inspired by him, Wittgenstein, according to his friend Paul Engelmann, "passionately believe[d] that all that really matters in human life is precisely what, in his view, we must be silent about."[11] The form of this silence is different for the philosopher and the artist or mystic, however, for in the case of successful expression of the aesthetic variety, "the unutterable will—unutterably—be contained in what has been uttered."[12] Thus, though Wittgenstein agrees with Moritz Schlick that "the doctrines of religion in their various forms had no theoretical content."[13] he was not in the least thereby denying the value of religion but was to that extent denigrating the importance of theory!

The principal consequence of the famous shift in Wittgenstein's thinking from the *Tractatus* to the *Investigations* is that he thus realized, toward the end of his career, a closer approximation of the goal announced at its beginning: "Whereof one cannot speak, thereof one must be silent."[14] The distinction between saying and showing that Wittgenstein had made so much of allows him to increase the ability to show by limiting further his ability to say certain kinds of things. The deletion of the doctrinal aspects of the *Tractatus* from his philosophic repertoire increased the understanding of philosophy as a manner of showing and being shown. And those few thinkers who are both familiar with Wittgenstein's philosophy and sympathetic to the mystical and aesthetic aspects of experience, may in fact see the manner in which these important aspects of his thinking are unutterably present in his philosophic utterances.

The consequences of Wittgenstein's methodological shift would have been extremely significant were it not for the fact that so few of his contemporaries were sympathetic to the project this shift realized. For to be silent about that which cannot be a candidate for discursive propositions is not the same thing as ignoring that domain of silence. Thus to note that the unutterable is present in the utterance of the artist or the mystic is certainly not to dismiss art and religious devotion as unimportant, it is rather to encourage the proper relationship between the activities of the philosopher and those of the mystic and artist. Wittgenstein understood the notion of limits, the intuition which, though expressed in a variety of ways by different philosophers, is the very ground of philosophic genius. And this understanding involves the knowledge that what limits not only *contains*, but (unutterably) defines the nature, character, and importance of what lies beyond.

Wittgenstein's primary contribution to contemporary philosophy is definitely not to be found in any of the forms of reductionism that have come to be associated, however indirectly, with his name. His great gift was his assessment of the intensive and extensive magnitudes of philosophy. The final achievement of the later Wittgenstein was in providing a way of envisioning the enterprise of philosophy which was con-sistently self-disciplined. The nonreductive character of the philosophic effort was thus ensured. Those things of which one could properly speak sorted themselves into a variety of idioms none of which could be reduced to any of the others. Each language game was thus ensured whatever autonomy its rules allowed. Of those things of which we could not speak at least this much was said with profound clarity: not only were they irreducible to the sayable, they could not be dismissed as irrelevant or unimportant aspects of our lives. Wittgenstein—with greater authority and alacrity than Kant—set limits to knowledge in order to make room for faith. But the faith for which Wittgenstein made room was not an articulated theological faith which advertises its dogmas through the construction of institutions and the enforcement of conformity in belief and action, but the *theorial* faith of what may not be said, only shown.

The principal criticism to be made of this vision of philosophy comes from the perspective of one who holds to the traditional view of philosophy as the ground of cultural consensus: the failure to provide an articulated stimulus toward the maintenance of those values which transcend direct propositional expression can easily lead to their being lost to general cultural consciousness. This is clearly a risk. But the response to such a criticism is equally cogent: if one begins to speak of that which cannot be uttered, one threatens to render transcendent interests subject to alien forms of thought and expression which effectively undermine their autonomy. This consequence can be illustrated by recourse to that contemporary thinker who most energetically sought to utter the unutterable. I refer, of course, to Martin Heidegger.

The imaginative boldness of Heidegger's attempt to reinstitute ontological investigations and to provide a deeper foundation for the speculations of contemporary philosophy provided an impressive corpus of philosophic writings which, oddly enough, demonstrate the same sort of shift from doctrine to vision, from substance to method, which is found in Wittgenstein's philosophy. The initial philosophic task, which Heidegger fortunately abandoned, was potentially more dangerous and destructive in its implications than that of the early Wittgenstein.

Wittgenstein's logical atomism of the *Tractatus* period was co-opted by the Vienna school and stood ready as a doctrine which could be wrongfully employed as a means of establishing material science as the paradigm for the acquisition and assessment of knowledge. The notion of philosophy as *scientia scientiarum* which had, since Aristotle, served to define the cultural role of philosophy was subjected to a reductio ad absurdum by the *Wiener Kreis*, obsessed as it was by the belief that philosophy had at last realized its immanent rationale through the unification of the ways of knowing by recourse to the method of the physical sciences. But even the science of physics is too haphazard an enterprise at the methodological level to become totalitarian. Among the positivists theoretical systems were replaced by efforts at encyclopedic collation. The *Encyclopaedia of the Unified Sciences* was rendered coherent primarily by its index.

The sort of consensus that exists at the strictly *theoretical* level of science is rather too vague and too abstract to serve as an overarching scheme in accordance with which a social and cultural consensus might be forged. For the scientific enterprise to become pernicious it must be married to the political structure of a society and made to serve its interests. The extreme danger of Heidegger's early philosophy, from the point of view of its totalitarian impulse, lies in the fact that it was connected, for systematically necessary reasons, to the language of a particular culture, German culture, and a particular political entity, the German state.

Heidegger's infamous discussion of the role of German philosophy in *An Introduction to Metaphysics* includes the claim that Germany is "the most metaphysical of nations," whose language is the heir to the philosophic Greek by virtue of its "power and spirituality." His assertion that "the destiny of a language is grounded in a nation's *relation* to *being*," and his belief that only Germany, the "center" of Europe, can save humanity from "the spiritual decline of the earth" together form a rather dismal instance of the political consequences of a certain kind of philosophy.[15] Heidegger's affair with the Nazi regime was not a consequence of compromise and weakness on his part, it was a direct implication of the kind of cultural role he conceived for philosophy.

Heidegger retreated from his political engagement with the Nazi regime in 1934, after "ten short hectic months."[16] And since the destiny of a language is determined by a nation's relation to being, his retreat to poetic mysticism after the defeat of his hope for the emergence of the "creative statesman" must have come from a new assessment of the relation of the German state and culture to Being. That is to say, Heidegger changed his mind soon after he claimed "the Führer himself and he alone is the German reality of today and for the future, and its law."[17] As a consequence, he had also to change his philosophy.

In *An Introduction to Metaphysics*, Heidegger saw only three possibilities for world leadership: Russia, the United States, and Europe (and in Europe, it is Germany, "the center of the European reality," which is the sole candidate for leadership). If in Russia and the United States he saw "the same dreary technological frenzy, the same unrestricted organization of the average man,"[18] Germany was the only hope. And if Germany fell victim to demonic forces, there would be no role left for the philosopher as a builder of cultural consensus.[19]

Since the failure of Heidegger's early cultural philosophy, there has been an increased awareness of the strange relationship between philosophic thought and political praxis. Defenders of Heidegger urge us to recall the fact that Plato as well sought out a tyrant and a dictator when he wished to implement his philosophic ideas. Such a tendentious analogy omits, of course, the kind of qualifications to totalitarian thought implicit throughout Plato's writings.

> We . . . can hardly help finding it striking and perhaps exasperating that Plato and Heidegger, when they entered into human affairs, turned to tyrants and Führers. This should not be imputed just to the circumstances of the times and even less to preformed character, but rather to what the French call a *déformation professionelle*. For the attraction to the tyrannical can be demonstrated theoretically in many of the great thinkers (Kant is the great exception).[20]

In fact, there are quite a few exceptions. Even if one forgets the ironic limitations of Platonic thought, the history of philosophy abounds with antitotalitarian thinkers. It is only if one believes that philosophy necessarily speaks German that one finds it difficult to note exceptions. In the twentieth century, thinkers such as Russell, Wittgenstein, Dewey, Whitehead, Sartre, and Camus more than suggest that the *déformation professionelle* is a condition limited to only some philosophers.

The question may in fact have become largely academic since the issue of hegemony has been reduced in most advanced industrial societies to a question of the interplay of technology and politics, and is being resolved without direct recourse to the philosopher's deliberations. Heidegger's *kehre*, which led him away from the desire to spread the cultural hegemony of Germany throughout Europe, turning him toward the quietistic, poetic mysticism of his later thought, was in large measure occasioned by his recognition that the technological virus had infected *all* political structures. There was thus no longer a cultural resource for the establishment of a meaningful consensus at the intellectual level. Heidegger's philosophy is a kind of thinking for an age to be born beyond the end of the technologically dominated era—if such an age there be. As the wisdom of the past was stored in jars and hidden away in caves or tombs, so Heidegger attempted to preserve something of authentic understanding in the vessels of poetic metaphor until such time as they should be uncovered and permitted to illuminate the world.

Meanwhile, Heidegger saw the technological domination of culture shaping an involuntary consensus, a structure of consent providing the presuppositions of thought and action as well as the grounds of anticipation. Heidegger by no means acceded to the phenomenon of technology on simple or unphilosophic grounds. Indeed, his analysis of the thought of Nietzsche, whose overturning of metaphysics laid bare the nihilistic consequences of the metaphysical tradition of the West, provided grounds enough for the pessimistic assessment he made of technological society.[21]

But in the light of our discussions of the distinctly European vision of the function of philosophy and its social mission, and of the nature of consensus as grounded (if only as a *déformation professionelle*) in totalitarian assumptions, it is essential that we recognize that such a holistic interpretation of technological progress may not be the only viable one. Before, however, we look at the more pluralistic and optimistic assessments of the technological phenomenon and its relation to the problem of consensus, we should examine some of the evidence which weighs heavily in favor of the Heideggerian view.

The most direct manner of indicating the influences of technology upon philosophic thinking is by noting that if the totalitarian interpretation of the technical phenomenon is accurate, the problem of consensus has been settled. Technology as *technique* as well as *tools* is capable of providing a framework for consensus in that it *preforms* and *predisposes*. Thus it cultivates and channels the energies associated with social action. It functions to generate alternative modes of plausible action and to set the priorities among them. What is missing in this form of consensual ground is the persuasive activity which introduces the consensual ground into a culture in a manner that presupposes the freedom of social beings. Thus the impositional character of technology is evidenced in the structure of means and forms which characterize advanced technological society. Turning away from theoria and holding praxis to be the sole arbiter of theory establishes the victory, in principle, of the technological state of mind. The efficiency with which technology seems to resolve the problem of consensus has made it heir apparent of the scientific enterprise as the putative ground of cultural coherence.

The scientific enterprise never constituted a monolithic set of activities. Idealists and pragmatists, as well as traditional mechanists, influenced the development of our contemporary scientific sensibility. Though the rhetoric of early twentieth-century science may still have suggested that something like a unified paradigm existed and was accepted within the so-called scientific community, the unity of science and its firm foundation in mathematics was collapsing significantly by that time. The unity of technological structures and means, however, was much more easily defended.

Technology, not science, is now accepted as the common schema within which there might be realized some degree of unity and coherence at the level of social practice. As a consequence of this development ideological visions are being forced to accommodate to the technological imperative. This results in the loss of efficacy of those ideologies at variance with the technological matrix. This accommodation is found to be fairly acceptable in Anglo-European cultures for the simple fact that each of the primary theoretical traditions can be expressed in technologically sympathetic ways without wholly losing their significance. Thus we have "conventionalism" replacing idealistic understandings; "behaviorism", as a set of technical procedures, replaces materialist and mechanistic theory.

The instrumentalist understanding grounded in a distinctly volitional vision is the dominant theory in our tradition. This is but to say that the ubiquity of technological activity in contemporary Anglo-European cultures is an outworking of a form of instrumentalism that was with us from the very beginning. This thesis allows us to understand how the history of our intellectual culture may be construed as a transition from theoria to theory and from theory to technological praxis.

The destiny of theory, as opposed to theoria, is technological praxis. In a technological society we are less involved as individuals in the pragmatic necessity of consensual thought and action since the consensus required is immanently realized through the coherence of the technological matrix itself. It simply matters less that we have theoretical or ideological disagreements, for either our ideologies can be expressed in terms consistent with the coherent order of technology or they have no real consequence, since the important consequences at the level of social praxis are consequences deriving solely from the technological matrix.

This fact is easily illustrated by the decreased importance of traditional values as the means of transmitting the grounds for coherent thought and action. Not tradition, but technology, is the principal guarantor of social harmony. In place of ritual, habit, and individually supported institutions charged with the transmission of cultural values, we have regularized forms of activity sustained automatically by the technological matrix itself.

I have been rehearsing some of the consequences of technological advance envisioned by those (principally European) philosophers who may be broadly associated with the Heideggerian analysis of the relations of philosophy and culture. The fact that philosophers do not, of course, all agree upon the nature and consequences of technological development is an important fact about the character of contemporary philosophic enquiry. Most interesting, perhaps, is the fact that attitudes toward technology are more often positive in the United States, the home of the most sophisticated technological advances. It is worth investigating whether the "dreary technological frenzy" that Heidegger found associated with life in the United States is quite as dreary, or as frenzied, as he seemed to believe.

I suppose it is truistic that one's attitudes toward the ubiquity of technological means which threatens (or is promised to) contemporary societies is a function of the vision of "meaningful human existence" antecedently entertained. If it is the case that one feels that the things which technological activity is apt to replace in human social activity are the very things that make us *human*, then we shall look dimly upon advancing technology. On the other hand, we may believe that just as "shuttles which weave of themselves" make slavery unnecessary, the tools and techniques associated with technological sophistication may serve primarily as means of freeing us from undignified burdens to which we have heretofore remained subject.

It is at the scientific and broadly ethical levels that technology is having its primary impact. In the sphere of science, technical sophistication provides that subtle instrumentation of scientific activity which ensures that understandings associated with technological means will be *instrumental* understandings. Tools, or instruments, are not only means through which knowledge is gained, they (and the specific forms of their interactions with the data investigated) are part of what comes to be known. Also, at the level of the moral interest technological advances alter the very basis on which ethical decisions have heretofore been made.

It is at the level of the interaction of technology and the sphere of public praxis we know as the "political realm" that the effect of the technical revolution is most importantly felt. As Karsten Harries has shown so clearly in his essay, "Heidegger as a Political Thinker,"[22] Heidegger's turn away from political engagement after the debacle of the thirties was associated with his recognition that National Socialism, which he thought could preserve humanness in the encounter with technology, was not the savior that he had imagined. Henceforth political leadership is interpreted by Heidegger as in the service of technological activity. The creative statesman who, along with the poet, Heidegger had given an important role in establishing the public realm no longer exists. Retreat from the public sphere is essential if authenticity is to be maintained.

One might ask if such a negative interpretation of the effects of technology is necessary. It certainly seems to be if humane existence is politically determined; if, that is to say, the public sphere is the sole realm wherein meaning may be created and/or discovered. Conceptions of human existence predicated, as is Heidegger's, on the existential problematic which conceives the human being as an empowered agent who construes the world from the perspective of the political sphere cannot but be undermined by advancing technology. But the retreat from the public sphere and the resort to a combination of metaphorical silence and disengaged ruminations is an eerie form of the licking-one's-wounds-while-nursing-one's-grudges sort of retreat. It inspires not hope but anxious anticipation.

The fault may lie in the classical distinction between the public and the private spheres of social existence on which so much classical political thought depends. This is itself a sophistic and existential mode of conceptualization. "Fame" and "greatness" are the humanizing values sought by those with "courage" and "good fortune." This vision is grounded in a trickle-down theory of meaning and value. The achievements of the truly great will flow downward to the masses who will receive a sense of standards and values which they can revere but never, of course, effectively realize. The leader's public presence will serve as the means through which a form of vicarious existence can be won which will prevent the failure of actual realizations to become altogether burdensome. And if we decry this trickle-down theory of meaningfulness in the name of a more democratic vision of life, we shall be told that without those who are willing to risk all in the search for greatness the masses shall never receive even their pittance of meaning and value.

The principal defect of such a view lies in its extremely narrow conception of meaningfulness which determines that power over others is the criterion which establishes one's value. The transvaluation of this conception which either denies the propriety of the distinction between public and private forms of social existence in the name of a more ecological vision of human environs, or which takes the individual's relation to this world as the foundation in accordance with which meaning may be established, would provide the basis for a significantly different evaluation of the technological phenomenon. The private mode of existence—the individual in solitary association with his distinctive environs—would now be the realm in which meaningful human existence is established. Politics, in whatever sense that term comes to be used after the technologizing of society, would be an activity which was undertaken not in order to achieve a meaningful life, but as a means of increasing human satisfactions and rendering more equitable the benefits accrued through social relations. Politics would be a realm wherein technicians and functionaries performed services rather than a sphere within which individuals sought to "realize" themselves.

The distinctly American interpretatoin of technology and its relation to politics is grounded on something like this latter interpretation of human existence. The tedious humorlessness of the Germanic analysis Heidegger provides is in contrast to the optimistic appraisal that comes from the pragmatic philosophers. This optimism is in itself enough to condemn it in the eyes of the brooding, world-weary thinkers of Heidegger's ilk.

For all Heidegger's wisdom and insight, he is guilty of a quite unacceptable combination of arrogance and ignorance (the unpardonable sin of the philosophic elite) when he attempts to interpret American thought.

> "Americanism" is something European. It is an as yet uncomprehended species of the gigantic, the gigantic that is itself still inchoate and does not as yet originate at all out of the complete and gathered metaphysical essence of the modern age. The American interpretation of Americanism by means of pragmatism still remains outside the metaphysical realm.[23]

One is reminded of Ortega's analysis in *The Revolt of the Masses* which finds that those profound notions such as technology and capitalism which define the essence of American life are distinctly European phenomena.[24] The assessment of pragmatism is what is important here, however. Heidegger dismisses the pragmatic interpretation (presumedly without bothering to read Peirce, James, and Dewey with the slightest care) largely because of his radically different interpretation of the technological phenomenon. Not requiring the Great-Man mentality as a basis for a philosophic anthropology, the pragmatists are able to escape from the special pleading that so unhappily enters into the Heideggerian analysis of the coming of the technological age. For the American thinkers there is no necessity for philosophy to retreat from engagement with the technopolitical sphere. That sphere is after all not essential to the realization of the ends of human existence. It is merely one possible organization of the means to those ends. And it is certainly an open question as to whether politics is the most productive organization of means.

The basis for the more optimistic appraisal of the technological phenomenon and of the belief that philosophy may continue to be engaged with the technopolitical realm has to do with the manner in which the tradition of American philosophy achieved an integration of the aesthetic and religious sensibilities into the interpretation of individual and social existence. As we shall soon see, this permits an understanding of human existence which does not depend solely upon the rational and ethical norms over which technology may exercise untrammeled influence. By refusing to define the meaning of human life in terms of the power of rational and moral efficacy, one need not be threatened by the advent of the technological era. On the contrary, if the aesthetic and mystical sensibilities are established as the primary conditioning factors in the realization of a fully human life, then a great deal is to be gained by the movement into the technological age.

In the American tradition the roots of an expanded vision of meaningful human life are to be found at the very origins of our philosophic speculations. The criticisms leveled by Jonathan Edwards against the thought of John Locke significantly broadened the meaning of "experience" in the Lockeian idiom and set the stage for the development of what eventually would be known as radical empiricism. For Edwards,

There is a distinction to be made between a mere notional understanding, wherein the mind only beholds things in the exercise of a speculative faculty; and the sense of the heart, wherein the mind don't (sic) only speculate and behold, but relishes and feels. That sort of knowledge, by which a man has a sensible perception of amiableness and loathsomeness, or of sweetness and nauseousness is not just the same sort of knowledge with that by which he knows what a triangle is, and what a square is.[25]

The "sense of the heart," that aesthetic sensitivity to beauty which Edwards ranged above propositional truth and ethical doctrine as the proper source for all intellectual endeavor, was a consequence of a bold attempt to ground theological understandings in vision as opposed to doctrine.

From the side of continental philosophy, specifically the romanticized Kant which was filtered through Coleridge to Emerson, American thought received a strong dose of intuitionist sensibility. For Edwards, the "sense of the heart" was limited to the elect whom God had chosen for salvation. Emerson democratized this aesthetic sense, urging all men to rely upon their intuitions and not upon the authority of tradition or of the "great minds" of the past. His conception of the ubiquity of the moral sense establishes a basis upon which consensus may be expected. In fact, Emerson's philosophic vision promotes a certain kind of pluralism and relativism at the level of doctrines and institutions while arguing for broad agreement at the level of fundamental moral intuitions.

Critics of moral intuitionism, particularly of the rather nontechnical variety championed by Emerson, sometimes forget that it is in fact arguably the case that there is less real divisiveness at the level of moral sentiments than at the level of doctrinal affirmation. There is some reason to believe that the conflict which exists among individuals and institutions concerning the most appropriate actions belies the true consensual understanding expressed in the forms of togetherness which establish the context for argument and conflict. Arguments, debates, disagreements are viable modes of interaction expressive of the moral intuition that, at the very least, the game is worth the candle. The nonpropositional source of moral insight is to be found in the empathic intuition of mutuality.

The structure and character of American philosophy, as one can begin to see already by the time of Emerson, sorts itself out in terms of the contrast of visionary and doctrinal perspectives. This theme is forcefully addressed by C. S. Peirce with respect to the subject of the hierarchy of normative sciences. For Peirce, logic constituted the science of rules or procedures for the attainment of ends or goals. Logic presupposes a grounding in ethics which establishes ends. But the ethical and logical norms which together define the means–ends spectrum in human experience can only find their justification in a general science of ends which considers that "state of things which is most admirable in itself regardless of any ulterior reason."[26] This is the science of *aesthetics*. There is, thus, a Platonic eros which leads from logic through ethics to the aesthetic vision of normativeness per se. And what is normative, ultimately, for Peirce is not unlike a "sense of the heart" that eschews the instrumental employment of reason as a criterion for deciding upon ultimate norms.

The conviction of William James, expressed in his *Principles of Psychology*, to the effect that "aesthetic and moral judgments express inner harmonies and discords between objects of thought"[27] takes on its principal importance from the corollary that metaphysical principles such as

> nature is simple and invariable; makes no leaps or makes nothing but leaps . . . express . . . our sense of how pleasantly our intellect would feel if it had a nature of that sort to deal with. The subjectivity of which feeling is of course quite compatible with nature also turning out objectively to be of that sort, later on.[28]

On this view what James will later term "the will to believe" is grounded in the aesthetic sensibility. The proper approach to metaphysical speculation, dependent as it is upon its own basic postulations, is one that ensures a prior adjustment to the world which precludes the kind of insecurity that leads to ontological obfuscations and defensive rationalizations. Philosophic vision is a kind of *seeing* grounded in *feeling*.

There is but a short step from these insights of Edwards, Emerson, Peirce, and James to the philosophy of John Dewey, whose concern with the aesthetic quality of experiencing is one of the most significant characteristics of his thought. In his *Art as Experience*, Dewey claimed that

> Not only is [the esthetic] quality a significant motive in undertaking intellectual inquiry and in keeping it honest, . . . no intellectual activity is an integral event (is *an* experience), unless it is rounded out with this quality. Without it, thinking is inconclusive. In short esthetic cannot be sharply marked off from intellectual experience since the latter must bear an esthetic stamp to be itself complete.
>
> The same statement holds good of a course that is dominantly practical. . . . The Greek identification of good conduct with conduct having proportion, grace, and harmony, the *kalon-agathon*, is [an] obvious example of distinctive esthetic quality in moral action. One great defect in what passes as morality is its anesthetic quality.[29]

For Dewey, both intellectual enquiry and moral action require the aesthetic quality if they are to be integral modes of experiencing. The consummation of an act of experiencing necessarily involves the aesthetic quality. This is the ground of Dewey's resolution of the dichotomy of theory and practice. Theoria and praxis are conjoined by *aisthesis*.

One of Dewey's principal concerns was to overcome the sharp division among types or modes of experiencing characteristic of modern philosophy from Descartes to Kant. Attempts to realize the aim of "philosophy as a strict science" both certified and ramified the distinctions among aesthetic, moral, and narrowly rational modes of experience and enquiry. Dewey recognized that merely developing a theory which precludes those divisions will not resolve the difficulties of overly specialized experience and expression characteristic of our Anglo-European culture. These divisions among types of cultural interest have become institutionalized in our societies in a variety of ways and the hierarchy of these interests provides the principal criteria in terms of which other modes of experiencing are to be assessed. Nonetheless, Dewey's vision of the aesthetic unity of experiencing permits him to consider the problem of consensus from a distinctive perspective.

> Philosophy has often entertained the idea of a complete integration of knowledge. But knowledge by its nature is analytic and discriminating. . . . Diversification of discoveries and the opening up of new points of view and new methods are inherent in the progress of knowledge. . . . Nevertheless the need for integration of specialized results of science remains and philosophy should contribute to the satisfaction of the need.
>
> The need however is practical and human rather than intrinsic to science itself. . . . The need for direction of action in large social fields is the source of a genuine demand for unification of scientific conclusions.[30]

Dewey well recognizes the dilemma of theoretical activity. In itself, theory does not require consensus for its justification. It is the sphere of praxis which cries out for consensus. Normally Dewey's thought is understood to require a methodological consensus. Treated as a kind of prototypical Popperian, Dewey, as Peirce before him, is read as seeking consensus with regard to rules of enquiry. This is to ignore the fact that, for both Dewey and Peirce, logical and ethical norms are rooted in aesthetic vision and value. The consummatory phase of cultural self-consciousness is the actualization of a ground for integral experience.

> Were there any consensus as to the significance of what is known upon beliefs about things of ideal and general value, our life would be marked by integrity instead of by distraction and by conflict of competing aims and standards. Needs of practical action in large and liberal social fields would give unification to our special

knowledge; and the latter would give solidity and confidence to the judgment of values that control conduct.[31]

Consensus is not primarily *propositional*, but valuational. We must seek the relevance of the known (which of course continually shifts and changes) to our beliefs about "things of ideal and general value." Though Dewey at times equivocates on this issue he seems, on balance, to believe that the role of the philosopher is not that of defining what those values are; neither is it the collection of the data comprising the body of the known. The philosopher, in his most positive activity, seeks to interpret the consequences of the results of responsible enquiry with respect to the values and purposes of a society. The recognition of the corrigibility of useful knowledge requires a pluralistic interpretation of theoretical activity. Scientific understanding is grounded in a reasonably uniform sense of the meaning of enquiry. But that understanding presupposes enquiry into the connection between efficacy and immediacy, between the instrumental and consummatory phases of experience at both the individual and cultural levels.[32]

The history of American philosophy from Edwards to Dewey traces the increasingly subtle appeal to the aesthetic sensibility as a means of broadening the characterization of experience and of providing a justification for the philosophic activity which eschewed the narrowly doctrinal or propositional interpretation of thinking. The distinctive problematic of American thought concerns the interpretation of pluralism in thought and action which leads to the enhancement of individual freedom. Thus the understanding of social and cultural pluralism as a harmony which draws its strength from the individuality of its component members is both cause and consequence of the importance attributed to the aesthetic interest in American philosophic speculation.

The emphasis upon the aesthetic modality of experiencing as a means of defining the substance and form of philosophic endeavor was continued in the thought of Whitehead who, though moving to America at the late age of sixty-three, is clearly within the tradition of American intellectual life beginning with Edwards and running through Peirce, James, and Dewey. Whitehead's metaphysical theory characterizes experience in terms of the notion of "aesthetic events" whose aim at "satisfaction" provides structure to the process whereby they come to be. In Whitehead's philosophy, Dewey's consummatory phase of experience receives an explicitly aesthetic characterization. But Whitehead carries further the peculiarly Platonic strain of philosophizing so influential among the principal figures of American philosophy by explicitly introducing the mystical element of the intellectual life that had been largely submerged in Dewey's work, as in Peirce's before him.

Whitehead's philosophy requires that a religious dimension of existence be recognized as the transcendent ground for the unity and harmony of aesthetic experiencing. Dewey believed that the harmony of immediacy and efficacy could be realized within a society through a cooperative effort of rational adjustment. Whitehead holds that such a belief is based upon an understanding of the aesthetic and religious modalities of experience which requires that the former do the work of the latter. Beyond the recognition of the self-justifying aesthetic enjoyment which rests in the immediacy of experience, there must be a sense of the value of any finite experience within the undifferentiated totality of experienced fact. This Whitehead terms the sense of Peace.

Whitehead characterizes the sense of Peace as a "trust in the efficacy of Beauty."[33] It is the sense presupposed by the drive of eros toward completeness of understanding. There must be some reason to believe that the finite activities of aesthetic events will be coordinated in such a manner as to prevent loss if there is to be continued motivation toward significant actions at the level of social praxis. The mystical sense is an intuition that there is, in the very nature of things, the promise of objective immortality for each instance of realized value.

The degree to which Whitehead depended upon mystical and aesthetic insights which seem to challenge rational articulation is often not appreciated largely because he insisted upon attempting to house these intuitions in an extremely sophisticated hypothetical-deductive system. The correct understanding of Whitehead, however, depends upon the recognition that for him no more than for Plato was systematic expression the ground or goal of philosophic enquiry. For Whitehead systematic philosophy serves to advertise the limited and tentative quality of thought. We can make this fact somewhat clearer by a brief consideration of Whitehead's vision of philosophic argument.

The first thing to say about Whitehead's method of argumentation is that in terms both of its problematic and its architectonic, philosophy is grounded in as broad a selection of evidences as are available to the responsible thinker. Whitehead offers his metaphysical theories in the systematic form illustrated by *Process and Reality*, as a complex proposition—that is, as a proposal for experience and interpretation. Four significant criteria are to be employed in testing philosophic propositions: *validity, truth, interest, and importance.* In the first place a philosopher ought to subject his thought to the tests of logical rigor. The systematic character of philosophy allows for the tests of logical consistency and coherence to be applied to the deductive and inferential moves of the philosopher or his interpreters. A philosophic scheme is meant to constitute a coherent set of propositions which permit valid inferential moves. The value of the systematic character of the scheme is that it allows the philosopher to "argue from it boldly and with rigid logic."[34] Thus logical rigor is an essential characteristic of all responsible philosophy.

In addition to the criterion of logical consistency, there is the test of truthfulness. This involves the continual comparison of one's philosophic propositions with the evidential sources from which they were derived. The conformation of statements with the facts or experiences they purport to describe, evoke, or classify is necessary at every step in the construction and subsequent employment of these propositions. Bare formal truths, however, even expressed in correct logical and syntactical form, are not yet full-fledged philosophic propositions, for "it is more important that a proposition be interesting than that it be true."[35]

The claim that "interest" is a significant criterion by which to judge the value of propositions, though initially striking, is rather obvious. Merely true statements are not necessarily interesting. Unless truths concern compelling issues or problems, those deemed relevant by individuals capable of understanding and analyzing or applying them, they will, of course, be ignored. For this reason, an interesting falsehood—simply because it occasions reflection, critical response, and otherwise stimulates intellectual activity—may turn out to be superior in philosophic force to a dull truth. Note that the test of interest is not a narrow one. It is not just that of *vested* interest. Interesting propositions occasion debate, enquiry, criticism, and, therefore, are conducive to the growth of understanding.

The final test to which philosophic propositions ought to be subjected is that of "importance." Importance is defined by Whitehead as "interest, involving that intensity of feeling which leads to publicity of expression."[36] In our culture, the various species of importance include the expressions of art, morality, science, religion, and philosophy which we have included as elements of the cultural sensorium. These species of importance are not defined in advance by philosophic theory. They constitute those cultural interests which have in fact come to possess *import* by means of their continued efficacy in the sphere of praxis.

Thus a speculative philosopher such as Whitehead is really a philosopher of culture who wishes to assess the relevance of any theoretical scheme to the important phases of human experience both as regards the question of the sources of evidence as well as in the application of the scheme. The ultimate test of a general speculative vision is its relevance to the width of civilized experience which contains the principal perspectives on the world provided by the various species of importance. Only if the philosopher seeks the widest possible relevance to the cultural matrix from which his scheme was born can he hope to promote the importance of his philosophic vision.

It is with regard to the issue of "importance" as a philosophic test of a speculative vision that we can understand the peculiarly pragmatic strain in Whitehead's philosophy. It is not within the purview of the philosopher to decide in advance just what constitutes the proper subject matter of philosophic analysis and construction. The speculative philosopher is a cultural positivist. Accepting the posited elements of the cultural milieu he constructs an interpretive scheme which may be used to integrate and enrich one's experience within that milieu.

Whitehead did not believe that the purpose of the systematic philosopher was first and foremost to "get it right." He was unsympathetic to the desire to make philosophy into a strict science. He certainly never thought that he had provided a theoretical scheme which would bring philosophic thinking to a close. All too many of his disciples hold views like these, but with absolutely no justification. Part of the reason for the misconstrual of Whitehead's principal project lies in the fact that he is neither a dogmatic nor a skeptical philosopher and, therefore, difficult to classify. His insistence upon system is grounded in a recognition of the bifocality of theory which directs it toward the sphere of theoria as well as that of praxis. For Whitehead, in precisely the same manner as for Plato, system ensures not only practical relevance, but provides the ground of self-transcendence.

If Whitehead is unclassifiable as either a dogmatic or a skeptical philosopher, neither does he fall into the categories of "systematic" or "edifying" philosopher recently developed by Richard Rorty in his *Philosophy and the Mirror of Nature*. In that work, Rorty attempts to develop a vision of the philosopher's role which eschews any obligation to construct a ground of cultural consensus. Rorty contrasts the "systematic" philosopher who, he contends, seeks "universal commensuration" as a means of putting philosophy on the "secure path of science"[37] and "edifying" philosophers who envision the latest systematic philosophy as "just another of the potential infinity of vocabularies in which the world may be described."[38]

Great systematic philosophers, like great scientists, build for eternity. Great edifying philosophers destroy for the sake of their own generation. Systematic philosophers want to put their subject on the secure path of a science. Edifying philosophers want to keep space open for the sense of wonder which poets can sometimes cause—wonder that there is something new under the sun, something which is *not* an accurate representation of what was already there, something which (at least for the moment) cannot be explained and can barely be described.[39]

Among the great edifying philosophers of our time Rorty lists Dewey, Wittgenstein, and Heidegger. It is to thinkers such as these that he looks for guidance in the understanding of the proper cultural role of the philosopher. The edifying philosopher functions best in his "protest against attempts to close off the conversation by proposals for universal commensuration through the hypostatization of some privileged set of descriptions."[40]

In terms of the arguments of this essay Rorty has misunderstood the cultural value of systematic philosophy by failing to see its theorial dimension. To the extent that Plato, for example, sought system he sought it as a means of ensuring the transcendence of the practical function of theory as a doctrinal ground of cultural consensus. For Plato, systematic theory as illustrated, for example, by the *Republic*, provided a superstructure enabling ascent beyond the sphere of praxis. Likewise, it is precisely the systematic character of Whitehead's philosophy which permits him to argue for its own transcendence in the continuing conversation of intellectual culture. This point is worth specifying in relation to Whitehead since Rorty explicitly excludes him from the privileged list of edifying philosophers.[41]

What makes Whitehead's thinking so difficult to characterize is that he has explicitly appealed to the broadest possible sources of evidence in the construction of his philosophic system. This means that in addition to the interests of science and ethical praxis he has employed aesthetic and mystical evidences in a manner that serves to qualify the sense in which his systematic philosophy is to be understood. As was the case with Plato, aesthetic and mystical evidences serve as limiting criteria with respect to any claims at propositional completeness. Whitehead's philosophy is a vision, not a set of doctrines.

At the close of *The Quest for Certainty*, Dewey appealed for the development of a "system of thought" which would promote the realization of a consensus concerning the relevance of knowledge to the needs of human praxis.[42] It is somewhat ironic that Dewey is seldom considered a systematic thinker in the same way as is Whitehead whose *Process and Reality* is thought to be a paradigm of systematic philosophy. The irony lies in the fact that Dewey's thinking is more dependent upon system than is Whitehead's since the submergence of the mystical element in his philosophy renders more difficult the problem of accounting for the coherence of cultural experience and activity. And for all his systematic appearance, Whitehead is much less concerned with the construction of cultural consensus. This is well illustrated in his attitude toward criticism. On an important occasion when Whitehead had the opportunity to reply to his critics, he offered the following remarks in lieu of a philosophic apologia:

> The progress of philosophy does not primarily involve reactions of agreement or dissent. It essentially consists in the enlargement of thought, whereby contradiction and agreements are transformed into partial aspects of wider points of view.[43]

Whatever consensus emerges in the history of thought is not one which is grounded upon successful dialectic and/or debate. The eros that animates the true philosopher is not that horizontal animus that seeks conformity among propositional assertions, but that vertical eros which realizes itself in the recognition of wholeness imaginatively achieved.

The transition from theoria to theory has led contemporary culture into a situation in which our increasingly articulated consciousness is experienced as fragmented by virtue of the conflict of the various theories we employ to make sense of our world. This situation dramatically illustrates the point we have been trying to make in relation to the immanent rationale of theoria as opposed to theory. Few seem able to appreciate the ironic fact that the aims of theoria and theory are no more in harmony than were the aims of theory and praxis, and this for the obvious reason that what we have come to know as "theory" is in fact nothing more than the reflective capacities of the human intellect reduced to practical activities. That is to say, theory is itself a form of praxis dominated by moral and scientific interests both of which have an instrumental grounding. The difficulty experienced increasingly in contemporary pluralistic societies is that, once raising to the level of consciousness the ineradicable conflicts of theory with theory we can no longer hope for a theoretical vision which promotes a coherent scheme of thought and action serving as the source of a privileged understanding of the way of things or as a repository of a coherent set of norms for action.

The difficulty in tracing the adventures of these ideas of theoria, theory, and practice is so great because of the extreme subtlety with which the motivation toward consensus must be analyzed. A theoretical consensus which permits the direction of social action may be essential to the ongoing stability of a given social entity. But there is no intrinsic connection between the desire for that kind of consensus and the aim at the completeness of understanding which is subject to the lure of eros. There is no gainsaying the significance of this latter desire for "consensus" as it operates in the spheres of aesthetic and religious sensibility. The variety of aesthetic and religious visions at the level of doctrine and theory is simply beside the point. No one really contests the compelling objectivity of aesthetic and mystical satisfactions which render all propositional description irrelevant and place all those who have so experienced in a community of shared realization. Who would be able to mount an intelligent argument against the possibility of a community of appreciation or of adoration which would unite those whose experiences of aesthetic or religious excellence was the sole binding factor? If Picasso and Leonardo were vouchsafed a moment together, would they really wish to argue about the relative superiority of aesthetic visions? If the Buddha and Jesus met would they not recognize their common sensibility?

Of course, neither the aesthetic nor spiritual elites strive for consensus in the traditional sense. The aesthetic elite is much more concerned with evoking the intensity of particular, idiosyncratic experiences. Art is fundamentally pluralistic. The dominance of a single artist in any given epoch does not lead other artists of real stature to imitate or to strive simply to fill in the details of a paradigmatic aesthetics. Such dominance in the aesthetic interest is itself a contradiction to the enterprise of art and results from wholly extrinsic causes. Art presses toward the appreciation of the particular. Consensus in the ordinary sense is contrary to its essence.

If construed in terms of its theological doctrines the religious interest seems above all to require consensus of the narrowest kind—namely, doctrinal orthodoxy. But the religious interest per se is not identifiable with doctrines and institutions. The mystical sense which defines the essential character of religion is an experience or set of experiences, which can be stipulated in alternative ways. Religious experience has no direct implications for practice, at least as that is normally understood. All religious descriptions are symbolic and any actions associated with religious experiencing are likewise symbolic. There are no criteria associated with propositional tests that allow for the judgment of one religious experience vis à vis another. Even the test associated with the "fruits of the spirit" must be held suspect if one identifies these fruits too closely with moral or ethical norms. And though there is obviously something in common between the various kinds of religious virtuosos, just as there is something in common among all artists and aesthetes, it is not something assessable in the way that propositional agreement or acceptance of common principles is. The character of spirituality shared by the Buddha, Mohammed, and Jesus is, perhaps, inexplicable in terms of concepts or propositions.

Insofar as it draws upon the aesthetic and religious interests for its primary inspiration, philosophy itself cannot be construed in terms of a search for consensus in the ordinary sense. One of the more interesting of the paradoxes associated with the role of the philosopher is that, while striving to convince others of his particular point of view, he, nonetheless, thrives on the dialectical differences which separate him from his peers. Nothing so characterizes the philosophical individual as his penchant for argument. And though argument aims at persuasion, its most enjoyable qualities are associated with the activity of thinking prior to any resolution of an issue. In short, philosophers love to argue—but they do not love to agree! This fact is the basis for much of the scorn directed toward the philosophic elite by those who presume themselves to occupy "the real world."

The collapse of the search for propositional consensus has seriously threatened the philosopher's consciousness of his cultural role. Rorty's conception of edifying philosophy as the model of philosophic activity is occasioned by the failure of classical philosophy to achieve its putative aim at cultural consensus. But Rorty's vision of edifying philosophy provides the philosopher with little more than the deconstructive task of criticizing the claims of the systematic philosopher. Little of a constructive sort remains for the philosopher to do. The major themes of the discussions sustaining intellectual culture have their origins beyond the philosophic interest. As a consequence the philosopher in his edifying role must always come late to the conversation. The contrast of systematic and edifying philosophy seems to have its origins in a failure of nerve in the face of the embarrassing history of systematic thought. The benign nihilism which results from this failure of nerve is doubtless one possible response to the challenge faced by philosophic speculation in our contemporary period. But it is, finally, the consequence of a misunderstanding of the true rationale of systematic thinking.

The benign nihilists among our philosophic elite have been confused in part by the attempt to understand the nature of "normal philosophy."

If, indeed, there is something like normal philosophy it is certainly a much more complex enterprise than that of normal science á la Thomas Kuhn. Normal philosophy is a mixed set of activities which contains at one and the same time both constructive and critical endeavors. Each of these types of endeavor has a long and noble history, of course, though the former has, largely for reasons extrinsic to the philosophic enterprise, tended to receive greater emphasis. The distinctive relationship between Socratic and Platonic philosophizing stipulates the manner by which these two phases of normal philosophy interact. The critical dialectician and his constructive counterpart comprise elements in the overall activity of normal philosophy which aims to keep the cultural conversation alive and lively.

The essential character of these two forms of philosophy was discussed previously with regard to the utopian and utilitarian modes of thinking. Normal philosophy per se might best be considered a combination of these two modes of thought. The utopian presupposes the concrete interactions which permit the justification and vindication of the metatheoretical enterprise. The utilitarian presupposes the existence of an unarticulated context within which conversation can take place. If the utopian philosopher allows his vision to be tested at the concrete sphere of praxis, it shall be found wanting. If the utilitarian thinker permits himself explicit appeal to the implicit context providing the ground for his pragmatic claims he finds the utility of these claims seriously qualified.

Doubtless one of the most important determinants of the relations between philosophic thinking and its cultural context is the manner of engagement between utopian and utilitarian thinking. In contemporary Anglo-European society philosophers have been unable to maintain the creative tensions between the two modes of normal philosophy. As a result philosophy itself has divided into two exclusive concerns. The inexorable consequence has been that "normal" philosophizing now consists in two forms of nihilism. Utopian nihilism finds it necessary to reject the belief in the ultimacy of any set of concrete circumstances; in its utilitarian form nihilism is expressed by the refusal to consider any theoretical context adequate for practical purposes. Both forms of nihilism result from the wish to affirm doctrinal over visionary modes of thought. When this is done utopias are literally construed and utilitarian principles become dogmatic methodologies.

If the sole relevance of intellectual pursuits lies in their germaneness to the sphere of public praxis then, clearly, the philosopher should be held up to ridicule, for the relevance of theory depends upon its application as a means of guiding or organizing praxis. Both tacitly and explicitly, however, philosophers tend to recognize the reference of theory as, ultimately, nonpraxial. The philosopher, in the act of scrutinizing the various subject matters he encounters "in benevolent disputation by use of question and answer without jealousy," aims at a realization of wisdom which cannot be expressed in any propositional form and cannot therefore *recognizably* serve as the ground of accord. Philosophers wish, through the activity of thinking, to realize the sense of eros which serves as the dynamic of thought itself. They cannot rest in consensus. Consensus per se precludes thought.

It is by advertising the oppressive harmony of doctrinal consensus that philosophy may best serve the sphere of public praxis. But the cries of "neti," "neti" do not always come from those who stand outside philosophic systems. If the theorial dimension of thought is to receive proper attention it is sometimes necessary to construct theoretical systems as grounds of their own transcendence.

One may recall the plight of the Arimaspians who, according to one version of he myth, possessed but one eye among them which they were forced to pass from one to another so that each could see. Their efforts to steal Apollo's gold were continually frustrated since, owning but one eye, they found they could not productively harmonize their individual efforts. Even when their persistence was temporarily rewarded, they could not enjoy their treasure fully. They had only one means whereby to see.

No more than the Arimaspians should we be content with such limited vision. Each of us who has eyes to see, let him see. No single eye, no single vision, can serve all. It is equally important to recognize that we are meant to see more than just those things close at hand. Our eyes must be turned not only outward but upward as well.

PART TWO
THE IRONY
OF EROS

CHAPTER FOUR
THE AMBIGUITY OF ORDER

The speculative philosopher Paul Weiss was once asked a rather whimsical question to the effect that, were he to hear a voice claiming to be that of God, how would he go about testing the claim. Without hesitation, Weiss replied, "I would ask for the solution to the problem of the One and the Many." Indeed! How, in some final sense, each object or event in the world, and the world per se, can be both many and one, in itself as well as in our understanding of it, is something even the most confident of philosophic spirits would concede, "God only knows."

Certainly philosophers will be forgiven their inability to resolve this problem once and for all. We ought not be quite so generous with our philosophic elite, however, when it comes to their failure to recognize the need for a parity of approaches to speculation concerning the problem. One cannot, after all, avoid the belief that for all their worry over the relations of the One and the Many, Anglo-European philosophers have, for the most part, been dealing from a stacked deck. The vast majority of thinkers, at least since Plato, have given priority to the One over the Many in their speculations concerning the nature of things. In our tradition, metaphysics, either as the science of first principles or as general ontology, seems to require that the actual world be one in the strong sense of constituting a Whole to which general principles, or the concept of Being per se, apply without qualification.

Only after considering the context within which the affirmation of the singularity of the Cosmos came to dominate metaphysical speculation shall we be fully prepared to realize that the problem of the One and the Many has for all practical purposes been reduced to the problem of how the one, singular Cosmos exemplifies the characteristics of manyness or plurality. The alternative question, "How are the many *Kosmoi* also one?," a necessary question if parity of the One and the Many is to be maintained, is seldom asked. That it was seriously asked once upon a time in our cultural tradition, and that it still forms the basis of the classical tradition of at least one exoteric culture, is largely ignored.[1]

The dramatic consequences of Plato's struggle against the "irrationality" of the *physiologoi* mentioned in Chapter 2 are well-nigh lost upon us precisely because of the complete victory of the Platonic vision of the Cosmos over the first natural philosophers. Plato's philosophic problem was to account for the existence of the one, solitary Cosmos ordered in accordance with the divine principle of normative measure. However much the essential aesthetic and ethical presuppositions of Platonic cosmology would be suppressed by subsequent natural philosophers, particularly after Galileo, the fundamental normative bias concerning the value-laden conception of order as intrinsically tied to unity and uniqueness remained. In this regard, therefore, the oft-quoted aphorism of Whitehead is perfectly on target: all of Western philosophy *is* a series of footnotes to Plato.

The first footnote, one which has from time to time successfully challenged the authority of its text, is that of Aristotle. The world which Plato viewed with a mathematician's eye Aristotle saw as a biologist. For the elegance and moral beauty of the concept of "normative measure" which Plato employed as a fundamental principle Aristotle substituted the notion of organic functioning. The order Plato envisioned by appeal to the ubiquity of mathematical principles, Aristotle realized through the notion of adjustment of ends or aims in nature. On the most crucial issue, however, Aristotle and Plato agreed: the Actual World is one. Whereas Plato's dialectical method guaranteed the unity and harmony of the unchanging world of forms, Aristotle's problematical method issued in a system of the sciences which ordered the changing world of natural processes.

In addition to his forays against the *physiologoi*, Plato maintained a concerted assault upon the Sophistic thinkers whose phenomenological account of the nature of things even more significantly challenged his ontological vision. Plato had to show that the forms are in the facts, that the flux of circumstance at the level of human existence provides a stepping-stone for the ascent to the vision of the Good. The alternative ontology of the atomists was simply so radically wrong-headed as to exist beyond the pale of significant dialectical engagement. Thus the ad hoc, positivistic character of Plato's arguments against the atomists.

A similar circumstance obtained with respect to Aristotle. He was not so seriously challenged by the Sophists, for their contrasting phenomenological description seemed to the other principal phenomenologist of ancient times so clearly false as to be quite easily refutable. His chief philosophic concerns were directed against the alternative visions of the atomists and the dialecticians. He had to show that there was no necessity to have recourse either to a world beyond this world of sense, or one "beneath" it. Neither an ontology of form nor of matter could be accepted in place of his functional organic naturalism. The result of the Platonic and Aristotelian successes in the criticisms of their natural philosophic enemies was that both of the logically possible means of defending Chaos against the finality of an ordered, structured cosmos were roundly defeated.

Plato's arguments against the relativism of the Protagorean principle and Aristotle's strictures against the contingency and accidental character of nature defended by the atomists combined to guarantee that the moral order of the universe and the scientific order of the natural world of process and becoming were firmly secured. By anticipation, Plato defended the Aristotelian phenomenology against the Sophistic alternative; Aristotle, in effect, promoted the Platonic ontology above that of the atomists. Aristotle's arguments with Platonism (at least regarding the notion of "order") turned out to be family quarrels.

The authority of Plato and Aristotle has been sufficient to occasion no little suspicion of the most radical consequences of the materialist and Sophistic philosophies regarding the notion of a plurality of worlds. The importance in our culture of the myth of Genesis in which an act of Divine Will creates our single-ordered world gives added support to the conclusions of the Platonic and Aristotelian visions of a single-ordered cosmos. It remains nonetheless true that from a strictly philosophic perspective there are two dramatically contrasting claims providing the parameters of cosmological speculation for our subsequent philosophers and scientists—one affirming the coexistence of a plurality of worlds, the other claiming that the Cosmos is one.

The character of our intellectual culture is defined by the complex of ideals, values, and interests determining our social activity and its products. The specific nature of our culture is a function of the important problems that have goaded and lured us to feel, think, and act in the manner that has given rise to the circumstances of our public life. In its most general character the cultural architectonic distinctive of Anglo-European cultures is consequent upon the cosmological problematic just rehearsed in terms of the Platonic and Aristotelian philosophies. But this cultural problematic, in spite of its massive and widespread acceptance, is not the only one available to us. The "many-worlds" view of certain of the *physiologoi*, later reflected in the relativism of the Sophists, is in fact the first problematic offered as an alternative to the mythical visions associated with the ancient religions. The second problematic, brought to fruition by Plato and Aristotle, must not be identified with philosophic understanding per se; rather it should be seen as but one mode of envisioning the foundation of cultural experience and activity. The preeminence of second-problematic thinking in our culture has, of course, clouded the most radical consequences of first-problematic thought, giving rise to the assumption that there is fundamental agreement as regards cosmological notions. A closer look at the sources of our classical understandings will permit us to see that this is definitely not the case.

The common ground that exists between the Platonic and Aristotelian sensibilities on the issue of the singularity of the world and the fundamental character of cosmic order is balanced somewhat at the beginnings of our classical culture by a commonality existing between the atomists and the Sophists on the notion of "convention." The Democritean dictum, "By convention sweet is sweet and bitter is bitter . . . in reality there are only atoms and empty space" is more than matched by the skeptical dicta of Protagoras and Gorgias. The ontological commitments of the atomists, given the fact the world(s) emerge(s) from "chance and necessity," do little to provide any single context within which truth could be sought. "In reality we know nothing," claims Democritus, "for truth lies in the abyss."[2] Or again, "We know nothing authentically about anything, but each one's opinions are simply what flows from him."[3]

The belief on the parts of Democritus and Leucippus in innumerable worlds is metaphysically grounded. Given the chance emergence of worlds from out of the vortex, there is no philosophic rationale for maintaining the uniqueness of the world in space or in time. Thus the "abyss" which holds truth is either to be identified with the ultimate unfathomableness of empty space itself, or is found in the variant cosmological structures evidenced by the plurality of worlds. There is either no truth to be found, or there are many truths derived from many worlds. This places the atomist in complete accord with the radical representatives of the Sophistic tradition. For these, likewise, there is either no truth, or there are many truths associated with many worlds. The fact that, for the Sophists, these worlds are constructs of human agency and intellect, rather than chance products of causal interaction, matters little when contrasted with the rather optimistic knowledge claims of the Platonic and Aristotelian proponents of a single-ordered Cosmos.

The essential traits of first-problematic thinking are to be derived from the notion that there are many worlds in some truly important sense. The first consequence of such a claim is to render problematic the notion of World itself. In the most direct ontological or metaphysical sense, there is no World, only worlds—no *Kosmos*, only *kosmoi*. It may easily be shown that the materialist and mechanistic metaphors that develop within the context of ancient Greek materialisms, grounded as they are in the denial of intrinsic relations among the atomic individuals and a fortiori among the constructs of such individuals, lead plausibly to the assertion of a plurality of worlds.

The conception of World or Cosmos, in any truly meaningful sense, requires the existence of a common patterning pervading the totality of that which is. If this structure is accidental or coincidental, as the atomists asserted, no intrinsic connections define the character of the totality and it is perfectly feasible to accept the existence of a plurality of complexes with coincidental and accidental regularities among which no meaningful interactions obtain. This extrinsic connectedness of alternative worlds existing within the same spatial void or serially throughout indefinite stretches of time would in no real sense constitute a meaningful totality answering to the notion of a single-ordered Cosmos.

The contrast between first- and second-problematic thinking is specifiable as the contrast between an-archist and archist forms of thought. An-archist sensibility is disposed to the denial of principles (*archai*) as external determining sources of order. Archists, on the contrary, find the affirmation of principles which ground the existence and meaning of things as the sine qua non of responsible reflection. In Anglo-European philosophy, there have been very few serious attempts to develop the anarchist sensibility in this fundamental form. Atomistic and Sophistic theorists have either ignored the basis for this enterprise inherent in their own sensibility or they have themselves been ignored whenever they have tried to forward such speculations.

Clearly, it is the assumption of the immanent character of principles which permits first-problematic thought. If the principles are atoms per se (and it was for identifying principles with matter that Aristotle criticized the atomists)[4] then the only meaningful way in which they may be said to transcend that which they cause is in the strictly derivative sense of efficient causality patterned by unalloyed contingency. The explanatory principles of the atomists must be grounded in the notion of the contingency of causal interactions. An indefinite number of atoms provides an indefinite set of principles and accounts for an infinity of worlds. Needless to say, this strains somewhat our traditional understanding of principles.

The analogous problem exists with principles if they are to be identified with individuals involved in social interaction. The Protagorean principle is not a principle in the classical understanding of the term derived from the second-problematic thinking of Plato and Aristotle. Individual human beings, as willful and capricious atoms, are the "principles" employed in Sophistic speculations. In this vision, order is reducible to the orders of our commanders; principles are immanent within efficacious princes; rules are the expressions of rulers.

The chaos of sensibility underlying both the Sophistic and atomist ways of thinking is hidden by the subsequent developments of the visions. In classical scientific materialisms the theological rendering of the views provides for, if not the metaphysial necessity of a single-ordered Cosmos, at least the belief in the priority of this actual world by virtue of its putatively unique relationship with its Creator. In the Sophistic philosophies, from Protagoras to Sartre, the persuasive activity of "great men" has determined that the human world would realize a relatively high degree of coherence because of the consequences of debate and conquest. The press toward unity is sufficient in either case to have obscured the first-problematic character of these styles of thought.

To uncover the radical consequences of first-problematic thinking one might have resort to the context within which these visions were discussed in Aristotelian metaphysics. The doctrine of the "four causes" provides an interesting means of understanding the nature of both first- and second-problematic philosophy. In Aristotelian causal language, the atomists stressed the material cause. Because of the immanence of material principles in the atoms themselves, however, strictly material-cause accounts lacked explanatory power. Materialists have traditionally had resort to the efficient cause to support their accounts of the nature of things. As became abundantly clear in Hume's philosophy, however, atomist metaphysics cannot provide a categorial ground for efficient causality. The fact that, after Hume's famous reductio of efficient causality, classical materialisms went blithely on their way, providing efficient-causal analyses of fundamental phenomena, argues persuasively for the dominance of second-problematic biases in our tradition.

Sophistic philosophies provide the basis for true efficient-cause explanations. The source of meaning and existence is to be discovered in the Protagorean principle. Volitional agency determines the character of the world in which we live. The family resemblance of the materialist and volitional thinkers, illustrated by their common appeals to convention, permits the materialist to mask the derivative nature of his efficient-cause explanations with some of the rhetoric of the Sophists.

Aristotle paid serious attention to the pairing of causes in philosophic explanations. The pairs of Matter and Form and of Activity and Aim are, of course, obvious. That it is futile to try to make sense of matter without structure, or of aim without activity, is a major insight of second-problematic philosophy. Plato's conception of the Form of the Good as final cause, and Aristotle's vision of the end of existence as the formal self-reflexivity of thinking per se combined to guarantee the persistence of this insight in the history of Anglo-European philosophy.

First-problematic thinking has developed either in terms of an indefinite number of blindly efficient material causes, or an indefinite number of efficient agencies relatively unlimited by material determinations. Second-problematic thinking is grounded either in formal structures the unifying principles of which serve as aims, or in the formal coordination of aims as functions of organic entities the relations among which provide the structure of the natural world. Whereas the senses of Form and End require the unity of structure and the coordination of ends, brute matter and mere activity may be more meaningfully separated one from the other.

If we look into the subsequent developments of philosophic thought in our tradition it is clear that first-problematic thinking, though philosophically viable as cosmological speculation, was never really accepted as a serious alternative to second-problematic thought. And the reasons for preferring the notion of single-orderedness seem to have had very little to do with the intrinsic philosophic excellence of the second problematic. Even those philosophers whose principles permitted them to take seriously the first-problematic sensibility did so, more often than not, in the most offhanded of manners.

Consider Newton's theological excursus at the very close of his *Optics*:

> Since space is divisible *in infinitum*, and matter is not necessarily in all places, it may be also allowed that God is able to create particles of matter of several sizes and figures, and in several proportions to space, and perhaps of different densities and forces, and thereby to vary the laws of Nature, and make worlds of several sorts in several parts of the Universe. At least, I see nothing of contradiction in this.[5]

Newton's accession to the plausibility of "worlds of several sorts" has very little to do with any claims concerning the omnicompetence of God, but a great deal to do with the materialist interpretation of matter and of space, and of the understanding of "laws of Nature" that derives therefrom. The sort of additional hypotheses necessary to transform materialist philosophy into second-problematic thinking Newton was, in *this* context, unwilling to feign. However, Newton's cosmology as it was transmitted to future generations did little to promote the notion of many-orderedness.

At the phenomenological level, first-problematic thinking is found in the distinctive thought of the essayist Montaigne. In that excruciating work of genius, *Apology for Raymond Sebond*, Montaigne states:

> Thy reason has in no other thing more of likelihood and foundation, than in that wherein it persuades thee that there is a plurality of worlds. . . . Now if there be many worlds . . . how do we know that the principles and rules of this of ours in like manner concern the rest? They may, peradventure, have another form and another polity.[6]

Unlike Newton, Montaigne's reason for affirming first-problematic thinking was not cosmological or ontological. In spite of the fact that Montaigne quotes Lucretius approvingly (and interminably) throughout this essay, it is the variety, complexity, incoherence, and inconsistency of life and circumstance that guide his reflections on the plurality and relativity affecting persons and nature. Montaigne was an apologist for the exceptions, anomalies, monstrosities, and prodigies which challenge belief in the principled order of things.

First-problematic thinking is not rightly to be identified with skepticism, however. It is rather a faith in the accidental character of things and in the seductiveness of "mere" coincidence. Montaigne's ironic gesture toward the acknowledgment of God's unlimited power as the basis for the plurality of things ("I do not like to have the divine power so limited by the laws of men's mouths") is not to be interpreted as a metaphysical or theological dictum, but rather as an appeal aimed at defending the infinite novelties of natural circumstance against the dictates of narrow anthropocentrisms.[7]

Perhaps the most serious attempts to speculate from the ground of the first problematic have been occasioned by the defense of what A. O. Lovejoy has called "the principle of plenitude." This principle requires that "no genuine potentiality of being can remain unfulfilled."[8] As long as this principle was affirmed *only* within the context of the belief in a graded hierarchy of perfections of being, the unity of the Cosmos was not challenged. It was among those thinkers who, to varying degrees and for various reasons, acceded to a principle of discontinuity, that first-problematic thinking came to the fore. The acosmical[9] thrust entailed in the denial of a graded hierarchy of being was, unsurprisingly, rare in that important period of cosmological speculation from Cusanus to Kant, though it was at least intimated at the beginning and end of that epoch.

Cusanus's claim that the Totality has its center everywhere and its circumference nowhere expressed the paradoxical acosmism which one can reasonably expect to arise from an intoxication with the infinite. Cusansus's aim was principally to be found in the affirmation of unfathomable complexity and of the human strategies required to face it. He sought to drive home the Socratic maxim of learned ignorance resulting from understanding one's limitations. Three centuries later, Immanuel Kant flirted with the notions of acosmism and first-problematic thinking when he claimed that there may be in Nature as a "Whole," "vacant and uninhabited regions, which are not, strictly speaking, made serviceable to the object of Nature, namely, the contemplation of rational beings."[10] But this is hardly more than a gesture toward the first problematic.

First-problematic thinking begins to become important in the modern period only when the arguments for continuity and a graded hierarchy of perfections are found difficult to sustain. The first step in this direction was taken through the emphasis upon temporal over purely logical or spatial conceptions of cosmic order. What Lovejoy has termed "the temporalizing of the chain of being" added a novel dimension to the consideration of continuity. Taking time seriously frees one from the necessity to argue for a plurality of worlds within a single cosmic epoch in order to make a case for alternative orders. Something like first-problematic thinking becomes more attractive if one is able to claim that a plenitude of perfections of being could be realized over vast spans of time. The first-problematic assumption of many distinct worlds strewn throughout all dimensions of temporal process did not take hold among the physical cosmologists of the modern period, however. It is to the Romantic reaction against the principle of continuity, as Lovejoy makes clear,[11] that one must look for the major illustrations of first-problematic thinking in the modern period.

The Romantic vision, chiefly the expression of poets and artists, but illustrated also in the thought of such philosophic theologians as Friedrich Schleiermacher, reintroduced the distinctly Sophistic form of first-problematic thinking into our cultural tradition. The stress upon idiosyncratic human experience and agency is the key to the understanding of the Romantics' partial conformity and partial disconformity to the principle of plenitude. To Novalis, "Man is the Messiah of Nature." It is his task to complete, to fulfill, to realize the plenitude of nature. The artist takes up his activity where nature ceases to operate in a direct sense. From the acorn, by nature, the mighty oak is made; and from the oak by virtue of *technē*, tables and cabinets are made. This vision differs from the similar view of the Aristotelian since, for the Romantics, the individual artists create the additional ends to be realized from the fructifying womb of nature.

The stress upon the individual agency of the artist reintroduces the Protagorean principle into intellectual culture, and with it comes, as a corollary, the principle of discontinuity. The qualitative uniqueness of the individual geniuses who aim to fulfill nature's press toward plenitude raised to the level of consciousness the fact that the presumed corollary of plenitude—namely, that of qualitative continuity—was, in fact, in contradiction to it. If the world is to be populated by entities possessed of self-identity in any strong sense, then clearly they must not merge into one another, but stand apart as distinctive loci of experiencing. If the plenitude of items in the world have as their principal instances human agencies, each possessed of his own experience, consciousness, and will, then the World is not a Cosmos but a congeries. Whatever unity or uniformity to be found in this world is authored by these agencies. The oneness of things is arbitrarily claimed, and with equal arbitrariness it is appreciated or understood. The World

> has the character and the range of content and of diversity which it happens to have. No rational ground predetermined from all eternity of what sort it should be or how much of the world of possibility should be included in it. It *is*, in short, a contingent world; its magnitude, its pattern, its habits, which we call laws, have something arbitrary and idiosyncratic about them.[12]

Reflection upon the Romantic reintroduction of first-problematic thinking into our cultural tradition permits us to see that the vision of many-orderedness entails distinctive psychologies as well as cosmologies. The creative imagination is the Chaos *terminus a quo* and the World(s) is the *terminus ad quem*, the polar character of which sets the permeable bounds to meaning and existence. Those sympathetic with first-problematic thinking ought not be overly eager to embrace the Romantic vision, however, for because of its cloying, tendentious, self-glorifying anthropocentricity, the infinity it praises is a false infinity and the diversity it serves up often masks a totalitarianism of the first water.

Both the materialistic and Sophistic versions of first-problematic thinking evidence serious flaws. The Romantic or Sophistic conception of first-problematic thinking accepts the imaginative capacities of the *human* agent, disciplined by volitional activity, as the basis for descriptions of the nature of things. An indefinite number of efficient agencies of a single type (namely, human beings) determine the complexities of the World by selecting from their imaginative resources. The materialists hold that things themselves, material units, scattered through the void by the winds of contingency, coagulate into various mutually uncoordinated orders the explanation for which is not to be discovered except by recourse to the bare facticity of the infinity of existents themselves. In each case there is manyness of a single type: a mere numerical manyness in the latter instance and mere qualitative diversity in the former case. This contrast is grounded in the more fundamental contrast of the strictly logical order of the materialist, and the narrowly aesthetic order of the Sophistic or Romantic vision. But the oneness-in-manyness and manyness-in-oneness which characterize the more general conception of order, and which render it irrevocably ambiguous, are to be realized only if order in any given instance (and a fortiori in the instance of world-orders) is construed as a polar concept.

The serious ambiguity involved in the conception of order, and the cosmological, sociological, and psychological consequences of that ambiguity, constitute one of the least celebrated scandals in the history of Anglo-European culture. The concept of order seems to be protected from rigorous analysis by a kind of gentlemen's agreement to avoid the nest of difficulties that any careful reflections would entail. That this notion can (and does) mean all things to all men for the sake of the gospel of rationality is more than evident from the slightest consideration of the concept. The chief embarrassment for anyone wishing to clarify the concept derives from the fact that we have no real means of distinguishing the normative conception of order from that of its murky contradiction, Chaos.

Uniformity of distribution (a condition for at least one oft-employed conception of order), were it to be realized in the physical universe, would entail maximal entropy and, therefore, the greatest amount of disorder. Thus the Second Law of Thermodynamics promises that physical systems will achieve maximal disorder in a final state of the physical world which, were it described in terms of simplicity, uniformity, and equilibrium, might just as well be called Absolute Order. Is Chaos, then, the state of confusion and irrationality so often associated with the term, or is it, indeed, the state of absolute uniformity? If we are to identify Chaos with the absence of potentiality for orderedness associated with the disorder of entropy, does it make good sense to claim that Chaos is the ground of cosmogonic acts of creativity? If, on the other hand, we claim that the confusion and disarray of Chaos constitutes the state of highest potential energy and thereby serves as the proper ground for creative emergence, does it make sense to claim that order was brought from out of the disorder of Chaos through cosmogonic activity?

The ambiguities in the concept of order will not be resolved simply by redefining terms. It is safe to say, for reasons immediately to be rehearsed, that no single concept of order and its conceptual cognates will serve to explicate the many important meanings associated with that term in the various intellectual disciplines that require it. On the other hand, unless a univocal concept of order may be provided at the very least within a single discipline, then no real clarification of the many cognate issues dependent upon that notion may be expected, and the coherence of that discipline is significantly threatened.

Consider the following statement of the physicist D. W. Sciama:

> A great complexity exists in the world. This complexity greatly complicates the physicist's task. Instead of matter consisting of a simple substance like hydrogen, it manifests itself in all the complex elements—about a hundred of them. And instead of being distributed uniformly it is clumped together into galaxies and systems of galaxies separated by distances large compared with their size. In many scientific problems such complications are a nuisance . . .[13]

A truly delicious statement! Were there only hydrogen atoms, and were they but spread uniformly throughout space, how much easier the task of the physicist. Unfortunately, not only would the fundamental problems of physics disappear under these ideal conditions, so would the physicists.

The universe is, by definition, complicated. Otherwise it would be totally meaningless. We must, of course, presume that Sciama recognizes the irony of his statement. But even if he does, the paradox suggested by this quotation remains. And it is one that inheres in all intellectual enquiry. The conditions giving rise to the serious problems which the scientist or philosopher finds most difficult and frustrating are the same conditions which permit of meaningful existence.

For the sake of speculation let us allow the circumstances entailed by a literal interpretation of Sciama's statement—namely, the existence of a thinker in a world possessed of a high degree of uniformity. In such a world, though an observing mind would have little by way of physical investigations to perform, the science of logic would be intact. Presumably the number and kinds of suggested uniformities would in fact increase with the increased uniformity of the world.[14] Thus a mind entertaining a totally uniform world could have unqualified logical enjoyment. Aesthetic enjoyment, however, would be lacking, since it is dependent upon the entertainment of the contribution each extant detail makes to actualized orders. For there to be aesthetic enjoyment there could not be uniformity as to the kinds of items extant. Each item should be unique by virtue of the contribution it would make to the unity it construes. In a world of absolutely unique individuals, logical understanding would be made more difficult, but it would not be impossible.

It is an interesting question whether the notion of order would apply to a logically uniform world in any meaningful sense. According to Peirce, in a world wherein bare logical relationships specify the types of uniformity,

> There is no possibility of a more or less degree of orderliness in the world, the whole system of relationship between the different characters being given by mere logic; that is, being implied in those facts which are tacitly admitted as soon as we admit that there is such a thing as reasoning.[15]

We invite confusion, in other words, when we identify order and uniformity. For order to make sense it must be the case that some of the kinds of uniformities that exist in nature be valued in some way by the individual entertaining them. We value a *kind* of uniformity (or a *particular* uniform distribution)—"All (or some) A is B," for example—when it has consequences we deem relevant.

Presuming the world to be of no existential value (as a whole or in any of its parts) by virtue of the fact that none of the uniformities could be of viable interest to the entity entertaining them, the world would be totally contingent. Or totally uniform. Or both. For if it is true, as Peirce suggests, that "the interest which the uniformities of nature have for an animal measures his place in the scale of intelligence,"[16] and if "the actual world is almost a chance-medley to the mind of a polyp,"[17] and if there are fewer interesting questions to ask of the world the more uniform it becomes, then the absence of significant questions would characterize two putatively distinct kinds of worlds—namely, one possessed of total contingency, the other of absolute uniformity.

The world is viably ordered if and only if it sustains at least the appearance of a mixture of chance and uniformity. Such a world is complicated in precisely the sense that gives rise to intellectual problems of the type that Sciama claims to be nuisances. The psychological response of the intellectual to the serious problems of his discipline perhaps contradicts his professional rhetoric in most instances. Would the scientist truly like to rid himself and his enterprise of all significant problems? Would the astrophysicist like to solve, once and for all, the problem of the origin of the universe? Does the philosopher really desire the solution to the problem of the One and the Many? The end-state entailed by the solution of all problems is that wherein no intelligence could exist. The activity of knowing begins and ends in ignorance.

We do not really want to be omniscient. Intellectual excitement results from the presumption that the answer to one question raises, in geometric progression, other equally profound questions *ad indefinitum*. And the sense of order presumed here is not one that requires a single-ordered world. Even if it were presumed that a final state of knowledge could be attained at some indefinite stretch of time in the future, would it be desirable? Perhaps to a polyp, or a stone. And if it is not generally desirable, should it serve as the implicit *telos* of intellectual endeavor? *Can* it so serve?

The question we are asking is whether omniscience could possibly make any sense at all. Or does the fundamental irony suggested by the necessary relations of knowledge and ignorance, an irony first celebrated by Socrates, express an essential truth about the character of our relationship to our world?

In one of his more bizarre tales, "Funes the Memorious," Jorge Luis Borges tells of a man who, after a fall from a horse, discovers that, though physically crippled, his mental powers have grown infinitely. He has developed the power of absolute and perfect recall. Not only can he recall everything he perceives, he can remember, as well, each time he has recalled a perception. The world of this prodigy is one comprised by the concrete data of perception and imagination. He owns no abstractions, no generalizations, no principles. He has no need for them.

The man was, of course, quite ignorant. For he was incapable of thinking in any meaningful sense. "To think is to forget a difference, to generalize, to abstract. In the overly replete world of Funes there were nothing but details."[18] One of the more impressive of the achievements of this knowledgeable idiot was the construction of a number "system" in which each number had a unique name.

In place of seven thousand thirteen, he would say (for example) *Máximo Perez*; in place of seven thousand fourteen, *The Train*; other numbers were *Luis Melian Lafinur, Olimar, Brimstone, Clubs, The Whale, Gas, The Cauldron, Napoleon, Augustin de Vedia*. In lieu of five hundred, he would say *nine*.[19]

This is not a number *system*. It makes little sense at all. What shall we say of the prodigious knowledge of Borges's character? Perhaps, that it was too prodigious. Without ignorance there can be no abstractions, no generalizations, no atemporal forms of definiteness patterning the mundane instances of perception and knowledge.

Omniscience involves not only the absence of discursive thought, but the incapacity to think at all. Complete understanding requires *both* the complete subjugation of the world and its components to principles, *and* the complete appreciation of each detail of the totality of things both in itself and in the concrete relatedness it maintains with respect to the myriad other extant details. The paradoxical condition for completeness of understanding is that the total number of principles must exactly equal the total number of existing things. At the extremes this condition is met either in a world comprised of but one kind of item, a totally uniform world, or by a world in which each item is unique and unrepeatable. In the first type of world there are as many kinds of order as there are logical patterns conceivable. In the second world there are as many orders as there are items, since the uniqueness of each item is determined in accordance with its construal of an order.

We find ourselves in the midst of these rather strange reflections because we tried to define order in some nonambiguous manner. This we obviously have not accomplished. One useful thing we have discovered, however, is that the conception of order must involve both uniformity and nonuniformity. Orderedness involves a mixture of (relative) pattern regularity and (relative) pattern irregularity. Second, we have found that the locus and character of regularity and irregularity are functions of the interest of the entity entertaining the order.

To the extent that order involves pattern regularity any recognizable order must involve some recognizable nonuniformity. Multiformity unconditioned by the criteria of pattern regularity employed in the appreciation of the order must be present in or to the given order. This most obviously occurs in ordinary instances of uniformity through the recognition of the mere approximative status of the order, as well as through the recognition of the specific context of relevance of the order. The "uniform" curvature of a line forming a circle drawn on a blackboard is tacitly accepted as an adequate surrogate for the construct as conceptually defined or as imagined. In formal instances the geometric concept of the circle is entertained in abstraction from the indefinite number of its concrete applications, and in isolation from its definite relations with alternative types of uniformity—for example, other members of the class of conic sections. The disordered background in relation to which the specific character of a single type of uniformity (or any instance or instances of that uniformity) is envisioned is essential to the appreciation of orderedness.

Some further clarification of the concept of order is possible if we make explicit the distinctive meanings of "logical" and "aesthetic" order which have been presupposed in the discussion thus far. This requires that we distinguish the sense of mere order from the notion of the enjoyment of order.

A logically consistent relation requires only that the conjunction of "A" and "B" is possible—i.e., $\Diamond(A \cdot B)$. An aesthetic relationship of orderedness exists when the following condition obtains: $A \cdot B$ iff C_r $(A \cdot B)$, where "r" = "is interested in," or "enjoys." Logical relations are abstract in the sense that the pattern regularities illustrated are applicable to all or some instances of the related entities. Aesthetic relations require focusing upon one specific complex of details.

If we identify *formal* abstraction as abstraction from actuality and what I shall call *selective* abstraction with abstraction from possibility,[20] we may see that in the former case increased abstraction involves increased indifference to the specific concrete details and the just-so-ness of the experience. In the proposition "A·B," an indefinite number of items or attributes may be substituted for "A" and "B." Selective abstraction, however, moves away from the realm of possibility to that of concrete circumstance which limits the number of actual relations. Aesthetic enjoyment, moreover, limits these relations even further. If "A" is "green of a particular shade" and "B" is "pink of a particular shade," any number of contexts could be imagined in which the conjunction of "A" and "B" would be aesthetic disaster. Aesthetic inconsistency is significantly related to the more familiar notion of logical inconsistency. However, aesthetic relations are relatively nonformal, involving mainly selective abstraction.

Just as it is possible to entertain aesthetically inconsistent items by virtue of formal abstraction from their details and from their perspectival relations to the act of aesthetic appreciation, so it is possible to entertain in the positive mode of aesthetic enjoyment propositions which, logically construed, may be inconsistent. The at least minimal interest shown in the "round square" or the "noisy triangle" at the level of imaginative sensibility illustrates this fact. The inconceivability of a notion does not preclude at least a minimum of interest, and interest in the fundamental form of aesthetic enjoyment.

The introduction of the notion of "interest" allows us to realize the important relations between logical and aesthetic notions of order. When Aristotle developed his notion of logical and scientific method in the *Prior* and *Posterior Analytics*, he was careful to distinguish the kind of knowledge associated with the truth of the conclusions of demonstrations from that attaching to the definitions and premises from which demonstrations proceeded. Scientific knowledge is of causes recognized through the relation of middle terms to the premises and conclusions of a syllogism. The syllogistic pattern guarantees the truth of the conclusion of a train of argument provided the premises are true. It is by intuition or self-evidence that we are assured of the truth of a premise or the adequacy of a definition. The understanding of the conclusion of an argument is a logical mode of understanding. But the grasp of first principles involves the recognition of novel patterns. This latter, intuitive act requires aesthetic appreciation. Syllogistic demonstration effects a kind of closure which guarantees the necessary relation of conclusion to premises; the assurance of the truth of first principles is an appeal to self-evidence which cannot result from the imposition of preassigned pattern but must be a kind of disclosure. Logic per se proceeds by way of attainment of a closed fact; aesthetic sensibility begins with the facticity of events or entities and seeks the self-evidence emerging from disclosure of details.

The obvious relation between logical and aesthetic order is evidenced by the aesthetic appreciation of bare logical and mathematical relations. The elegance of a particular proof, or the beauty of a curve evincing a "tang of infinity as it journeys off into uncharted space"[21] is aesthetically enjoyed. And it is the particularity of the whole (the particular proof, the particular curve) and the disclosure of the necessity of the finite details to the integral whole which are affirmed. Aesthetic interest is at the heart of the logical enterprise; without it we should not be motivated to lift our pencils or chalk to perform the logical operations.

The somewhat less appreciated relation of logic to aesthetics is to be found in the necessity of closure in art and aesthetic activities. However much we may scorn the development of styles of art, or schools of art, as somehow challenging the originality of the aesthetic enterprise, it is essential to have some degree of closure, some notion of preassigned pattern, if there is to be the cultural enterprise of art at all. But it is not just in relation to technique, or schools, that the logical impetus is to be discovered in art. Some artists resort to the logical perspective through the employment of preassigned patterns for the coordination of vast details simply because they are inundated by the variegated complexities of experienced circumstance. Logical relations per se may serve to discipline the overly rich imagination sufficiently to allow the aesthetic sensibility to be exercised in a healthy manner.

However much we appreciate the relationship between logical and aesthetic orders, we should realize that the former has as one of its prime rationales the avoidance of inconsistency, whereas the latter celebrates the fundamental fact of inconsistency. Abstraction from actuality yields increased possibility for consistency by virtue of the employment of patterns which are putatively generic. General patterns restrict the entrance of de-selected details. Irrelevant details being absent, inconsistencies are less in evidence. The more we are concerned with a particular relationship or particular things, however, the fewer entities are able to realize that relationship.

Because of the formal character of conceptual understanding, it is difficult to see how one might achieve the highest degree of selective abstraction. The aim of such completeness of selective abstraction is to realize a thing in and for itself (and in its totality of relationships to all entities comprising its environment) as an instance of aesthetic disclosure.

> Thus in proportion as we penetrate toward concrete apprehension inconsistency rules. Namely, all entities, except one, are inconsistent with the production of the particular effect which the one entity would produce. In proportion to our relapse toward [formal] abstraction, many entities will alternately produce the same abstract effect. Thus consistency grows with abstraction from the concrete.[22]

One lesson to be learned from the contrast of aesthetic and logical orders is that classical thermodynamic interpretations of cosmological order, irrevocably conditioned by the concept of entropy, are productive of a great deal of confusion. We may accede to the fact of entropy, but it is essential to clarify the meaning of order before we take the naïve step of contrasting entropy and order. It may be true that, for all X, if X is the ordered consequence of ordering activity, X involves an increase in entropy, but this proposition obscures the fact that, for *some* X, if X yields an entropy increase, X is ordered, while for some (other) X it is disordered. The transition from a complex order to one of relative simplicity (provided both are balanced, equilibrated) yields an entropy increase. Likewise the sudden collapse of a complex order into a congeries of uncoordinated suborders has the same result. Thus, on a scale of predictability or measurability, there is some sense in which the extreme cases at either end of the scale are entropic with respect to those cases nearer the mean.[23]

The tension between types of order highlights a characteristic dilemma of philosophic thought. This dilemma is illustrated by the fact that though the most adequate accounts of the relations of the parts in an ordered unity seem to require that both aesthetic and logical value be provided categorial status, the attempt to do so appears always to end with one mode of value being stressed at the expense of the other. My solution will be to argue that this dilemma is not metaphysically grounded. The aesthetic interest must take precedence over the logical.

Perhaps Whitehead's greatest gift to philosophic speculation is his insight that a complete account of the nature of a thing requires recourse to both genetic and morphological modes of analysis. These modes indicate, respectively, what a thing is for itself and what it is for environing others. Most philosophers are not as sensitive as was Whitehead to the distinction between the *analysandum* and the *mode of analysis*, however. In the genetic process of experiencing there is a many becoming one; in the enjoyment of that experience the sense of unity precedes the enjoyment of details. A logical patterning per se constitutes a unity comprised by the relations of its components. In the understanding of that pattern the component details as a many are enjoyed as permissive of that given set of relations. There is thus a multi-valent set of relationships between the genetic and morphological constructions and enjoyments. Both genetic and morphological orders may be considered from genetic and logical perspectives.

The kind of orders associated with genetic processes are paradigmatic illustrations of *aesthetic* order whereas the constructions resulting from these processes, in their objective character, are illustrations of *logical* patternings. Logical order is extremely abstract since the pattern regularities it illustrates may be constituted by an indefinite number of entities. Aesthetic relations require focusing upon one specific complex of details. In the broadest sense a logical perspective involves the coordination of details in conformity with a preassigned pattern. The aesthetic perspective involves the emergence of a complex whole by virtue of the insistent particularity of essential details. Logical construction and enjoyment merge when one begins with many things and seeks their unity in accordance with a preassigned uniformity. Aesthetic sensibility begins with the one thing and finds the occasion for enjoyment of it in the balanced complexity for which the ingredient details are differentially responsible. The act of aesthetic enjoyment depends upon the fact that these details maintain their individuality with respect to the harmony of the whole. Logical enjoyment depends upon the recognition of the fullest possible coordination of the ingredient details.

It is not only confusing but impertinent in the strictest sense, to attempt the analysis of an order which ignores either its logical or aesthetic dimension. Order is a polar concept in which the oneness and manyness of things inhere in direct and nondetachable manners. The discovery of logical order requires an act of *closure* in which a given pattern is seen to be illustrated by related details. Aesthetic construction involves closure as well. This time, however, the many details are gathered into a novel unity. Aesthetic enjoyment, as opposed to construction, celebrates the *disclosure* of the insistent particularity of those details in tension with the unity initially entertained, whereas logical enjoyment depends upon the recognition of the character of those details as abstractions comprising the given pattern. Logical disclosure is the disclosure of unity; aesthetic disclosure reveals insistent particularity.

One conclusion to be drawn from this discussion is that the complete understanding of an order requires the consideration of its aesthetic and logical characteristics, both from the perspective of its constitution and the perspective of our enjoyment of it as constituted. It is essential that the simplicity of logical uniformities be appreciated along with the complexity born of the insistent particularity of extant items. It is equally essential that the act of appreciation itself include aesthetic as well as logical construal.

Aesthetic characterizations depend upon the fact that at the level of percipient experience plurality must be conceived as prior to unity, disjunction to conjunction, and inconsistency to consistency. If one were to accept the view that the harmony of a definite thing is a contrast of its constituent elements, then the analysis of things or states of affairs would lead from pattern to pattern, from contrast to contrast, from one type of togetherness to another, one unity to another. The importance of the insistent particularity of self-existing things would be mitigated. This would be tantamount to the denial of aesthetic order as a fundamental fact. The traditional understanding of harmony in contrastive terms tacitly assumes the priority of consistency, conjunction, and unity over their opposites. This tacit assumption is both cause and consequence of the belief that norms, or pattern criteria, exist independently of the flux of passing circumstance and function as forms of togetherness characterizing the harmonies we objectively experience.

In the truest sense process understandings must have the notion of insistent particularity as both ground and goal. Process and particularity are mutually implicative. If there were but one kind of entity, uniformity would be complete and the varieties of logical order (the sole object of enjoyment in such a world) could be enjoyed in abstraction from the entertainment of any actually existing thing. Any item in such a world could serve as surrogate for any other. Total stasis would be the rule. In a world of insistent particularities persistence is less valuable. Items and their complex unities must move off the scene to make way for other items and complexes incompossible with regard to the former. Particularity argues for process if the fullest values are to be realized. And process, if it is to be more than a shifting of components and patterns (whose *possible* existence is thought to be as rich as the actualities so patterned), requires particularity.

The mutual entailment of process and particularity leads to the affirmation of inconsistency and disjunction as fundamental forms of relation. A particular item, simply by virtue of its particularity, excludes other particulars. If we are solely concerned with the conception of alternative components in an artistic or mathematical composition, it is logical consistency or inconsistency that is at stake. Aesthetic inconsistency is recognized when one senses that only that single extant detail could create the effect it in fact achieves. Thus aesthetic inconsistency is a characteristic of actualities as self-existent particulars.

The stress upon contrastive harmony leads to the overvaluation of unity and consistency and, thus, is nothing less than the logical construal of aesthetic order. If unity and harmony are the primary criteria in accordance with which value is assessed, then individuals tend to be construed as for the sake of the order and harmony they support. Thus the denial of insistent particularity threatens individuality at the level of social praxis. The stress upon the notion of contrastive harmony permits one to argue for a metaphysical ground of moral value and our discernment of it. However, it exacts a tremendous price. Such metaphysical moralism is well-nigh fatal to the aesthetic sensibility. Such a vision denies the primacy of process, usurps the fundamental reality of present experiencing by shifting much of its intensity to the past and the future, and construes the insistent particularities of experience merely as singular abstractions forming components in the harmonies which constitute the putative objects of aesthetic and moral discernment.

The grounding of the aesthetics of process upon the notions of inconsistency and plurality entails the view that harmony is a constraint against which the details struggle. Unity is a transitory condition grounded in the mutual deference of the components. The harmony of a unity is the gift of the individuals which comprise the elements of the contrast, not the gift of the contrast. Unity is the price paid for the maintenance of insistent particularity. It is, in fact, the reason for the insistence. The mutuality required for there to be harmony is the luxurious by-product of process, not its end. Ontological individuals, uniquely self-existent, envisioned as creating their worlds rather than being created by them, are the final realities as aesthetically constituted.

Thus far my remarks have consisted in nothing more than a challenge to the moralistic emphasis upon logical over aesthetic understandings. Nothing I have said could be construed as much more than a statement of my preference for aesthetic over logical modes of analysis. Clearly my arguments in favor of aestheticism are simply beside the point if I remain content with chiding the moralist for mitigating the aesthetic interest while I, for my part, attempt to undermine the arguments supporting the moral interest merely by challenging the value of logical understandings. My claim against the moralist can be responsibly sustained only if I can demonstrate that aesthetic value has a metaphysical grounding which must be denied to moral value.

Aesthetic experience is the immediate enjoyment of the relations of an object or event functioning as a finite detail to the rest of the natural world that it inexhaustibly construes from its own perspective. The enjoyment of "B" by "A" recognizes the self-existence of "A" as an insistent particularity constituting the complex relations of the items comprising the world it construes. Perceiving in its generic sense is the recognition of the natural relations one has to the world as an object of entertainment. At the most general level, this requires an ontological reference since the most profound relationship of perceiving event to its world is that which defines its uniqueness through the contrast of the solitariness of its character as foreground and the indefinite character of the world as background. The perceiving event per se is unique; it is the final piece in the puzzle which is the totality of things. The contrast of individuality and totality construed as completeness and unity is the source of mystical experiences of union. Alternately, if the individuality of the perceiving event, or of any finite particular in a complex unity, is envisioned as constituting the formative element of a complex whole, there is aesthetic experience.

Both mystical and aesthetic intuitions deal with the ontological characteristics of things. Cosmologically, the perceiving event and that which is perceived are construed in terms of the assignment through physiological, linguistic, or rhetorical operations of a pattern of meaning which constitutes one set of relations that can be said to exist among the items entertained and the manner in which the context so conceived determines the character of the items forming the context. It is at this level that morality is grounded. The references of the aesthetic and religious senses are, each in their own ways, more fundamental than that of the moral sense. Morality concerns the contrast of the individual with a finite selection of others construed solely within the cosmological context defining kinds and degrees of order associated with the beings involved in the moral experience. The ontological reference which undergirds the ultimacy of aesthetic and mystical experiencing is not a part of the moral experience.

In discriminating value experiences we must understand that the sense of the immediate enjoyment of self-existence (value for oneself) is differentially related to the sense of being one for a many and one for the indefinite totality of things. The one-some-all matrix of value experience is the basis of the discrimination of types of value. If he is to defend the objectivity of value, the metaphysical moralist must argue that the value a thing has for itself is identical with the value it has for others. The analysis of value experiencing suggested here would make this true only if the "others" included *all* others—that is, if they constituted the totality rather than any discriminated portion of it.

One implication of the understanding of value experience discussed above is that morality is a penultimate experience associated with certain contingent cosmological characteristics of the world conceived as an indefinite totality. Insofar as these characteristics may be transcended through aesthetic and mystical experiences, morality may be seen as differentially reducible to the claims of art on the one hand or religion on the other. Morality constitutes a comfort station at the point of no return between the aesthetic and religious termini of experience. Just as the *felix culpa* argues against the assurance of consistency between the claims of religion and morality, so the confinement of many of our more avant artists to bohemian ghettos argues against the necessary harmony of moral and aesthetic values.

The principal burden of my arguments thus far has been to show that historically, our culture provides evidence of a cultural problematic at variance with that which has served us from the beginnings of our intellectual tradition. I have named this alternative first-problematic thinking. It is the presumption that no single order can define the nature of that which is. I have also sought to show that there is a serious ambiguity in the most general conceptions of order. Implicit in these arguments is the conviction that the ambiguity highlighted is a consequence of a one-sided emphasis upon second-problematic assumptions. In the following pages I hope to show that, for a variety of reasons, contemporary thinkers are beginning to research novel conceptions of order as a means of attempting to resolve serious problems arising in their disciplines. This provides the opportunity for looking into the manner in which first-problematic conceptions of orderedness may contribute to contemporary intellectual resources.

In this century there have been a number of major assaults upon the notion of a single-ordered cosmos that underlies second-problematic thought. The hypotheses of biological evolution, particularly those which emphasize emergence, stress the likelihood of the creation of radically novel orders over a sufficient span of time. The completeness of the world is challenged by this notion. Abstracted from its strictly biological context, the concept of emergent orders has taken on such significant theoretical forms as that of Whitehead's vision of "cosmic epochs," cosmological orders of a dissociated and radically novel sort successively realized over vast reaches of time,[24] and that of Karl Popper's somewhat less ambitious notion of the discontinuous emergence of sentience, consciousness, and language.[25] Each of these instances dissociates the concepts of order and predictability and, thus, challenges the knowability, and, therefore, the strict meaningfulness, of the notion of a single-ordered world.

The name of Sigmund Freud is associated with a vision requiring the reduction of reason to certain phenomenological manifestations of rationalization. The deterministic substratum of the Freudian theory doubtless is in conformity with the classical vision of single-orderedness, but the psychological implications relative to the human organism work to undermine the confidence in the rationality of the cosmos in much the same way as the views of Democritus and Lucretius had done. The conventional nature of human understandings does not reach the actual way of things. Orderedness, its construction and its appreciation, are functions of the psychological needs of the organism, and are not primarily to be considered apart from the psychic function they serve. Cosmological theory is as much a sublimated product of libidinal drives as is any other cultural product.

Relativity theory has seriously challenged traditional conceptions of order. By denying absolute simultaneity, special relativity leads to the rejection of the notion of the universe as in any sense a *stasis*. In the realm of Einsteinian cosmology the concepts of order and measurement are intrinsically tied. This dissolves the Order of Nature into a complex of shifting frames of reference. The dominant interpretation of general relativity requires local distortions of Euclidean space by gravitational forces. This notion frustrates any conception of space serving as a container within which to chart the order of things. Matter and space are each dissolved into relationships of a dynamic sort. Local distortions of spatiotemporal fields require us to believe that neither is space uniformly curved nor does time uniformly flow.

Relativity theory has complicated the notion of order enormously by requiring that the observer be taken into account, because of the necessity of specifying frames of reference as conditions for measuring activities. Quantum theory, in its major forms of interpretation, makes of the observer a conditioning participant. Descriptions of particle interactions at the quantum level require recourse to the relationship between an observing system (an individual plus his experimental apparatus) and an observed system (specific particle interactions). More importantly, the conceptualizations of the observer, and the specific character of his apparatus, are both habituated to and conditioned by the apparent causal regularities of the macro-world. These regularities are describable in terms of classical physics and its attendant technologies. The observed system, however, dissolves into the fuzziness and uncertainty of probability situations which require a mathematical formalism of a type which does not (yet?) answer to the intuitive or conceptual equipment of the observer, armed with his sophisticated apparatus. The dissonance set up between the observer and the observed can be only partially resolved and this *partial* resolution means that the experimental observation, to a presently unknowable degree, determines the character of that which is observed. The transcendence of this inherent limitation in atomic physics requires the development of something more than more subtle instruments or more precise experimental parameters. What is required is a demonstration of the nature of the connection between the important characteristics generalizable from the observing system and those discoverable in the objects observed.

The consequence of such a theoretical determination would be that we should be able to answer the question of the nature of the relationship between the world within experience and the world beyond experience. Ultimately, this requires that we hold as axiomatic the proposition that the logical and aesthetic relations to be found in nature are also to be found in our experience of nature.

In the original Aristotelian sense of the term, an axiom is that which must be known to be so if anything else is to be known. The divorce of mathematical formalisms from intuitive experiencing, which has reached its grandest extremes in certain theories of quantum relativity, has led to a condition in which we know less and less about more and more. As such, atomic physics is reducible, with little of significance remaining, to a set of techniques or technologies the instruments of which provide us with only *instrumental* understandings.

If science and philosophy are to remain important perspectives upon the world, maintaining the privileged place that the search for important knowledge requires they maintain, two heuristic assumptions must be functionally axiomatic: first, orders discoverable within the experience of an individual observer must be demonstrably commensurate with orders beyond the immediacy of experiencing; second (this is likely entailed by the first), we are required to affirm a heuristic panpsychism in which the relation of "world within" and "world without" is reflected in the polar relationship of the oneness-in-manyness and manyness-in-oneness of order as at once logical and aesthetic.

The mutual relations of psychology and cosmology as the sources for the *terminus a quo* and the *terminus ad quem* of the notion of order provide the primary ground for the necessity of this heuristic panpsychism. For the only significant means of taking into account the relationship of knower and known which ultimately does not require a reduction of knowledge to the conditions of knowing is by recourse to the fact that the self-world polarity defines the character of both selves and worlds. Psychology, in its broadest sense, entails cosmology, and cosmology grounds psychology. In the words of Whitehead, "The world within experience is identical with the world beyond experience."[26]

Perhaps the most fruitful contemporary discussions of the concept of order are to be found among the quantum theorists and the brain physiologists. The reason that this collaboration is so interesting lies, of course, in the fact that the brain is the principal element in the observational system entering into every instance of observation at the quantum level. If a model of the brain can be discovered which correlates meaningfully with a model of nature as observed, then it will be possible to approach more closely to a concept of order which viably combines the logical (observed system) and the aesthetic (observing system) aspects of the term. Briefly examining instances of novel conceptions of order from physics and psychology will permit us to make a case for the importance of the first-problematic thinking in contemporary culture. It will also set the stage for any subsequent speculations concerning the social applications of first-problematic thinking, since social theory involves mid-range considerations that fall between the conceptualizations relevant to cosmology and psychology respectively.

Doubtless the best example of first-problematic thinking in our contemporary period is to be found in the work of the physicist David Bohm. Bohm argues for a conception of the natural world as an undivided whole which he terms the "holomovement." Entities and their interactions, as considered through particular scientific observations and theories, are explicated with respect to the total implicated wholeness which is the ground of all order. Bohm uses the hologram as a model for the universe thus construed.

The character of holography is such that a picture taken of a particular object contains the entire object represented in each segment of the hologram. Thus the segment of the hologram analyzed out from the gross representation will, on detailed consideration, be found to have implicated within it the entire structure of the hologram. Each part of the entire structure at the gross level is spread throughout each other part in such manner as to present an indivisible whole.

Bohm outlines a simple experiment which illustrates the manner in which the notion of implicated orders is to be understood.

> Implicate order can be demonstrated in the laboratory, with a transparent container full of a very viscous fluid, such as treacle, and equipped with a mechanical rotator that can "stir" the fluid very slowly but very thoroughly. If an insoluble droplet of ink is placed in the fluid and the stirring device is set in motion, the ink drop is gradually transformed into a thread that extends over the whole fluid. The latter now appears to be distributed more or less at "random" so that it is seen as some shade of gray. But if the mechanical stirring device is now turned in the opposite direction, the transformation is reversed, and the droplet of dye suddenly appears, reconstituted.[27]

Several important points may be gleaned from this illustration and from Bohm's subsequent discussion of it. First, the ink can exist either as explicit in the form of a droplet or in various degrees of implication. Second, if we were to add other droplets of differing colors we could implicate the droplets with respect to one another. If the droplets were added at different moments in the process of turning, we should have a very complicated structure in which the droplets were implicated in relatively different degrees. The structure of the whole (i.e., the measured orders established by the various relations of implicated droplets) would exist both among droplets of the same degree of implication and of differing degrees. For example, assuming this model, the structure of the realm investigated by microphysics would involve the relations of wave phenomena and particle phenomena which exist with respect to one another in relatively different degrees of implication. The principle of complementarity would then apply to a structured whole, distinctive "parts" of which would be illustrated by waves and particles.

If the structure of the totality of things is an undivided whole consisting of an arrangement of orders of varying degrees of implication with respect to the observer-participant, then the conceivable limit of such a structure is illustrated by the proposition, "$p \cdot \bar{p}$," where p has an implicate order of 1 (I_1)—that is, is explicit—and $\bar{p}$ an implicate order I_N, where $N \to \infty$. Thus there is a way of speaking of the structure of the whole which consists in overlapping orders of various degrees of conceptual compatibility. The whole is, thus, *Chaos* in the sense of that term heretofore presupposed.

Conscious perception is grounded on the p and $\bar{p}$ contrast in which the negative judgment serves as the background for the positive form of the perception. The recognition of p as $\bar{m}$, where p is the color blue and m any other color, is a simple instance of such negative judgment. The most radical form of negative judgment is found in dialectical thinking at its most general extreme where $\bar{p}$ is generated with every entertainment of p. The Platonic insight, "Not being has a kind of being," may be interpreted in the following manner, using the notion of implicate and explicate orders:

$$p = \bar{p}\,(I_N) \cdot p\,(I_1)$$

where
$$\frac{\bar{p}\,(I_N)}{p\,(I_1)} \to \infty$$

and "p" is any factual proposition.

Speculations of the type instanced above are not restricted to physical cosmology. If we recall that one of the distinctive features of quantum relativity is that it requires that the observer and the observing system be taken into account in the most intimate way, we can easily see how it is essential to supplement novel cosmological understandings by equally novel psychological speculations. For certainly the most important aspect of the observing system is the brain (mind) of the observer-participant. If we could understand the brain functionings relevant to the observation of the phenomena at the level of quantum relativity we should progress a long way toward sorting out the meanings of the phenomena into which we seek to enquire.

Recently, theorists of brain functioning have developed significant and dramatic hypotheses concerning brain activity which lead to a number of interesting conclusions relevant to the understanding of order in nature. Karl Pribram, for example, has appealed to the model of the hologram to interpret certain brain functionings which had long been resistant to adequate explanation.[28] For example, memory processes seem to be spread across the whole brain such that a given memory trace may be contained in every part of the brain just as the whole figure in a hologram is contained in its entirety in every part of its complex. There is at present no sound evidence to the effect that the hologram model may be generalized with respect to all, or even most, of the activity of the brain, but the suggestiveness of this model is sufficient to increase our understanding of the nature of the observational system not only with regard to the phenomena which occur (presumedly) outside the brain cage, but with respect to the observation of the brain itself as well.

The reason one may wish to call into question some of the findings of the neurophysiologist who claims that the brain is a hard-wired mechanism with processing systems similar to those of digital computers lies in the fact that the functioning of the so-called dominant left cerebral hemisphere is supplemented by the activity of the right cerebral hemisphere whose manner of entertaining the world seems so radically distinct. The linear, causal, temporal, and discrete processing characteristics of the left hemisphere contribute to understandings of the world which well match our classical scientific visions. The less articulate, more implicit acausal, analogical renderings of the right brain challenge these classical understandings.

If it is the left brain which examines the whole brain, then one would expect the hard-wired mechanistic and causal model to dominate our speculations concerning brain function. But if we ask the right brain for advice on how to understand the whole brain, the linguistically mute right hemisphere might provide us with intuited orders which, though incompletely expressible in propositional form, nonetheless indicate, via metaphor and allusion, that the world has a radically different character.

The brain as the primary component of the observing system in the development of physical theories may be thought to have two subsystems relevant to the observation. The dominant left brain is an explicating system which details via analysis the character of things as discrete entities with causal interactions. This left-brain process may proceed with varying degrees of contribution from the nondiscursive right brain. The right hemisphere tends to be an implicating system which eschews causal analysis in terms of holistic explanations. These two subsystems are themselves related as explicate and implicate with respect to one another. In terms of Bohm's interpretation of order as undivided wholeness, the right-brain evidences are given priority at the level of understanding. At the level of practice, relevant forms of explication would be stressed. This latter consequence matches well our understanding of the brain as a consequence of evolutionary development in which the survival needs of human beings are most closely dependent upon left-brain functionings that help to organize behavior at the level of cultural praxis. The world insofar as it transcends the direct experiencing of the human organism may best be understood in terms of criteria developed from attendance to right-hemisphere evidences. In particular, if more intuitively grounded mathematical models begin to dominate the more discursive forms of propositional language in our theoretical descriptions of the way of things at the microphysical level, models of understanding more closely associated with right-brain patternings will be required.

We should not lose sight of the purpose of instancing contemporary understandings of the observer and the observed at the levels of physics and neurophysiology. The strategy with which I began this discussion of the ambiguity of order was concerned with the attempt to illustrate historically, as well as in abstract conceptual terms, the ambiguity of the concept of order and the way in which that ambiguity has clouded our understandings of that concept in ways precluding the richest possible understandings of the nature of our world and the form of our presence to it. A significant conclusion to be drawn from this discussion is that the most relevant approaches to the understandings of order in our contemporary world are those grounded in what we have called first-problematic thinking. For, paradoxically, the holographic model of the totality of things does not lead to the notion of a single-ordered world with a single complex of pattern regularities associated with a single set of laws. The world itself is, as Bohm indicates, "not limited in any specifiable way at all. It is not required to conform to any particular order, or to be bounded by any particular measure. Thus, *the holomovement is undefinable and immeasurable.*"[29]

I have certainly not attempted to chart each of the classical and contemporary challenges to the concept of a single-ordered world. I should, however, round out this rather loosely concatenated set of forays into the issue of the ambiguity of order with a brief consideration of the strictly philosophic perspective on the issue of cosmological order.

As our review of the earliest philosophic cosmologies has shown, the presumption of single-orderedness is just that—a presumption. The early victory of second-problematic thinking "settled" the issue for some time. Clearly, the thousand-year subservience of philosophy to theological doctrines ensured the simple givenness of the notion of the World as a created product the coherence of which was guaranteed by the Mind and/or Will of God. Modern philosophy, however, began by raising to the level of cultural awareness the question of God's existence. This could only eventuate in raising the question of the status of "the World" as well.

The most significant philosophic assault upon the integrity of the notion of the World was entailed by Descartes's attempt to make the viability of the physical universe depend upon the certitude of God's existence which in turn he grounded upon the certainty of the *cogito*. The seeds of solipsism contained in such a project have been harvested in any number of ways in contemporary thought. The existence of God and a fortiori of the physical world were not found to have the same authoritativeness as that of the existence of the self. No less important in this light was Leibniz's endeavor to ground the coherence of the World Order on the principle of sufficient reason. By raising to the level of consciousness the questions of the existence and coherence of the world, Descartes and Leibniz transformed the "naïvely given" into the "intuitively given." And once a thinker claims intuitive certainty for any principle or doctrine, he challenges his colleagues to test that claim by recourse to their own intuitions. The collapse of consensus is almost surely the consequence.

On the empirical side, Locke and Hume did much to cast doubt upon the conception of a single-ordered cosmos. Locke's "something we know not what" that served him as the putative substratum of ideas, and Hume's notions of "custom" and "constant conjunction" by which he sought to characterize metaphysical beliefs, seriously qualified the reasonableness of speculative philosophy. Locke's queries raised doubts about the notion of general substances and, a fortiori, about the notion of the general be-ing of the cosmos. Hume's attack upon the necessity of cause–effect relations seriously challenged the grounds for rational belief in the interconnectedness of the world.

It was Kant's radical solution to what he perceived to be the defects of modern philosophy from Descartes to Hume that set the context for the final collapse of philosophic visions of the strict unity of the World.

Practically all of the contemporary debates concerning the viability of the notion of the World derive from the distinction between "things-in-themselves" and the schematizing activity of the Understanding. For it is precisely this distinction which undergirds the contrast between facts and theories, givenness and interpretation, a priori and empirical truth, the World and visions of the World, and so on. This latter point has been most succinctly addressed by Richard Rorty in his article "The World Well Lost."

> Since Kant, we find it almost impossible not to think of the mind as divided into active and passive faculties, the former using concepts to "interpret" what "the world" imposes on the latter. We also find it difficult not to distinguish between those concepts the mind could hardly get along without and those which it can take or leave alone. . . . But as soon as we have this picture of the mind in focus, it occurs to us, as it did to Hegel, that those all-important a priori concepts . . . might have been different.[30]

This insight that "it might have been different" undergirds the pragmatic thrust of much contemporary philosophy, significantly determining the sort of limitations one wishes to place upon the construction of cosmological theories. For philosophies such as these the World becomes the putative object of subsequent enquiry. It is, in one sense, the taken-for-granted background of all acts of knowing; in another sense it is the variety of types of togetherness associated with the kinds of unities that emerge from enquiries.

For James, "it is possible to imagine alternative universes to the one that we know, in which the most various grades and types of union should be embodied."[31] The reason such imagination is possible to James is that the unity of the world is the unity of *belief*. That is, the world hangs together precisely to the degree that it is known to do so. The world, in fact, "is growing more and more unified by those systems . . . which human energy keeps framing as time goes by."[32] The world of our inner lives is as little unified as can be; the world of our public, consensual beliefs is as ordered as it can be.

Opening the World to a variety of conceptual interpretations makes of it a vague "something we know not what" passive to numerous theoretical interpretations. Finally, the World becomes "worlds" once the distinction between that which is given for interpretation and the interpretation itself can no longer be persuasively defended. A given remains, of course. It is the vague and indeterminate something which we characterize through our interpretive activity. But it is a mere teleological notion. The only coherent concept of World is one which exists by virtue of a complex of beliefs concerning that which is.

Thus, for Rorty, " 'the world' is either the purely vacuous notion of the ineffable cause of sense and goal of intellect, or else a name for those objects that inquiry at the moment is leaving alone."[33]

The pragmatic conception of the world eschews cosmology by rejecting the notion of the world as the vague object of theoretical articulation, accepting that whatever coherence the world has is a consequence of currently unquestioned beliefs. I have accepted as an essential part of the enterprise of philosophic understanding the first concept of the world as a balance to the second. The world is both the indeterminate something which serves as the putative goal of enquiry and, equally, the set of determinations that exist at various levels of articulation from the lowest level of mere association related to the unshared contents of our imaginations to the intersubjective ideas and convictions that form our cultural *communis sensus*.

Contemporary philosophy is a victim of its own tendentious rigor. Impatient with the ambiguities encountered in the search for a univocal sense of order as the consequence of acts of knowing, contemporary analytic philosophers have sought to abolish the ground of that ambiguity by denying the Kantian distinction of the thing-in-itself and the schematizing activity of the mind. This denial has paved the way for Quine's attacks upon the distinction between a priori and empirical truth and Sellars's analysis of "the myth of the given," in much the same way that, a generation before, it had grounded Dewey's assault upon the distinction between the genetic-functional and mathematical-formal methods of enquiry.

Quine's assault upon the "dogmas of empiricism"—namely, the distinction between the analytic and the a priori, and the reductionism attendant upon the verificationist theory of meaning—results in what he holds to be a logical extension of the presumptions of a thoroughgoing pragmatism. For Quine, "each man is given a scientific heritage plus a continuing barrage of sensory stimulation; and the considerations which guide him in warping his scientific heritage to fit his continuing sensory promptings are, where rational, pragmatic."[34] C. I. Lewis had sought to relativize the Kantian distinction of the analytic and the a priori by introducing the notion of a shifting set of a priori languages and concepts. Quine completed this move by claiming that "the totality of our so-called knowledge or beliefs, from the most casual matters of geography and history to the profoundest laws of atomic physics or even of pure mathematics and logic, is a man-made fabric which impinges on experience only along the edges."[35] In such a world there is no room for a radical disjunction between matters of fact and matters of language. Experience does not count for or against individual matters of fact since "no particular experiences are linked with any particular statements . . . except indirectly through considerations of equilibrium affecting the field as a whole."[36] All beliefs, whether in the reality of physical objects or of Homeric gods, are grounded in "cultural posits." This makes of any claim to have discovered, in this or that instance, a distinction between necessary and contingent truths, a truly tendentious assertion which attempts to make what is only a question of *degree* into a question of *kind*.

The epistemological holism exemplified by Quine's philosophy strongly suggests (if not to Quine, certainly to some of his more insightful interpreters) that "reality" or "the world" must be viewed as a richly indeterminate surd serving as a radically underdetermining cause of any particular theoretical vision.[37] For if one eschews any one-to-one correspondence between facts and propositions, then a variety of world visions can be sustained. No stipulated segment of the world can be distinguished in accordance with which the truth of a particular theory may be assessed.

Wilfrid Sellars's criticism of "the myth of the given" parallels this Quineian endeavor. Sellar's epistemological holism is expressed in much the same way as that of Quine:

> the conceptual framework of persons is the framework in which we think of one another as sharing the community of intentions which provide the ambience of principles and standards (above all, those which make meaningful discourse and rationality itself possible) within which we live our individual lives.[38]

Sellars's denial of the plausibility of any form of absolute givenness as a ground for knowing means that the "community of shared intentions" is the sole source and authority for the justification of true belief. Knowing, therefore, involves the placement of one's knowledge claims in "the logical space of reasons" constituted by the conceptual framework of the community.

Like Quine, Sellars is concerned to appropriate for the community of shared intentions the methods, principles, and interpretations of the scientific community, that prestigious subset of the broader community of shared intentions forming the common-sense world. And though he at times seems to wish, again not unlike Quine, to provide scientific understandings a privileged status within the community of shared intentions which grounds our knowledge claims, he finally accedes, as on his principles he must, to the same cultural positivism as that of the most committed of the pragmatists.

Consistent with his stress upon the cultural importance of science, Sellars articulates what he calls "the scientific image of man" and suggests that it might properly be joined to the "manifest" or more broadly consensual image which is present to us by dint of long tradition and reflection. He is not concerned to replace one image by another but to provide the grounds for some kind of coherence between the images. His motivation is, of course, pragmatic. We do have these two images, born of the "two cultures." The authoritativeness of a community is undermined if prominent images compete one with the other. And since "the aim of philosophy . . . is to understand how things in the broadest possible sense of the term hang together in the broadest possible sense of the term,"[39] Sellars is but fulfilling his philosophic duty by seeking coherence among apparently disparate understandings.

Taking the notion of a community of shared intentions in the broadest sense, it becomes quite feasible to develop distinctly "aesthetic" or "mystical" images of persons and the world born of exoteric communities which could be creatively conjoined with the images from our indigenous community. For once the notion of givenness is relativized in the manner required by this form of cultural positivism there can be no a priori limit to the variety of images which ultimately inform a community of shared discourse. Interest and importance become the principal criteria by which one selects viable images.

There can be no theoretical limits set to the variety of types of schematization possible to the experiencing being. Nor can we establish priorities among sorts of things-in-themselves. The products of past acts of interpretation are as much a part of that "collateral contemporaneity"[40] which is our world as are the inventory of "raw feels" thought (naïvely) by some to be free of interpretation. Thus, "the myth of the given" is essential to the enterprise of knowing at least in the sense that "something" is insistently present in any act of perceiving and understanding. But the given need hardly be construed as a primitive surd. What is given in experience is precisely that which is initially *other* in the sense of being offered for the remolding activity involved in every act of intellectual entertainment.

What is clearly at issue for the cultural positivists is not this or that image or theory, but the notion of *framework* which structures the world in the broadest sense and allows us to see the way in which it "hangs together." Nelson Goodman has explicitly addressed this issue by exploring the variety of ways in which worlds are constructed. Goodman remains himself uncommitted to any final articulated notion of the World, nor does he even feel that he must claim that the World exists. He follows an altogether pragmatic route strongly reminiscent of William James.[41] He sees that "many different world-versions are of independent interest and importance, without any requirement or presumption of reducibility to a single base."[42] There is no more an absolutely given for Goodman than there is for Sellars or Quine. "Worlds" are not made from various "stuffs." The stuffs are made *pari passu* with the making of the worlds. And "worldmaking, as we know it, starts from worlds already on hand; the making is a remaking."[43] Thus the given is an already-taken.

Goodman's views permit him to say that the variety of descriptions, envisionments, pictorial depictions, and so on which constitute our repertory of world-versions are complementary. They cannot, however, be rendered coherent simply by recourse to an effort of theoretical conjunction. "We cannot conjoin a paragraph and a picture."[44] Nor can worlds be reduced one to another. "How do you go about reducing Constable's or James Joyce's world-view to physics?"[45]

Quine, Sellars, and Goodman all share that cultural positivism characteristic of the pragmatic thrust of contemporary philosophy. With Quine and Sellars there is a clear preference for the evidences of science in the development of concepts of the nature of things. And it is a distinctly moral concern which leads them to derive the grounds for legitimate theorizing from the "community of shared intentions." Because of his background in art and art criticism, Goodman is slightly more sensitive to the contributions of strictly aesthetic criteria in the construction and criticism of world-versions.

In this chapter I have sought to provide evidences from the history of philosophy and contemporary culture which would support first-problematic thinking. The last few pages have been dedicated to sketching the manner in which philosophic speculation grounded in cultural positivism leads to the denial of a single-ordered world. Contemporary rejections of the search for "one best theory" or a single world-version, or single world-order, have opened thinking to the richness of cultural evidences drawn from the entire breadth of civilized experience. It remains to show how one might proceed to exploit this complex variety of "cultural posits" for the development of the most adequate of philosophic visions. The sort of vision to be sought cannot be *theoretical*. Rather, in the idiom of this essay, it must be a consequence of *theoria*.

CHAPTER FIVE
THE METAPHORIC MUSE

Our discussion of the "office of philosophy" in Chapter 3 pointed away from the classical search for consensus as a means of grounding social and political thought and action and directed us toward a renewed stress upon the original function of philosophy in its guise as theoria. The analysis of the notion of "order" in the previous chapter provided some evidence for the promotion of theorial, as opposed to strictly theoretical, reflections. We are now prepared to ask after the sort of language available to us for the exercise of such reflections.

In classical philosophy the conflict between the idealist and the realist has most often been expressed in terms of the relative independence of the objects of knowledge from the knowing process. Realisms stress the belief that what we know has, in some significant sense, existence independent of the act of knowing; idealisms claim that the act of knowing is largely constitutive of that which is known. The question as to what, if anything, the knowing subject contributes to objective knowledge is ultimately unanswerable, unless of course some intellect qualitatively distinct from the human could be called upon to arbitrate the issue.

One of the reasons the question is so complicated is that knowing necessarily involves both rational and aesthetic activities. For in addition to the objective content of experiencing, we have also to consider the character of the subjective form of feeling in accordance with which the content is grasped. For example, from the idealist perspective, the objective content of perception resulting from a schematizing activity on the part of the experiencing subject includes an aesthetic contribution via a distinct subjective form of feeling the world. Putatively scientific accounts of experience, even those idealist in character, ordinarily concentrate upon the objective contribution to experiencing construed in terms of broadly rational activity. Seldom is the aesthetic character of knowing assumed itself to have objective—that is, generic or universalizable—qualities. Indeed, objective knowledge, on the scientific model of understanding, is taken to be the result of that kind of knowing in which, by definition, "subjective" contributions play a minimal role.

The question of the aesthetic element involved in the knowing process is certainly not excluded from realistic theories. If the *ens realisimum* has a fundamental aesthetic character, the noetic grasp of it must include aesthetic feeling as a datum. And though in the discussion which immediately follows we shall be more concerned with aesthetic modes of entertainment per se, it is important to recognize that the aesthetic feelings associated with fundamental acts of knowing are presumed to have their source in the distinctive character of the experienced world.

We may begin to investigate the aesthetic contribution to the knowing process on the hypothesis that there is a subjective mode of understanding in terms of which our knowledge of the world could be justifiably grounded. This is perhaps not as controversial as it might initially appear. Clearly, any act of knowing presupposes the fact of *interest* directing attention to that which is to be known. Absolute boredom promotes no new understandings of the world since that which may be known is literally invisible to a bored individual. When Whitehead claimed that "it is more important that a proposition be interesting than that it be true," he was maintaining at the very least that the truth or falsity of a proposition will remain undetected unless our attention is directed to it by virtue of the subjective form of aesthetic interest. Interest, therefore, serves as a categorial grounding for any act of knowing. Our question concerning the possible contribution of the subjective form of feeling to the process of knowing can now be put in this fashion: "Does it make sense to say that there are various modes of interest, some or one of which is superior to others in providing us with fruitful understandings of the way things are?"

Though this question may seem rather ambiguous, it is sufficiently clear to direct us in a search for those species of interest constitutive of the activity of knowing. Homely examples of such types of interest come immediately to mind: the optimist sees his wineglass as half full whereas the pessimist sees it as half empty. Such contrasting interpretations of the objects of one's experience are not in any meaningful sense dependent upon either "facts" or "theories." The glass is both half full and half empty. And though that statement as to the relativity of factual knowledge in relation to the glass of wine may be construed as a theoretical statement it does not provide any suggestion as to the normative means of construing the event in pragmatic contexts. For, clearly, the statement "What, ho! My glass is both full by half and empty by half" itself involves a subjective form of feeling, one we should probably identify as the mood of the ironist.

Mood is hardly a trivial accompaniment to the act of knowing. It is absolutely essential to our understanding of the character of an event. Of course, even if one's mood could be shown to be consistent with a theoretical vision of the world, it would remain to be demonstrated whether the prior factor is the vision of the world in propositional form or the subjective form of feeling found to be consistent with it. It seems prima facie the case that if moods have any noetic significance at all they must be foundational rather than consequential in relation to theoretical visions. For the fundamental characteristics of a mood are its pervasiveness and its simple givenness in experience.

Fortunately, we do not have to stop short with such mundane examples of the importance of mood to the knowing process. Indeed, in Unamuno's "tragic sense of life," Freud's vision of Eros and the Death Instinct, Heidegger's notion of "Care" (*Sorge*), Polanyi's concept of the "tacit dimension," and so on, we can easily discern modes of philosophizing which celebrate the contribution of feeling to the act of knowing. None of these philosophers eschews the importance of ideas in the confirmation of one's sense of the world, though each would doubtless agree, *mutatis mutandis*, with Unamuno's claim regarding the tragic vision: "This sense does not so much flow from ideas as determine them."[1]

The contributions of these thinkers to our understanding of the aesthetic dimension of the knowing process are not in themselves sufficiently fundamental to characterize the point I wish to make. They all share a form of antirationalism which requires them to construct their theories over against the presumed defects of the principal rational accounts. What is required is not so much a critique of reason and rationality (though this may, in fact, be a prerequisite of more constructive operations) but a consideration of the meaning of knowledge which is naïve with regard to the dialectical disputations among rationalists and antirationalists that have patterned recent philosophic controversies.[2]

What would be the consequence of assuming the activities of perceiving and knowing to be construable in terms of moods as species of interest? Take the presumption that at least on some occasions we have knowledge of the facticity of events in nature. Such a presumption may be said to be grounded in a "literalist" sense of the world. This mood may be characterized as one which presumes a certain univocity as regards the objects of knowledge. On this view, "facts" are as they present themselves. As data (that is, as *given*) they serve as evidence for the construction of contexts of understanding (theories) but are not themselves presumed to be dependent upon theories for their facticity. In propositional form, facts secure the world for knowledge since they point to certain self-evident characteristics of it. They are literally "the case." Whatever may be said about the vagueness or ambiguity of some other events or phenomena, we can at least be sure of these givens in experience.

Carried to the extreme, the literalist sense finds the meaningfulness of experience in the facticity of some (or all) events in nature. Whatever is held to be nonfactual, in the sense of being neither a fact nor immediately derivable from facts, is thought to be meaningless. In this sense, facts need not be limited to empirical data, but may as justifiably be illustrated by the self-evidence of principles which are subsequently employed to develop theories of the ways things are. Thus facts range from mundane examples such as, "I have a nickel in my pocket," to the relatively esoteric, "*Cogito ergo sum*." The principal characteristics of facts as given are, to borrow phraseology from the most famous discoverer of the latter fact, "clarity and distinctness," which characteristics presumedly guarantee certainty.

But the literalist sense per se is not usually found among those whom we recognize as theoreticians. For the theorist, facts are held apart from theories, and our disposition toward the recognition of facticity is to be distinguished, at least initially, from the dispositon to view the world as a coherent whole. Mutual consistency is a primary quality of objects of knowledge viewed in the mood of the literalist. Inconsistency, construed either as incompatibility or contradiction, is to be avoided at all costs. The literalist sense expresses itself as a discriminating attitude that promotes the understanding of isolated and autonomous data involving a relative detachment from coherent theories of the way of things.

The obvious criticism to make of the literalist sense of the world is that it can be sustained only if the constitutive character of those contexts which provide the meaningfulness of the facts entertained in this mood is ignored. Informal contexts, such as those promoted by the language, customs, institutions, and value-orientations of a given culture, as well as more formal contexts such as "the scientific community" with its conventionalized language, serve as stipulative contexts permitting the assumption of the univocity of at least some data. There is certainly no great value to be found in making a direct and detailed appeal to the stipulative context each time one wishes to make an assertion . On some occasions, particularly in the more formal types of stipulative contexts, it is clear to all communicants precisely what kinds of stipulations are involved. A scientific community is involved in the use of terms as conventional stipulations. Literalists among scientists would hold that such stipulated words may be tailored so as better to fit the form of the realities they purportedly name.

However we speak of facticity, the fundamental situation remains the same: theories, as informally or formally articulated visions of the way things are, serve as the stipulative contexts within which facts or data are found to be literally the case. Furthermore, the relative fluidity of language in its ordinary form prevents the propositional statement of a fact from maintaining its univocity under conditions of careful scrutiny. The literalist sense, which seems to be the basis of common-sense understandings of the world, may serve as a motivating factor in the development of theories since the attempt to overcome the fluidity of language, and thus to pin facts down, requires resort to more formal contexts of stipulation.

The literalist appetite for univocal facts is satisfied under the following conditions: those items of experience which are unremarkable or uninteresting may survive in their putative univocity precisely because of the vagueness engendered by their uncontroversial character. Once a fact becomes interesting, however, its vagueness gives rise to a recognition of the fluidity and ambiguity characteristic of all natural language. In these cases the contexts of stipulation become more formal. But this press toward theory as a means of protecting the univocity of experienced data hardly solves the problem. For when it becomes necessary to raise to the level of consciousness the theoretical context supportive of the facticity of one's most cherished data, facticity itself is undermined.

Facts are found to be fluid in two principal ways. In the first manner, the propositions which house them are found to grow in meaning through time. The hermeneutic school, initiated in large measure by Wilhelm Dilthey, seems perfectly on target here. It does make sense to say that later generations can come to understand a thinker more completely than he understood himself. Plato or Aristotle, Kant, or Locke would each be surprised (but not altogether displeased) by the state of scholarship regarding their particular philosophies. Propositions held to contain univocal terms within their theories will, with only unremarkable exceptions, now be found to have accrued enormously richer significances during the periods intervening between their respective philosophic activities and the present. Thus theoretical propositions grow in meaning with interpretative distance from their origins.

This concept of the growth of propositions means that natural language systems can, in principle, escape some of the strictures placed upon algebraic systems by Gödel's theorem which claims that no hypothetical-deductive system can be in the fullest sense complete. Thus a system of propositions, if expressed in algebraic form—that is, in the form of univocally defined connectives and real variables—cannot refer to significant aspects, objects, or events logically presupposed by the system itself. Apparently, insofar as algebraic form is essential to a given proposition, Gödel's theorem must stand. However, clarity in any form is achieved at the cost of certain rather obvious facts concerning the meaning of meaning. Natural language, for example, always tends to suggest meanings beyond the boundaries set by and for propositions. However much we might wish to expel occult significances, they continue to plague us. The paradoxes of language which frustrate the mathematician and delight the mystic must not be ignored.

One difficulty is the seemingly innocent assumption that, though it is language and only language which means, meaning transcends language in at least two senses. In the weak sense, a linguistic expression may be said to mean what its expresser intends it to mean and what the receiver understands it to mean. That these two meanings are ever identical is unlikely. Either the expresser or the experiencer of language may intend or understand more than the other. In a second, stronger sense, meaning transcends language in that no presently conceived set of meanings can exhaust the possible meanings of a proposition. Language, once accepted as symbolic, is opened to a wide range of possible significances. Apart from arbitrary limits placed upon the meaning of a proposition, it makes little sense to speak of limits in regard to its meaning. All this is truistic. If it is forgotten, however, clarity, or certainty, or specificity (which always means clear, or certain, or specific enough for present purposes) will be inordinately valued.

The second manner in which formalized facts are fluid as regards their meaning is this: because of the existence of alternative, often incompatible theories with "the same" subject matters, we must assume that intertheoretical communication (if it exists at all) takes place in part because the putatively common terminology may be presumed to be common only in the sense that there are overlapping significances involved. That is, at least some of the meanings associated with a term in one theory may be naïvely held to be attached to that term in the alternative theory. (This is, of course, to express the situation in an extremely simpleminded manner.) In this second sense, the fluidity and ambiguity of language is recognized in the fact that the broad range of significances associated with a given term permit incompatible and even contradictory significances depending upon the character of the alternative contexts within which the meaning of the term is stipulated.

The existence of alternative cultures, ideological movements, or theoretical visions frustrates the literalist in his search for univocal data. Fated to defend the most important of facts by appeal to dogmas which themselves require protection within formal theories found to conflict with other theoretical understandings, the literalist is forced to cultivate narrowness, blindness, and defensiveness as a way of life.

The sophisticated thinker who comes to recognize the plight of the literalist will not for long be tempted to give up the idea of facts and univocity altogether. After all, if the literalist sense of the world leads in every important instance into contradiction and self-referential inconsistency, the nonliteralist is no better off. Difficulties involved in the valid statement of a skeptical epistemology aside, we do seem to depend upon at least the presumption of facticity in any important theoretical endeavor. Even if it were desirable to develop a theory of the world which denied univocity and literalness as important notions, what specific sense would it make to say that every proposition in a theory is symbolic, or ambiguous, or metaphorical? It is perhaps too obvious to need stating that symbols carry weight partly because of the presumption of literal truth at some level, and that ambiguity functions in relation to the norm of univocity. In a like manner, expressive metaphors extend the significance of principles whose facticity is affirmed as the basis from which metaphorical deliverances can be fruitfully made.

Univocity, literalness, facticity are a cluster of notions which are found well-nigh impossible to defend in any given instance, but which must at least be posited as norms for certain types of discourse if we are to make sense of communication. The theoretical proposition, "There are no facts," on the other hand, is itself impossible of consistent defense. We find ourselves in the strange situation of being able to defend facticity at the theoretical level but not at the level at which the facts are presumed to exist. Contrariwise, we can discover any particular fact to be corrigible but cannot meaningfully assert this of facts generally.

If we raise our discussion to the level of speculative theory we are no better off. Rational, systematic visions of the world depend upon categorial notions which ultimately lead to extratheoretical entities or concepts. The Form of the Good (Plato), Prime Matter (Aristotle), God

(Spinoza), Creativity (Whitehead) are examples of such notions in their metaphysical form. Leibniz's Principle of Sufficient Reason provides perhaps the best epistemological illustration. Each of these notions functions, *mutatis mutandis*, as a fact with respect to the particular theoretical vision with which it is directly associated. So-called empirical facts are immanent in the sense that they can exist within at least one stipulative context. Theoretical assumptions are transcendent in the sense that they are not exhaustively stipulated by the theory for which they serve as ground. The appeal justifying theoretical assumptions of the categorial variety is broadly intuitional.

No ultimate distinction may be made between the facticity of immanent and transcendent facts. Some mid-range scientific theories, for example, may employ an appeal to common sense to justify facts presumed to be transcendent of the theory in question, but necessary to the grounding of the theory. In the case of these mid-range theories, however, a more general theory would render both classes of fact relative to the more formally abstract speculative context. The result must always be that even the most general speculative vision must employ at least one notion as a transcendent datum.

When the justification of a categorial assumption is sought, it is certainly possible to assert that the vision permitted by the categorial assumption(s) may claim preeminence by virtue of its clarity, cogency, elegance, or (what is more likely) its pragmatic consequences. But this does not satisfy the literalist sense which requires that a datum be accepted as evident by virtue of the self-presentation of certainty. For this the appeal to intuition is necessary. The rationalist mood, on the other hand, is satisfied only if the facticity of the categorial assumption is guaranteed by explicit recourse to the theoretical vision itself. Apparently the rationalist sense of the world must be frustrated in at least one (extremely important) instance—namely, with regard to the transcendent category or categories, ontological or epistemological, which ground the rational vision.

The situation is this: the literalist sense of the world has as its dynamic a concern for securing the facticity of data which leads to the development of theories of a more and more general sort until a cosmological vision is expressed which requires resort to one or more categorial assumptions found to be defensible solely through an appeal to intuition. The facticity of the caterory(ies) depends upon whether or not one can successfully claim to intuit the truth or importance of the categorial assumption(s). The testimony of the history of speculative theorizing is, of course, that intuitions differ dramatically. At the level of empirical facts such relativity has required theoretical activity promoting stipulative contexts serving to articulate and to defend the facticity of data.

What recourse does one have with regard to metaphysical categories which transcend speculative system? Classically, the principal response to the relativity of categorial assumptions has been a combination of dialectical refutation of alternative speculative visions and philosophic reconstruction in response to such dialectical activity when directed toward one's own systematic vision. Thus the history of speculative philosophy.

An obvious conclusion of even this slightly whimsical examination of the literalist mentality is that it seems inevitably to lead to a vacillation between skeptical relativism and provincial dogmatism. The literalist as theoretician finds that unless the scope of his theory is sufficiently narrowed he cannot avoid confrontation with the plethora of world views characteristic of a sophisticated social milieu. Such a narrowing of his theoretical perspective results in the most pernicious forms of provincialism. Broadening one's vision, however, requires engagement with the wealth of alternative theories. The ultimate consequence of such encounters is usually a capitulation to the more or less skeptical form of relativism which eschews claims to adequate knowledge.

The most prominent feature of speculative activity in contemporary culture is that it is patterned by the same kind of relativity of theoretical perspectives as are the special sciences. Idealisms, materialisms, naturalisms, existentialisms vie for our attention and commitment. Each type of theory contains an explicit or implicit critique of the alternative points of view. No two of these types of speculative theory can be said to be mutually harmonious. Indeed, each constitutes a categorial context within which the principal concepts applied to the understandings of our world receive a distinctive characterization bringing it into semantic conflict with its alternative renderings.

One of the least dubitable of facts concerning the history of intellectual activity is that theoretical conflict originated along with theory per se. In our Anglo-European tradition, the story of so-called pre-Socratic philosophy is a tale of conflicting visions grounded upon alternative means of construing the world. We might wish to enquire into the reasons for this apparently unavoidable development of theoretical relativity. Why was singularity of philosophic vision not characteristic of the origins of theoretical activity?

Presumably the felt immediacy of our fundamental senses of the world prior to the emergence of articulated consciousness provided an imaginative substratum in terms of which language, in both its naïve and sophisticated forms, engaged. The recognition of a discriminated environment occurred, we must assume, through the utilization of at least the following primitive elements: *objects*, as those items of experience which can be encountered as other—as, that is to say, ob-jective to us; *ideas*, as mental figurations of these objects which permit us to manipulate our environment in absence of immediate experience of it; and *words*, functioning as names and descriptions, which allow us to share our experienced encounters with others.

The experience of our ambience as other is very complex, of course. For it is possible to sense varying degrees of otherness. That which is experienced as independent of us altogether—for example, rocks and other such material objects—ranges at one end of the spectrum; organic structures, as functional interrelations of parts characterized by identifiable purpose or aim, fall near the other end. Organisms are possessed of an "inside" in addition to an "outside" and promote the possibility of more complicated forms of interaction than those anticipated in relation to wholly material objects.

The felt sense of immediacy from out of which emerged the sense of causal efficacy and, finally, of the conscious entertainment of the world, is the source of all of our theoretical visions. But the intuitive immediacy of the aesthetic sense has a unity and completeness about it which is soon lost once the importance of consciousness and concepts is recognized. Materialist and mechanistic theories select the sense of outsidedness possessed by the objects of the material sort as expressive of the real character of things. Idealism characterizes the world in terms of the patterns emergent from, or reflective of, the figurations of objects originating in the imagination. Organic forms of naturalism construe objects with the inclusion of significant internality characterized by the possession of a unique function or purpose. Finally, volitional theory accepts the instrumental use of language as the means of grounding our characterizations of the world.

Seen in this fashion, the development of alternative theories of the way of things came about from the utilization of elements of a primary semantic context serving as the source of the whole complex of meanings available to the human being. This is but to say that the sophisticated speculative enterprises associated with various traditional modes of understanding are metaphorical activities in the sense that each construes the whole from a part.

Philosophic theories may not seem to function metaphorically in the usual sense since comparisons of a whole-part form are more often thought to be forms of analogy having a degree of explicitness normally absent from our understanding of metaphor. But analogies of the type which ground philosophic theories are, in fact, disguised metaphors, even if construed in terms of their abstraction from a primary semantic context. This is because of the vagueness of such primitive terms as "object," "idea," "organism," "words." The significant depth of these terms, their semantic richness, means that analogies which lead to the construction of world views by recourse to selected elements of a primary semantic context have about them the same vagueness (and, of course, "richness") as do more ordinary forms of metaphor. The use of the term "root-metaphor"[3] made famous by Stephen Pepper in his metatheoretical analysis of general philosophic visions is quite apt even if these metaphors are themselves grounded in an imaginative source which loosely and vaguely relates them one to another.

Pepper's root-metaphor theory of metaphysics provides an argument for the complementarity of speculative visions. Pepper believes that "one way, and perhaps the only way, in which metaphysical hypotheses can be derived is through the analysis of a selected group of facts . . . and the expansion of that analysis among other facts."[4] Speculative theories are distinctive forms of perspective abstraction permitting access to "the World." "A world theory is autonomous in its interpretations of facts and autonomous in its criticisms of interpretations; [thus, for example,] the only legitimate criticism of idealism is in idealistic terms."[5]

A metatheoretical vision of this type requires that one view theories either as completely separate and compartmentalized visions, or as complementary perspectives upon a rich and indeterminate world. The argument for the latter approach over the former is simply that individuals of different theoretical persuasions do interact at the theoretical level. Thus one may presume at least some ability to move from one theoretical context to another as would be required were one to have any hope of understanding the world view of another. Clearly the eclectic alternative is unsatisfactory since by combining inconsistent doctrines in an ultimately incoherent way the richly varied worlds constituting the subjects of various ontologies are reduced to no world at all. "Eclecticism is . . . mixed metaphor."[6]

Though I am not concerned here to argue for the strict incommensurability of world views, I do believe that the apparent incompatibility of our principal speculative theories, which receives its prima facie defense in the obvious conflicts among the theoretical visions arising from each of these selected elements, argues at least for the view that there is no level of experience or expression at which we can demonstrate freedom from metaphorical meaning. If we are indeed bound to metaphor, it is in part because any given act of understanding or articulation can, and perhaps must, have a metaphorical dimension.

To say that every expression is potentially metaphorical is to point to the nature of language as a means of expressing the immediacy of our experiencing of the world. What is explicitly and/or literally the case within one context must be but metaphorically understood in other contexts. The assumption of the mechanists that the world *is* a vast machine ensures that the constituent parts, as merely externally related objects, are literally extant. But these same objects seen from the perspective of a formalist, field-oriented theory must be construed metaphorically. Likewise, "ideas" as categorial patterns or structures of meaning are literally the case from the idealists' perspective, whereas they have only metaphorical meaning within a mechanistic world view. If, in the classical scientific manner, we tend to view theories as either true or false in their roles as descriptions of the world as it really is, then our particular metaphysical commitments will lead us to see each of the alternatives to our own vision not as metaphorical, but as false.

But what of the view that all theories function metaphorically? This assertion, with which I have great sympathy, is, in fact, easier to make than to defend. Where does one stand while making such a claim? Standing within a theoretical context, excepted from the complex of alternative theories which one is considering, may involve the presumption that each of the alternative theories is but a complex metaphor. Even if one denies standing within any theory when making such an assertion the question still arises as to precisely what kind of world it is wherein all significances are metaphorical. The obvious way out of this difficulty is to see that one always implicitly or explicitly has a theory which serves as the context for one's proposals about the world, but that one is not bound to have the same theory all the time. That is, it is possible to shake oneself loose from untoward philosophic commitments by maintaining a certain flexibility which allows one to shift from one theoretical context to another whenever circumstances permit.

It may be fruitful to see various speculative theories as complementary in somewhat the same way as one sees the wave theory to be complementary to the particle theory in microphysics. The principal difficulty with such a view is obvious, however. When discussing differences among metaphysical theories we are operating at a significantly different abstractive level than when discussing distinct alternatives within a single specialized cultural interest.

The principle employed by Niels Bohr in his development of the notion of complementarity was that "a complete elucidation of one and the same object may require diverse points of view which defy a unique description."[7] His assumption that the princple of complementarity might be extended to theoretical conflicts beyond the realm of physics has, however, been criticized by those who claim that complementary characterizations may be given adequately only if they are of the same entity and are of the same logical level or type.[8] It would be extremely difficult to develop a metatheory which would permit one to demonstrate how these conditions are met by alternative metaphysical visions such as materialist and idealist systems. In spite of the difficulties such a metatheory provides the most promising way of conceptualizing alternative philosophic visions. The principal alternatives are either to consider one theoretical tradition essentially right and the others wrong, or to see other views as special cases, or approximations, of one's own view, or to claim that there are no coherent relations among speculative visions. These approaches seem altogether too naïve to hold much promise.

All that is required to make the presumption of complementarity reasonable with respect to alternative speculative theories is to indicate how one might see these theories as applying to "the same entity." This is obviously the putative assumption of metaphysical theorists who wish to give a characterization of that which is. If the object of speculative theory is presumed to have any existence at all independent of the theory, then it is a reasonable assumption that these theories may in fact aim to characterize the same indeterminate entity. The necessity that these theories express the same "logical type" seems inapplicable to speculative visions since, unlike the notion of the World which serves as the putative object of metaphysical speculation, the issue of the logical level at which a theory is expressed, or the logical type or types it may adequately represent, is a question only answerable within the given theory. From the general metaphysical point of view we may, indeed, require a complementarity of logical types as a necessary condition for the existence of adequate descriptions.

Ultimately, of course, the question as to whether two or more theories apply to the same entity is a context-bound question and is undecidable except by recourse to a more general theory. But surely we can say this much: with regard to speculative theories of greatest generality the putative, presystematic subject of the theory is the World as richly indeterminate. Theories are versions of the World. The effort to discover a single coherent scheme within which to discipline the variety of world-versions must inevitably lead to reductive endeavors which dissolve all aberrant data into the same theoretical type. But the ontological richness of the World as the putative object of the variety of world-versions depends upon a presumption of parity among ontic commitments. The analysis of our languages, including the languages of art, ethical activity, and religious devotion, reveals the nature of these ontic commitments. Any subsequent attempt to render such commitments coherent cannot but seem arbitrary to those whose ontology is thereby impoverished or rendered unacceptable.

The majority of theoretical accounts possessing any significant degree of generality must function reductively with regard to at least some other theories or theoretical concepts. For a great deal of our explanatory activity per se consists in accounting for the place of theoretical claims within an alternative theory. For example, we can easily encounter numerous theoretical accounts of the phenomenon of "neurosis." Theorists often simply forget that neurosis is an abstract, theory-born notion and approach it as if it were an empirical phenomenon to be interpreted theoretically. In a relatively complex culture the more interesting notions are often those constructed by formal theory. It is these notions, detached from their originating context, which become candidates for alternative explanations.

Pure explanations must be teleological. That is to say, they must characterize the meaning of a concept in terms of the theoretical context which originates the notion. Thus both Platonists and Sophists employ the term "freedom." The cause of philosophic conversation is hardly advanced, however, if the alternative theories utilized by these opposing types of philosophers are merely used to reduce the terms of their opponents to an alternative context. The Sophist must be prepared to argue on Platonic terms, and vice versa. Of course the very purity of such teleological activities may itself preclude productive interactions beyond relatively straightforward exercises in semantic clarification.

Clearly, we have no means of testing the viability of a consistent theoretical vision other than its application to the sphere of praxis. The difficulty arises upon realizing that the sphere of praxis is itself comprised primarily of abstract artifacts of alternative theoretical explanations. The theoretician per se may remain relatively pure, satisfied with teleological vindication. The more practical sorts, however, insist upon applying the theory. Such applications are little more than the painting of gray on gray which results in the thick and crusty veneer of advancing cultural expression. For in applying a theory in order to interpret what is in truth but an artifact of an alternative theory we manage only to promote the forms of theoretical reduction expressed in the construal of one theory in terms of another.

The wiser and more chastened among contemporary philosophers recognize the necessity of explaining theoretical relativity in a nonreductive fashion. It is no longer fashionable to look for "the best theory." The pragmatic among our thinkers ground theoretical relativity in the notion of ontological relativity. Accepting a notion of reality sufficiently rich and indeterminate to permit—indeed to require—alternative theoretical constructions, pragmatists claim that ontological statements are context-bound. It is possible to characterize the ontology of a given theory either teleologically or through comparative statements concerning the ontologies of two or more theories from the perspective of an alternative context serving as theoretical background. True propositions are those which stand the judgment of "the tribunal of sense experience."[9] It is essential to understand, however, that this tribunal itself serves the ends of the cultural sensibility of an intellectual epoch comprising the "web of belief"[10] patterning experience in its most fundamental way.

In this way our cultural positivists have attempted to make a virtue of the necessary conflict among theoretical visions. This view argues for some sort of richness and indeterminancy as regards Reality, or the World, as the putative object of theoretical constructions. Whatever the difficulties such views have with respect to the question of the assessment of "good" and "bad" theories, they are not nearly so great as those involved in the attempt to clear away the problem through the strategem of reductive assault. We are left with the notion that the coherence to be discovered among various theoretical visions must be a function of their complementary character as explanatory constructs.

If we accept as a reasonable assumption the relevance of the principle of complementarity in our understanding of the coexistence of alternative speculative visions of the world, we shall succeed in "saving the appearances" in a way that could not be so on other grounds. For the persistence of alternative metaphysical theories throughout the history of our theoretical efforts is one of the most obvious of the phenomena characterizing our cultural existence at the intellectual level.

If we isolate the history of scientific theory since the Renaissance we are likely to see the resort to complementary descriptions of microphysical phenomena as but a transitory episode in the history of science. For should we not expect, sooner or later, that a coherent vision of the microphysical realm will be developed, and that we shall no longer have to have recourse to alternative descriptions such as the wave and particle theories? Surely the testimony of science demonstrates analogies to our present dilemmas which were successfully resolved by a single coherent vision. One might see in the conflicting characterizations of the meaning of "space" contemporaneous with Descartes's philosophizing an instance of theoretical conflict which was resolved adequately by the Newtonian paradigm. On the other hand, the fact that there was not the explicit recognition of complementarity at the time may be simply a function of the fact that scientific research was operating at a much less sophisticated and well-integrated level, and the pressures which would have led to the institutionalization of complementary visions were not present. But Thomas Kuhn, by seeing the history of science in terms of transitions among research paradigms, is led to argue that the persistence of such conflicting models of understanding in this or that area of science is but a symptom of a crisis in research activity which promises the construction of a novel coherent view resolving the crisis.[11]

Though we should certainly not seek to use the principle of complementarity as a means of closing us off from the search for more coherent visions, we should at least note the consequences of accepting that principle at the level of metaphysical alternatives. It is much more difficult to accept this metaphysical complementarity as a transitory episode in the history of thought. For at the level of speculative theory there has never been a time when a single vision operated as the sole coherent paradigm normalizing philosophic reflection. Perhaps the closest we have come to this is scholastic philosophy employed as the handmaiden of theological analyses and reflection. But even here we not only see perhaps a much greater diversity than in the history of scientific activity, but we are easily led to understand the underlying unity of speculative endeavor in terms of ideological factors extrinsic to the nature of philosophy per se.

A consequence of the vision of normal philosophy developed in Chapter 3 is that both utopian and utilitarian options must be kept alive. The tensions which exist between these ways of approaching the activity of thinking are essential to the maintenance of viable philosophic activity. By characterizing the relations of mutually contradictory visions of the way of things in terms of the concept of complementarity, we can take a significant step in the direction of protecting the creative tension between utopian and utilitarian modes of thought.

Though the concept of metaphysical complementarity argues against both consistency and coherence as final philosophic aims, it need not promote irrationality, contradiction, and paradox as ends in themselves. It is more properly to be understood as an argument in favor of the rich and fluid character of language which allows the construction of alternative metaphorical visions of the world that celebrate the significant depth of our experience of it. Theories are complementary in much the same way as poetic constructions may be said to be complementary. We do not search for a single poem which may be claimed superior to all others by virtue of its expression of the nature of things. We accept the variety of poetic figurations as constitutive of a mosaic of significances which together suggest a general meaning associated with our articulated aesthetic sensibility.

The convergence of so many of our best minds upon the problem of language and consciousness is highly suggestive of the sense of crisis and transition that we are currently experiencing with regard to our form of participation in the world. The nineteenth century saw the culmination, in principle, of the dominance of the mechanistic world view in science. In place of the world as a Great Machine, we now experience, at least vicariously through our scientific minds, the sense of the world modeled in fields and patterns associated with mathematical formalism. More importantly, we are required to take quite seriously our own participation in this world if we are to understand it and ourselves. Though, as I have indicated before, this anthropocentric conception of participation is not altogether adequate, at least it can serve as the beginning of the re-cognition of the organic relation of each percipient in his particular ambience. Along with the denial of strict objectivity, the literal-mindedness which is its essential attendant is also passing away. The increasing interest in the metaphorical and symbolic nature of language is an attempt to provide some means of gaining insight into the character of our understandings of the experienced world in something other than descriptive terms.

Taking seriously the metaphorical character of our theoretical understandings of the world leads us to that kind of reflection which renders possible a return to theorial participation. And though there is no sense in which we can or ought return to our initial modes of relatedness to the world through unconsciously and uncritically authoritative myths and rituals, there is a sense in which our emergent form of relatedness to our experienced ambience can share some of the qualities of our culturally primitive experiences. The difference between our primordial past and the contemporary modes of participation is, perhaps, best expressed in terms of the increased consciousness of the distinct factors comprising our most articulated experiences. This is illustrated very well by the importance of theories of the unconscious, theories of metaphorical and symbolic functions of language, and theories of theories.

Theories of the unconscious, classically expressed by Freud and Jung, make a subject of theoretical reflection precisely what by all accounts ought to be free from conscious intervention. Theories of metaphor provide a set of conscious reflections upon what was itself unconsciously employed. Metatheoretical activities lead us to recognize that, rather than envisioning the world, we need to envision our ways of envisioning. This increased consciousness which has taken the element of reflexivity as the primary component of our intensionality finally leads us to recognize that systematic, rational, and coherent understandings of the sort upon which we have come to depend are products of our own particular concerns for praxially relevant meaning. This is certainly a means of recognizing that we do indeed participate in the world, but this understanding of participation is quite different from the actual experience of participation which must have belonged to the primordial past. For in the modern sense not only do we participate on our own terms, we are unable to participate on any other. We are trapped by a "web of belief" which we ourselves have spun.

This recognition, born of the contemporary return to the Protagorean principle, is often celebrated as an advance over the objectivist mode of thinking which divorced the observer or knower from that which is observed or known. But there is a certain poignance in the Protagorean insight which, in effect, reverses the polarities of the theorial experience and replaces wonder by construal. The initial manner of participation was doubtless more direct and intense at the beginnings of human consciousness. We must presume that the human individual in fact fabricated himself from out of a sea of unarticulated aesthetic feelings associated with dreams and imaginative figurations serving as his primary modes of being in the world. The sense of self-consciousness was doubtless emergent from the sense of generalized consciousness which did not promote a discriminated intuition of the distinction of self and other. The movement from *being at one with*, to *being in wonder of* names the transition from preconscious or vaguely conscious experience to the experience of theoria. The further transition from theorial to theoretical understandings carried this process to its conclusion.

In the ordinary consciousness of most contemporary human beings there is doubtless a disposition toward the denotative, extensional uses of language and away, therefore, from the connotative and intensional significances of terms. Naïvely we assume that meaning depends upon reference. One of the first things we ask for when hearing a new word is for an instance or example. The ostensive definition of a term is likely to carry the most impressive significance. If asked for the definition of "baselisk" we are forced to point to myth, legend, and literature rather than to a perceptual object in "the real world." By so doing we can dispose our questioner to classify the meaningfulness of the baselisk in accordance with a somewhat less prestigious realm of fantasy objects. We may scoff at the Homeric account of the gods, or the medieval literature concerning angels, because we have no other way of approaching such discourse than to ask whether it is "fact" or "fiction." It is highly unlikely, however, that Homer or Saint Augustine would have accepted the existence of gods or angels on the same kind of terms that we today accept the existence of airplanes. Our literal-mindedness leads us naïvely to believe that the Homeric Greeks, the medieval artists, the Taoist sages, and so on hold to the same literal mode of conceptualizing as we.

It is not impossible, however, to recognize that there are modes of reality or realization which are not necessarily to be construed in terms of physical instantiation. Believing in angels is not only possible to sophisticated thinkers whom we might think ought to know better, it is an extremely reasonable belief assuming a Neoplatonic universe in which beings form a continuum of existences manifesting the strictest obedience to the principle of plenitude. It is only if we insist upon seeing angels as either corporeally recognizable beings or mere products of fruitless speculation and fantasy that the belief becomes absurd. We might make some progress toward understanding possible alternative modes of consciousness if we realize that the literal-minded belief in the concrete reality of material objects as given perceptually in human experience has as bizarre a flavor to the true Neoplatonist as does the acceptance of angelic hosts to the rabid materialist. What is obvious at the philosophic level, however, may not be so at the experiential level. For if asked whether angels are real or not, the medieval artist or philosopher could well say, "Yes," meaning all the while by the term "real" something which is so experientially foreign to our sensibility fed by the bias toward facticity as materiality, that we could hardly be expected to understand his meaning.

There is an interesting example of the effects of the literal-mindedness of rational consciousness to be found in the discussion surrounding the ontological argument for the existence of God. Kant's refutation of one form of this argument depended in part on the denial that existence could be legitimately predicated of an item in the same manner as could other qualities. What does existence add to the object as a significant state of affairs? In one sense, of course, it adds everything. But on analysis we find that the additional character given an object by virtue of its existing rather than not existing has nothing at all to do with the meaning of the object only with its use, its instrumental value. The increased significance which a "real" twenty-dollar bill seems to have when compared to an imagined note of the same value is, of course, only an increased instrumental or pragmatic meaning. After all, I can purchase imaginary goods with my fantasized money just as I can buy real goods with real cash. The extra prestige accorded real as opposed to imagined objects is not in the least a function of intrinsic significance, but of consequential value.

It is too simplistic, of course, merely to maintain that literal-mindedness promotes instrumental or practical value more than does allegorical, symbolic, or metaphorical thinking. For we can easily imagine the existence of a culture which promoted the pragmatic value of relatively nonreferential meanings. Major forms of the Buddhist tradition, for example, wish to produce a detachment from cosmological commitments which undergird the belief in facticity. The doctrines of codependent origination and of the emptiness of all phenomenal existents challenge literal-mindedness in the sharpest possible manner. Indeed, poets and artists even in our own culture may be more relevantly associated with fantasized objects than with the factually existent objects of the consensual realm.

One of the consequences of ignoring aesthetic and religious evidential sources to the degree we have in fact done in Anglo-European culture is that we are increasingly unable to appreciate modes of reality which contrast with those which are physically or referentially characterizable. We are not apt to appreciate the instrumental value promoted by metaphorical language if the ends to be realized are other than those associated with the spheres of ordinary consciousness.

Thus metaphor can be employed instrumentally, as a means of realizing ends beyond those of immediate enjoyment. With some metaphors, however, the question of reference is so little stressed, and the issue of the immediacy of felt significance is so much the point of the experience, that there is less room for the instrumental employment of the experience at the level of concrete praxis. The shift away from the intrinsic to the extrinsic functioning of language is certainly much older than the development of our modern scientific and technological forms of rationalization. It is as old as articulated cultural experience itself. Though it is tempting to see in the mythical visions which ground our cultural understandings etiologic accounts celebrating our original forms of participation in our world, there is already in the construction of these mythical visions an instrumental and pragmatic motivation which threatens the theorial attitude. We can see this clearly if we focus upon the philosophic variations on the principal mythical themes. The metaphors which ground the types of philosophic theory are not exclusively metaphorical in their functioning for, in addition to serving as a general matrix of meaning and significance which grounds one's sense of the meaningfulness of things, they remain, for the most part, quite passive to the rationalizing and literalizing activities associated with the development of Anglo-European consciousness. This is attributable, of course, to the fact already noted that the transition from *mythos* to *logos* was motivated by the *mythos* itself. Our cosmogonic myths are myths of construal which employ reason, volition, and eros as variant types of ordering principles. The "myth of the literal" has disciplined most of our metaphorical deliverances.

Of course literalization is only one form of the disciplining of metaphor. In our culture it has been combined with the process of institutionalization. The myths which undergird our theoretical visions are themselves constructed as a means of promoting ritualistic and other forms of institutionalized activity which further one's practical engagement with the world. And though it is doubtless true that the mythical underpinnings of philosophic visions contain a great potentiality for aesthetic enjoyment, the history of their progressive development into theoretical understandings argues for their practical use.

The bifocality of theory urges the recognition of the aesthetic and religious modalities of experiencing as relatively detached from the instrumental motivations associated with narrowly rational and moral sensibilities. This bifocality is an argument in favor of increased recourse to what we recognize as imaginative capacities. The original, and originating, activity of the imagination was doubtless the source of our cultural visions and values. It can be our principal re-source as well. Upholding the autonomy of the imagination as a means of enriching the sources of cultural evidence requires that we have recourse to aesthetic and religious experience in their most direct forms, since both art and religion (unlike morality and science) involve the experience of a kind of harmony which transcends principled order. Both art and religion have occasion to celebrate the paradoxical character of that which is. Each sees in the mundane world of consensual understandings a "mis-shapen Chaos of well-seeming forms,"[12] and attempts to evoke an alternative sense of positive Chaos as the sum of all orders. Art does this from the perspective of the experiencing subject, religion from the point of view of that which is experienced.

One way of beginning to grasp the distinctiveness of the aesthetic and religious interests is by reflection upon the distinction between the "mystical" and the "mysterious."[13] In the aesthetic experience there is always an element of the mysterious in the sense of the inexhaustible, the unfathomable, or the paradoxical (and therefore irresolvable) character of things. In religion, characterized in terms of the experience of the holy, the mystical intuition involves a sense of being at one with the Totality. This intuition of experiential unity which forms the apex of religious experiencing does not dwell immediately upon the mystery of the unity but upon the sense of at-one-ness. In aesthetic experience the sense of immediacy is felt internally, or with reference to the experiencing subject. The world experienced referentially in an aesthetic act is then sensed as inexhaustibly replete with profound significance.

I am not claiming that any particular artist or religious virtuoso must be limited to his respective mode of experiencing. That would be quite silly. Poets can certainly experience the holy through the occasion of the writing or reading of a poem, just as holy individuals can enjoy the mysterious character of the world as a satisfying experience referred to one's immediate subjectivity. But even though aesthetic expressions may be characterized as means of moral inspiration, or media of religious insight, and so on, clearly, the most fruitful analysis of a work of art is a strictly aesthetic one. Such an analysis envisions the art object as the locus of and occasion for the experience of insistent particularity, of just-so-ness, of uniqueness, the meaning of which has only indirect reference to the world beyond. Religious experiencing directly unites the experiencing subject and his world in a single experience. Here uniqueness and particularity are felt by virtue of the contrast of the individual and the Totality.

The relations between art and religion are analogous to the alternating relations of figure and ground in a gestalt. In the aesthetic experience the finite immediacy of the experiencing subject is the figure and the totality of factors or data is ground. In religious experiencing the gestalt is transformed, the Totality coming to the fore as the figure of the experience in relation to which the experiencing subject serves as ground. Classical descriptions of religious ecstasy in which the individual literally stands outside himself and finds the focus of experience beyond his own presented locus suggest this interpretation of religious experiencing.

The ineffability of religious experiencing is in part a consequence of the fact that the experience is complete in itself. To the extent that we think of language in terms of the coordination of meaning and reference, therefore, the experience is meaningless because it has no isolatable referent. Descriptions of mystical experiencing then are aesthetic in character, employing metaphor to evoke some sense of the experience. Most understandings of these descriptions of mystical experience by non-mystics would in fact be aesthetic understandings in the sense that what is most likely communicated is the mysterious depth of the experience, not the sense of mystical union.

Aesthetic experience is not ineffable in precisely the same sense as is the experience of mystical union. The works of the poet or the painter may in fact communicate the inexhaustibly mysterious sense of things which is the immediate context of aesthetic experiencing. Thus, metaphorical deliverances are constitutive of art in a way that they are only instrumental in religion.[14] That is, in religious articulation the characterizations of the ineffable experience are meant to point beyond to the object of the experience. Strictly aesthetic metaphors, however, evoke an immediate experience of the mysterious which is, in fact, the direct content of the metaphors employed.

It is obviously difficult to distinguish between aesthetic and religious experiencing with any kind of finality. For what may be an aesthetic proposition for one individual can easily be a religious proposal for another. If an art object, a painting, for example, is experienced as suggestive of the immediate sense of the mysterious depths beneath and beyond the finite subject of the experience, it makes all the difference in the world whether one celebrates the unique individuality of the object or allows the experience of the object to be an instrument through which one gains a sense of the mystical unity with the totality of experienced fact. Whether we focus upon the aesthetic or the religious mode of experiencing we still must understand the subject of experiencing in terms of its *terminus a quo* in the chaos of sensibility which I am identifying as the imagination as well as in terms of the *terminus ad quem* in the chaos of factors constituting the flux of passing fact which I am calling the World.

The attempt to express the ineffable has as its goal the evocation of the experience of mystical union. Religious language is formally the same as aesthetic language, but rather than serving as the immediate occasion for self-enjoyment, it is instrumentally employed as a means of attaining an experience of ultimacy. It is certainly possible to articulate a religious experience in other ways. For in addition to the twofold allusiveness of art and religion, it is often the case that we may seek interpretations of these fundamental experiences. Theological articulations characterizing the source or occasion for religious experiencing in terms of theistic concepts are, in fact, concessions to the concern for systematic coherence and rational consistency which meet our rational interests.

Thus religious communities which stress the importance of belief in articulated theological propositions tend to tie the imaginative expressions of religion to strictly rational interests. A further consequence of this tendency is that the affective experiences associated with these theological propositions tend to be aesthetic rather than religious since, instead of promoting a mystical intuition, they celebrate the mysterious otherness of the interpreted source of religious experiencing.

One final implication of this tendency should be noted: if it is held that belief in theological propositions should find its ultimate justification in practical actions in the realm of praxis, then the strictly moral component of experiencing is allowed to discipline the final meaning of the mystical experience. In this sense, then, to amend slightly Matthew Arnold's description, religion becomes "[science and] morality tinged with emotion." And the emotion is aesthetic, not religious, feeling.

Straight indeed is the gate, and narrow the way that leads to the realization of mystical union, and few, very few, there are that tread that path. And, if religious experiencing is so often derogated in our culture, we are only slightly more open to the mysterious character of experience. Again, this is because of the inordinate emphasis placed upon the moral and scientific interests. Theoretical activity for the most part serves to defend the facticity of the data encountered at the perceptual level and to promote the coherence of principles which may be employed in the controlling of our ambience construed as a sphere of technical and moral praxis. The individual, accidental, unique, just-so-ness of things is continually abstracted from in order that we may manipulate our world as a complex of instances, or types, contributing to our rational and ethical behaviors.

The only purely participative grasp of the world is the sense of Chaos as nonordered, the original sense of the formless, the empty, the void. It is that experience which in our culture has repeatedly given rise to myths of the construal of order from disorder, of the conquest of reason over contingency and confusion, of the overcoming of the yawning gap separating the elements of the ordered world as we subsequently have come to know it. Chaos is the source of meaningfulness in the sense that it is the occasion of the development of mythical and theoretical articulations as descriptive of the order of the world itself. Ironically, it is this attitude which leads us to a loss of participation in the world of experience. The *philomythos* participated, we presume, theorially through the mythical vision, and practically through ritual. As long as it was remembered that the purpose of the ritual was to celebrate a temporary victory over Chaos, one which required continued reversion to the experience of Chaos as the source of all meaningfulness, participative experience was assured.

We have at last reached a point in our discussion where we may productively draw upon the analysis of "order" provided in the last chapter. Two distinct theories of language may be gleaned from the consideration of logical and aesthetic orders. The logically oriented theory is grounded upon statements of relations as paradigms from which extensions of meaning may be made. Metaphor, on this view, is the key to the extension of significance beyond the literal. From the aesthetic perspective, so-called metaphors are not to be interpreted as extensional but as intensional. They are not intended to stretch the literal sense of a term but to serve as the ground in accordance with which other, more literal or instrumental, employments of language are to be understood. Not only do aesthetically oriented individuals take metaphors more seriously than do literalists, what literalists must mean by metaphors (namely, locutions extending the sense of words or concepts beyond their literal significance) is not at all what the aesthetically oriented mean by the term. In aesthetic uses of language, metaphors are the very foundation of meaning.

These two understandings of the function of language can be contrasted in terms of what we may call the "expressive" and the "allusive" visions of communication. In the logical view the purpose of language, both literal and metaphorical, is the expression of meaning; in the aesthetic interpretation words are allusory and suggestive. "To express" derives from the Latin *exprimere*, meaning "to press out (or from) a particular thing." Ex-pressing involves a representing of a thing by pressing out a meaning from it. Expressive acts of communication suppose the legitimacy of such direct forms of channeling meaning from one communicant to another. "To allude," on the other hand, means "to play with" (*alludere*), "to touch lightly upon." Communication through allusion always involves indirect reference, the sidewise glance. Expression has the directness of a statement; alluding, on the other hand, suggests the indirectness of "mentioning."

In the world patterned primarily by logical order, expression would be the paradigm form of communication. If, on the other hand, communication is to be considered primarily within the context of an aesthetically ordered world, then one must be content with allusion. Logical theories of meaning and truth are associated with cosmological orders in which the pattern of relationships among things establishes the data which are to be communicated. These patterns are expressible through logical forms which are universal with respect to this type of relation. Meaning is expressed by characterizing a given set of relations.

On the aesthetic model, however, meaning and truth cannot be expressed since the truth of the thing is its ontological reality. There can be no preassigned patterns through which the meaning of aesthetic orders can be expressed. In this case, one can only allude, glance out of the corner of one's eye, touch lightly upon, mention, suggest.

In the allusory theory, general propositions cannot be true. Truth requires the kind of subtlety that is to be found in the allusiveness of any reference to the world. Were we to read the parabolic sayings of Chuang-tzu or Jesus with a logical eye, we would be able to abstract from them a set of apparently important principles: "Be spontaneous"; "Avoid rationalization"; "Act always in accordance with the true natures of things." But surely this would be silly. Such translation permits the parabolic utterances to be placed in logical contexts which require the use of class concepts of a very general nature, and this involves relative indifference to the peculiarities of experience and the assignment of meaning in accordance with a preselected pattern of significance. Such generalizations, by applying to everyone indifferently, apply to no one in particular.

The paradox, of course, is that allusiveness leads to the appreciation of details each for its own sake. And, equally significant, the true reference of allusive propositions is to the individual who understands the proposition. He who has ears to hear, let him hear. The allusive character of language permits truth to be truth only if it is realized in the communicant. The parable is true because it is *striking*. One can tell the truth only if that striking is *telling*. A true proposition is a *telling* statement. And it is not telling because it is true, but true because it is telling.

The theory of truth to be gleaned from the aesthetic and mystical visions of the world is an ontological theory. Truth is the reality of a thing. But the aesthetic interpretation of order permits no single privileged order, nor any coherent complex of orders, to define the nature of the world. Truth of an ontological sort is always individual. The general laws of nature cannot be true; universal moral principles cannot be true; standards of truth and ugliness cannot be true. Truth is particular. And how does one express the particular? Obviously, that is impossible if by "express" we mean to convey the significance of an item in terms of its qualities or characteristics since these characteristics and qualities are class concepts. Communication must be allusive, quite subtle, merely suggestive. We can only hint.

The systematic, intransigent ambiguity in the concept of order precludes the development of a language satisfying the demands of both logic and aesthetics. The recognition that both demands exist and lay claim to our sense and sensibility is essential. Ontologically, the truth is to be found in the unique reality of a thing, which cannot, of course, be named. Cosmologically construed, truth is context-dependent. To repeat the relevant statement from Chapter 4, cosmological truth is dependent upon "the assignment through physiological, linguistic, or rhetorical operations of a pattern of meaning which constitutes one set of relations that can be said to exist among the items entertained and the manner in which the context so conceived determines the character of the items forming the context."

Both the logical and the aesthetic visions require that, as Chuang-tzu insisted, "Words are not just wind; words have something to say."[15] The problem is that they have altogether too much to say. They express, but they also allude. Thus the infinite plasticity of verbal forms. If we seek expression as the primary communicative act we soon discover that there is truly no limit to the meanings that may be expressed, for just as "a road is made by people walking on it; things are so because they are called so."[16] The natural world is passive to an infinite set of patterned relationships. The frustration of the attempt to express *the* truth is that one finally must accede to the conclusion that "there is nothing that is not so."[17] Each truth we express is met, in due time, by its opposite which is also claimed to be true. Viewed cosmologically, the world is not a Cosmos, but a congeries patterned by the extreme relativity of facts and values.

Driven beyond this relativity we may seek "a state in which 'this' and 'that' no longer find their opposites."[18] The world of ontological particulars, where each thing is just itself in its insistent particularity, is just such a place. The unique items comprising such a realm cannot, of course, be directly named. But their uniqueness can be approached through allusion.

When we try to understand metaphorical communication it is important that we be able to distinguish those metaphors which tend more toward expression and those which function allusively. It is safe to say that because of the literal-mindedness that has dominated our consciousness since the transition from theorial to theoretical understandings we are apt to misunderstand the consciousness of those periods of our culture and history less literal-minded than we.

Language, at its source, is allusive. It is meaning-disposing. Through explicit acts of expression a meaningful pattern is brought forth from the Chaos of nonorderedness. Only at our great peril, however, can we forget that to experience the allusive ground of language we must have continual recourse to the Chaos from out of which it comes. An active interest in the disordered, confused, contradictory, paradoxical opacity of experience is essential to our participation in the real world which is Chaos Itself. The experience underlying both the creation of mythical visions and the development of theoretical perspectives is the sense of the Chaos as an infinitely allusive matrix within which all potential patternings are contained. The character of the response to this primordial experience of Chaos indicates the path a culture will take in the development of the complex of meanings and values instantiating its mode of existence.

In Anglo-European culture, cosmogonic myths stress the notion of the construal of order from disorder. The Chaos of voidness, or of confused disorder, or of separation, constitutes the source from out of which our volitional, rational, and affective capacities as human beings have received their primary interpretation. Because we have been prone to interpret God's will or reason or love in terms of a dualistic relation with the created order motivated by the overcoming of Chaos, we have been disposed to interpret human action, thought, and passion in the same fashion. The sense of enmity expressed toward our natural ambience is a consequence of our belief that the order of things is the product of an act of construal. As representatives of the Divine we are surrogate artificers who objectify our world because only in that fashion can we reduce it to the possibility of understanding and control. But there is doubtless something alien about this world if for no other reason than we fear a reversion to the primordial Chaos out of which it was made. Unable to accept the multifariousness of items in the inexhaustible depth of their significances, we reduce the inner complexity of things in themselves to the outer simplicity of objects which, though they object to us in their construed existence, can nonetheless be overcome as was their parent, Chaos, in the time of beginnings.

The dominance of interests of control illustrated by scientific and moral reasonings is not a necessary condition of human culture per se. Indeed the acknowledged importance of the aesthetic element in Oriental cultures seems to go hand in hand with a deemphasis upon classically Western conceptions of science. Likewise, the peculiar importance of religious experiencing as intrinsically related to aesthetic experience, illustrated by classical Chinese Taoism or Ch'an Buddhism, entails a mitigation of the importance of purely ethical values. Not only are these traditions excellent samples of the consequences of the stress upon aesthetic and religious modes of activity in a culture, they also demonstrate by contrast the important consequences of our Anglo-European stress upon moral and scientific interests.

If we take the cosmogonic myths patterning our tradition seriously they may be seen to indicate at the cultural and psychological level the possibility of the experience of rational order as a second-stage phenomenon. The fundamental sense of the world is of disorder, confusion, voidness, separation, and alienation. Cosmogonic myths provide a means of overcoming that original sense of Chaos by recourse to the conception of a primary creative act. But Chaos, and the attendant anxieties associated with its existence as the fundamental matrix out of which, in accordance with which, or over against which the creative act was initiated, is not forgotten. For the ritualistic behaviors associated with the cosmogonic myths as they appear in our primary religious traditions celebrate the victory over the evil of Chaos, as if to provide a recurrent reminder of the fact that the "forces of order" are still in control.

It is important to note that there are alternatives to this type of radical cosmogony. The principal alternative entails the consequence that Chaos, as the original or pervasive character of the world, is a harmonious matrix of complex orders functioning as the source of alternative meanings, an allusive gestalt which serves as the paradigmatic experience of meaningfulness. Those traditions which do not depend upon radical cosmogonic speculation believe that the world is spontaneously ordered, so that no act of Primary Creation is necessary. In our tradition there are, of course, strictly philosophic theories such as the Aristotelian which offer no cosmogonic speculations per se, but which find in the relations between God and the World a timeless interaction that permits God as Supreme *Archē* to function as the principle of order and harmony. But in the Taoist tradition, for example, there is not only no need for a Primary Creative Act, there is no need to appeal to a Supreme *Archē* as guarantor of order and harmony in the world. For the Taoist, and similar traditions, which find the experience of positive Chaos to be fundamental, the alternative to artificially construed order is not dis-order and confusion, but is spontaneous, uncreated harmony.

The phenomenal chaos of modes of thought and activity expressed in our conflicting theories, ideologies, and systems of value argues for the celebration of primordial Chaos as the sum of all orders. This permits the appreciation of the contrasting interpretations of the world leading not to rejection, refutation, or dialectical sublation, but rather to the attempt to harmonize them through an intuition of the allusive significance of the source of all orders of which each separate ideology, theoretical system, or plan of action is but a single finite manifestation.

The source of meaning is Chaos. But there is no hope, nor should there be any desire, to construe that Chaos as a single-ordered Cosmos whose privileged order can be defended rationally and politically. It is not Cosmos as a single-ordered matrix that we should be defending; rather we should be employing our energies in the nurturance and protection of Chaos as the infinitely allusive source of meaning and value which promotes all of our finite endeavors of understanding and action.

My plea on behalf of Chaos should not be taken amiss. I am not urging the abandonment of rational order and instrumental praxis. I merely wish to defend a broadened conception of theory. To the understanding of theoretical principles as primarily for the sake of rational understanding we must add the notion of theory as functioning allusively with regard to the nature of the reality it purports to interpret. The understanding of the allusiveness of theory is the gift of eros-returned, of the reversal of eros and its redirecting capacity exercised within the realm of praxis. The aesthetic form of the religious intuition of completeness is expressed as a horizontal transcendence of facts and theories complementing the vertical transcendence provided by spiritual insight.

Horizontal transcendence teaches us that the finite facts, propositions, hypotheses, and theoretical systems which pattern the realm of human praxis must be understood as functioning allusively with regard to the reality they are meant to describe or interpret. The intuition of completeness precludes our simple ad hoc rejection of one theory in favor of another, or of one class of facts over another. The condition of relativity at the level of praxis is such that fidelity to the intuition of completeness experientially realized at the mystical level must be expressed through the mysterious depths of existence advertised by the conflicting variety of perspectives which constitute theoretical activities at the level of intellectual culture. The absence of a single vision which adequately encompasses all other theories is reason enough for us to see the relation of these theories one to another, and to the reality each attempts to capture through its explanatory principles, as an allusive relation.

In more formal language we might say that in addition to the understanding of our intellectual endeavors as productive of facts and theories functioning in the aim of the control of experienced processes, we must see the metaphorical function of language as providing significant depth and vagueness to our world such that we shall not be tempted to lay claim to certain knowledge where none in fact exists. Whereas facts find their proper home within theories which account for and justify their facticity, theories may find no common basis if each of two theories lays claim to metaphysical generality. Two putatively general metaphysical theories functioning in a realm of common discourse function metaphorically with regard to one another. The attempt to establish a common ground for communication among conflicting theoretical systems must involve more than the endeavor to refute one theory from the perspective of another, or by a dialectical strategem which attempts to interpret one theory as a special case of another. Though this on rare occasions may be acceptable to both parties in a theoretical dispute, the far greater likelihood is that these attempts at refutation or sublation will be met by an equally cogent counteroffensive on the part of the theorist initially under attack.

The data-bits which we often presume to be lying around for our dispassionate inspection are the products of perspective abstractions from experience which do not so much justify our theoretical endeavors as they stand in need of justification from them. And theories, once they reach the generality of speculative systems, cannot themselves be justified within theoretical contexts, but must find their justification in the categorial intuitions which ground them. If we seek literal understandings we shall always be frustrated by reflection and critical enquiry since they will inevitably call into question the incorrigibility of facts and theories.

The proper response to the unavoidable consequence of the extreme theoretical and valuational relativity patterning contemporary culture is to recognize the ultimately metaphorical character of all attempts to express the final character of the nature of things. Theoretical propositions which, from a literalist point of view, are thought to describe the nature of the relevant subject matter in fact only allude to that subject matter. The allusiveness is characterized by an indefinite complexity which serves as the context within which one participates in the significance of that to which one alludes.

Analyses of works of art as cultural objects illustrate the allusive potentialities of language. The meaning of a painting does not have primary reference to the paint and canvas as a perceptual object. Analyzed simply in terms of the physical substratum constituted by the artist's materials or the impression made upon the senses, a work of art is a natural object among other such objects. It becomes an aesthetic object when it attains a significance with an affective depth. When the object as physical datum is transmuted through the introduction of affective referents, organized through a single intuitive grasp of the interfused occasions for that introduction, a cultural object emerges. The most primitive aesthetic experience occurs in the reorganization of focus upon an object in the perceptual field which brings to bear upon the object the affective significance of its physical components as alluding to significances inexhaustibly present in the object. Cultural objects establish a virtual intersubjectivity between the object "out there" and some selection of the significances potentially present within the object and open to enjoyment by the observer. Such observations are in fact participations.

Such an interpretation of aesthetic experience depends upon the presumption that our fundamental form of being in the world is that of participation in the components of our ambience in a direct and primitive sense only hinted at in the ordinary acts of sense experience. An object qua object is the consequence of an act of objectification. But the existence of the object in this objective mode does not exhaust its being. Neither the realist notion of the act of perception as a recognition of data intuitively given nor the idealist assumption that the act of perception constitutes the object is (wholly) correct. The object is constituted, to be sure, but the end result of that constitution is a perspective abstraction involving the selection of components from that which is present to us and a transmutation of that object which allows us to see it by resourse to this abstractive mode as if it subsists in that mode alone.

To presume that an object is in fact that which we transmute is a judgment of an uncritical sort which, while serving some practical interest, belies the deep complexity of our experienced world. Even the most critical reevaluation of our perceptual entertainments, however, would never allow us to exhaust the indefinite variety of perspective emphases possible in relation to an object. Literal, conceptual, imaginative, and metaphorical language, as repositories of the results of these abstractive emphases, and as a means of achieving these emphases, is inexhaustibly vague when it becomes the object of interpretation and reflection.

We are by no means led to the conclusion that we are trapped inside our language, unable to appreciate the infinite complexities and nuances of the experienced world. Our language itself is inexhaustibly significant. There are an inexhaustible number of facts, as well as an indefinitely large number of concepts, because language has the potentiality of indefinite expansion by recourse to the allusiveness of metaphor.

The claims made here are, of course, truistic in a very real sense even though we tend to forget them when enchanted by the pragmatic successes achieved whenever we take the objects of experience as exhaustibly present to us through acts of theoretical construction. The progress of scientific understandings of the world tended toward the reduction of the objects of perceptual experience to externally present factors in fact. It is this that has been most determinative in the mitigation of the participative mode of thinking associated with metaphorical expressions. We come to believe that our consensual understandings have a certain directness and adequacy which vaguer forms of experience do not have. But the presence of aesthetic metaphor and religious symbolism continues to mean that we are always called back from a final capitulation to the literalist mode of entertaining the world.

The history of the transition from theoria to systematic reflection is a story of the decreased recognition of the mode of participative thinking. That we have decreasingly recognized the importance of this mode does not mean that we are any less involved in acts of participation. We are, however, less able to enjoy this intersubjective experience of our world. What this means is that we have increased the distance between ourselves and the objects of our experience by refusing to take responsibility for the constitution of the objects while trying to take control of them as if they stand over against us, objecting to our presence. The polar relation of self and world has been construed as dualistic, and the alienating consequences which are advertised in our obsession with techniques of organization and control at the level of understanding and action are evident for all to see.

The principal functions of theory—the delimiting, integrating, describing, generating, interpreting functions[19]—do not well suit the aims of participative thinking. To delimit is to define the sphere within which concepts and principles will be operating. The integrative function of theory depends upon such limitation. A theory integrates data by providing a coherent set of abstractive procedures which serve to specify the organic relationships of both the elements of the theory and the data to which the theory applies. These relationships are emergent from the specific kind of abstractions employed. They provide a matrix which describes adequately only those events or entities in the experienceable world which are, at least potentially, termini of the same form of abstractive procedures. Interpretation, as opposed to mere description, depends upon inferences legitimated by the theoretical context construed as a consistent complex of logical propositions and/or upon analogical relations obtaining among the propositions and items of experience which would give rise to similar or isomorphic propositions if themselves directly described. Theories qua theories generate new data by pointing out the consequences of the relations among the logical propositions of the theory, or by suggesting the existence of novel phenomena by virtue of the application of the theory as a matrix in accordance with which one might see these novel data as the termini of the given abstractive procedures.

Though the interpretative and generative functions of theory often involve the use of metaphor, it is expressive and not allusive metaphor which is employed. The allusive character of theoretical language has, in our tradition, been ignored for the most part. Indeed, stressing it to any profound degree would lead to the loss of the sense of consistency and coherence upon which the other functions of theory so obviously depend.

The problem lies in the very nature of the apologetic enterprise. It may indeed be mistaken to seek theories of the way of things which try to remain theories in the classical sense while drawing upon aesthetic and religious sensibilities. For it is in the very nature of the theoretical activity as opposed to the theorial that there is already present a tendency toward the domination by moral and scientific sensibility. Myth and metaphor, as modes of participative thinking leading one to a directness of the experience of the world, tend of necessity to be eschewed in rational, systematic, principled modes of thought since the rational means of appropriating the character of things is at variance with the means provided through art and religion.

CHAPTER SIX
FROM OTHERNESS
TO EMPTINESS

A persistent theme throughout this essay has been the issue of theoretical relativity. So many philosophic visions compete for attention and commitment that the professional philosopher cannot but continually be threatened by embarrassment. For either he falls prey to the eclecticism and dilettantism consequent upon the refusal to opt among competing philosophic views, or he is forced into a dogmatic, provincial narrowness if he does choose from among conflicting claims. The hope that a new systematic vision will emerge which contains both the virtues of consistency and coherence on the one hand, and adequacy to the complex welter of individual, social, and cultural experience on the other has been all but abandoned. The few such speculative endeavors that have been forwarded by contemporary philosophers to meet our chaos of sensibilities have not been accorded respect, or even much attention, by the individuals or enterprises they purport to engage. Equally ineffectual are the wheel-spinning varieties of philosophic discourse which eschew grand issues and content themselves with fragmented endeavors at analysis or description.

It would appear that the relatively recent introduction into this cultural setting of yet other philosophies drawn from the exoteric cultures of India, classical China, and Japan could only exacerbate our present difficulties through the addition of novel visions to our already unbearable confusion of tongues. But, ironically enough, the stimulus provided by the challenge of Oriental philosophies has promoted a concern for the development of comparative methodologies relevant not only to the East–West dialogue, but to intertheoretical communication per se.

One of the primary conditions for the existence of that kind of meeting which results in significant communication is the presence of a psychological tension among communicants deriving from a sense of distance, difference, or otherness. The crucial element in significant communication is the tension predicated upon the need to share feeling or fact. If the condition of sharing already obtains there exists a communion with no necessity for further effort or articulation. If, however, novelty is introduced into a context of communication, there is something there to be *learned*. Significant communication always involves learning, and learning requires change, movement, alteration of sensibility, reorganization (however slight) of patterns or priorities in one's thinking.

One of the consequences of the fact that tension based upon otherness is essential in acts of communication is that we often find ourselves unable to learn from our friends. At least we do not learn those things we might expect to learn from authorities and experts. The cliché "Familiarity breeds contempt" all too often applies to communication among familiars. Indeed, just as a prophet is seldom honored in his own country because of the condition of familiarity, so lovers often find it difficult to learn the most obvious things from one another, and parents find it extremely challenging to be teachers of their own children. What is presumed missing in failed attempts at significant communication among familiars is the element of tension which breeds attention. In competitive societies, significant communication (at least of the type that involves formal learning) most naturally takes place in contexts of conflict and competition, in which we find ourselves at odds with one another. When, therefore, friendships are formed on the basis of seeking respite from the discomforts of such conflict some opportunities for learning seem to be lost.

In our technologically advanced societies, communication difficulties are in large measure the result of the abstractness of social relationships. First, there is that abstract equality we experience by virtue of membership in an ostensibly democratic society. This stipulative equality relieves all parties in a relationship from the necessity of deference essential to significant communication. In formal institutional settings there is a stipulative *in*equality as abstract as the relation of equality in more informal public settings. The active contempt associated with disrespect, antipathy, or utter indifference is often the consequence of alienation from authorities whose claims to their authoritative role are justifiable solely by appeal to the abstract inequality established by the fact of office or title.

Somewhere beyond the communal comforts which offer sharing without learning, and somewhere between the forms of active and passive contempt bred by the abstract equality and inequality of ordinary social relations, lies the possibility of significant communication. But we are hard pressed to say precisely where that possibility is to be found. Each relational act, each event of potential communication, is *sui generis*, and must finally be assessed on its own terms. Abstract equality no more promotes communion than abstract inequality guarantees learning. And, to further complicate what appears to be an already impossible situation, the greater number of presumedly concrete situations of conflict and disagreement in our culture are in fact communal in character. Having agreed to disagree, old enemies rehearse a ritual of conflict which cannot, of course, serve the ends of communication but does in fact promote the communal feelings associated with participation in a common rite. Habitual conflict among nagging couples or warring ideologies is maintained in part because of the comfort and security obtained from the background conditions of mutuality.[1]

Philosophic communication is beset by the same difficulties I have just attributed to informal acts of communication. Philosophers sharing a common set of assumptions seldom learn anything of significance from one another since they have already agreed that they possess the truth in all things essential. Writing for their colleagues, their works take on the form of interoffice memos rather than serious attempts to confront difficult issues. Real disputes among philosophers seldom take place since truly conflicting thinkers are not disposed to engage one another since they already know what the course of the dialogue will be—namely, the mutual reduction of theoretical propositions by recourse to alternative methodologies. When a philosopher does in fact attempt to critique an alternative point of view, his remarks are usually read only by his sympathetic colleagues and are either ignored by thinkers against whom they are directed or are met with counterbombast. The comfort of communal feelings associated with the rehearsal of common views within one's consensual group, or the more stylized ritualistic communion resulting from the rhetorical fireworks launched by ideological opposites, are the most characteristic phenomena in so-called philosophic dialogue.

The crisis in philosophic communication in Anglo-European traditions is largely attributable to the self-consciousness of our contemporary intellectual culture. Having raised to the level of consciousness what we presume to be the principal theoretical visions, we are skeptical of discovering anything like novel approaches to our perennial philosophic issues. The stimulus provided by transcultural and intercultural communications is significant since the claims of the alternative theories in such interchanges are still relatively unfamiliar one to the other, and, therefore, mutually intriguing. The otherness experienced in inter-theoretical communication between Oriental and Western philosophies is a creative otherness which lures the communicants into a context of promising dialogue. In at least this sense, the form of the East-West philosophic dialogue may be seen to provide a model for all types of intertheoretical communication.

In the absence of any sophisticated reflections on the matter, we presume the event of communication to be aimed at provoking understanding: an act of communication is a kind of *praxis* conditioned by *theoria*. We perform that others may be informed. This is communication stripped of any specific pragmatic ends. The expressive undertaking which initiates communication may involve gestures or other nonverbal cues; direct expressions in verbal form; indirect expressions such as the writing of a letter, or, still more indirect, the composition of a pamphlet or a book. Pragmatic uses of language involve, at least initially, the provocation of understandings, emotions, or actions which are directed by, or focused upon, the purposes of the expresser. Passive enjoyments or understandings, as well as playful activities, are the products of simple communication. The more communication serves the ends beyond those of immediate enjoyment, contemplation, articulation, or play, the less is the event of communication conditioned by theoria, and the more by notions of practicability of purpose.

In what follows I shall examine some of the consequences of the view that the act of communication is, ideally, noninstrumental and that the aesthetic character of communication, as distinct from its merely pragmatic or rational character, names what is essential to every communicational event. We may begin by reflecting upon a model of learning and communication developed by Gregory Bateson which employs a set of distinctions germane to our previous discussions.[2] Bateson offers a hierarchy of types of learning or (since learning is a "communicational phenomenon") of communication. Learning involves a kind of *change*. "Zero-learning" requires a specificity of response which is not open to correction. Examples of learning, or communication, which approach zero are highly stereotyped responses such as those determined by genetic or structural rather than experiential factors. The best illustration Bateson provides of this type of communication is that of simple electronic circuits in which the causal links are not open to alteration via feedback circuits or mechanisms. In zero-learning there is a simple kind of "communion" which does not, therefore, involve a learning.

For learning to take place there must be change. Level I, or the first level of what we may presume to be significant communication, consists in "*change in the specificity of response* by correction of errors of choice within a set of alternatives."[3] The set of alternatives is determined by a context which grounds the proper interpretation of the data confronted. Level I is most obviously associated with phenomena such as classical conditioning involving behavioral reinforcement, rote learning, and so on. In classical conditioning, a dog may learn to salivate at the sound of a buzzer at t_2 which did not stimulate salivation at t_1. The buzzer as stimulus must be presumed a constant from t_1 to t_2, as must the laboratory conditions which constitute the context.

Obviously this type of communication is best adapted to explain digital rather than analogical forms of experience and expression. At the sophisticated levels of human communication digital learning and communication involve the assumption of facts as isolated data-bits which may be learned and communicated without taking into account the theoretical context establishing their facticity. Level-I understandings are the bases for the most naïve forms of empiricism associated with the belief in the total objectivity of sense experiencing.

Level-II understandings involve a change in the conditions of Level I. That is, they require a correction of the set of alternatives determining the context of choice. Level-II communication involves primarily analogical components since we are concerned with the transition from one type of context to another, presumedly similar, type. Psychological transference, according to Bateson, is an illustration of Level-II communication. The relational context deriving from the patient's unconscious infantile past (if we take the Freudian sense of transference) is projected (most likely inappropriately) upon the behavioral context represented by the patient–therapist relationship. Thus, unlike Level-I understandings, Level II involves at least minimal awareness of theoretical principles or hypotheses which may be applied beyond the context from which they were initially derived.

If Level-III communication is to be achieved there must be a change in Level II such that one alters one's perspective upon theoretical contexts. Normally, one must experience the change of contexts as either appropriate or inappropriate. Learning III requires the transcendence of contexts in the sense that one experiences indifference to the selection of theoretical background. The fundamental aim of learning at Level III is freedom from bondage to the contexts of Level II.

Learning the fact "The earth revolves about the sun" does not necessarily involve explicit awareness of any particular heliocentric theory, though obviously that fact does depend on some such theory. Likewise, to know that "The sun revolves about the earth" does not require explicit recourse to geocentricity as a theoretical notion. Learning I goes on within contexts but without explicit awareness of contexts. Learning II proceeds in accordance with some theoretical awareness. At Level II one knows "The earth revolves about the sun" or "The sun revolves about the earth" by virtue of an appeal to principles which define a given theoretical context. Learning III requires indifference to contexts. Thus at this level one may know both of the facts cited above. And this knowledge includes awareness of the theoretical dependence of each fact.

Here we must be careful to distinguish Level-III understandings from a Level-II phenomenon which seems to approximate it—namely, the simple shifting from one theoretical context to another. At the level of logical system, there can be only one of two or more conflicting visions internalized at a time. It is obviously possible to be converted from one set of assumptions to another. This can occur either spontaneously as in the case of spiritual conversions, or somewhat more artificially through certain therapeutic procedures, or it can be the result of a rational critique of the inadequacies of a given philosophic vision. The Wittgenstein of the *Tractatus* may be understood as having a distinctly different world view from the Wittgenstein of the *Investigations*. With perhaps less justification, Saint Paul may be said to have entertained an alternative systematic understanding to that of Saul of Tarsus. Taking a more extreme case, it might be said that the individual sustaining multiple personality patterns, each one unconscious of the others, is employing a plurality of systems of psychic orientation alternately. The aesthetic visionary of Level III, however, is distinguished from the systematic thinker of Level II by virtue of the fact that he experiences the parity of alternative contexts.

In the case of the astronomical theories instanced above, the aesthetic visionary may claim that each fact cited is true or theoretically viable by appeal to the notion of relativity. If he does so without reifying some relativity theory as a rational system which competes with other systematic explanations then he has achieved the beginnings of Level-III understanding. Conventionalist approaches to scientific facts which appeal to convenience, efficiency, simplicity, elegance, and so on as grounds for choosing among apparently conflicting facts are grounded in unarticulated forms of aesthetic vision. From the aesthetic perspective, the earth *does* revolve about the sun and the sun *does* revolve about the earth, and in manners required by the Copernican and Ptolemaic theories, respectively. Moreover, these facts are on a par one with the other. Obviously the cosmos which permits of the kind of ontological parity suggested here is not the traditional cosmos, but is, rather, *Chaos*—the sum of all orders.

The assertion that one may hold conflicting and even contradictory visions of the world is doubtless quite bizarre from the point of view of the rationalist. From that perspective it is, in fact, impossible. But what are we to make of the claim of the classical Christian mystic that the world is both finite and infinite entailed by the explication of the God–Soul identity state? Or what of the assertions of the nature mystic to the effect that the world is fundamentally One and Many? Or what of the testimony of the microphysicists that natural events are patterned by both particulate and wave characteristics; are both localized and nonlocalized, both spontaneous and absolutely determinable? The aesthetic visionary sees in paradoxes of this type the suggestion that the actual world is not single-ordered but is, in fact, a sum of overlapping orders.

Intellectual sophistication of the type that allows one to remain indifferent to contexts establishing the facticity of facts is extremely rare. Indeed, it is not at all possible as long as one continues to hold rational criteria to be the principal means whereby to establish the viability of a general theoretical vision. For even the principle of sufficient reason is a context-bound notion since its ultimate satisfaction requires the assumption of a single-ordered Cosmos.

Clearly, Bateson's three levels of learning and communication constitute a kind of Platonism in which the Divided Line is employed in a truncated fashion. In terms of the vocabulary used in this essay Bateson's three levels conform to the factual, theoretical, and theorial modes of understanding we have rehearsed at some length. The aesthetic and mystical motivations which lead to the transcendence of theory and the exercise of the theorial impulse are here again to be contrasted with the moral and rational motivations which tie one to facts and theories. Placing the discussion of the theorial impulse within the context of the understanding of types of communication renders obvious some of the more significant of the consequences of the inordinate dependence upon factual and theoretical knowledge.

The primary instances of theorial learning and communication are to be found among mystics and Zen masters, as well as some artists, since they are not burdened by the necessity to hold rational or logical order more important than aesthetic order. The prestige of rational conceptions of order in the West has caused even the mystical tradition to be disciplined by theological principles which are grounded in theoretical understandings. Not content with the acknowledged ineffability of the mystical experience, confessors and theological systematizers have molded the reports of the mystics into patterns of theological orthodoxy, doing no little violence to the mystics' experience.[4] The desire for propositional expression and systematic coherence and consistency which has dominated our treatments of the mystical tradition since the beginnings of Judeo-Christianity has precluded the general recognition of theorial visions.

Buddhist and Taoist traditions are not nearly so plagued by this press toward theoretical orthodoxy. More comfortable with paradox and the threat of logical contradiction, such traditions have provided articulations of the mystical experience which suggest a type of learning and communication qualitatively distinct from that demanding rational or logical forms of order.

One of the main reasons Anglo-Europeans find it difficult to take seriously Oriental thinking in its more aesthetic forms is grounded in the necessity to hold fast to a substance view of the self. It is the persisting self, in some real sense identical through time, that is perhaps the fundamental dogma of Western philosophy. It is the datum which thinkers in the West are least likely to yield. Theorial understandings must, ultimately, lead to the surrender of the concept of the self as possessing any ultimate ontological character. The self is, after all, but a complex of characteristics qualifying the context of theoretical activity. As Bateson shrewdly notes, " 'I' am my habits of acting in context and shaping and perceiving contexts in which I act."[5] The transcendence of these contexts required by theorial forms of communication entails the transcendence of selfhood.

The claim that self or self-consciousness persists as the ground of mystical experience, if justified, all but assures the victory of the exponents of the doctrinal ground of mystical experiencing. For if, as such proponents claim, mystical states are "not the ground but the *outcome* of the complex epistemological activity which is set in motion by the integrating character of self-consciousness employed in the specifically mystical modality,"[6] then it is clear that the relativity of linguistic and conceptual structures associated with the variety of mystical traditions must come into play. If "these constructive conditions of consciousness produce the grounds on which mystical experience is possible at all,"[7] then mystical experience is but a way of knowing which is variously influenced by the specific problematic from which the experience begins. This makes of nirvana, Tao, the Uncreated Essence of the Holy Trinity, distinctly different experiences as well as different doctrines. A consequence of such an interpretation of mysticism is that all experiences of the mystical variety are context-specific.

The claim of W. T. Stace and Aldous Huxley, among others, to the effect that all mystical experiencing has a "universal core" leads to a preference for Oriental over Anglo-European forms of mysticism. This is because of the Eastern attitudes toward language and toward the substance view of the self. In Buddhist and Taoist mysticism the self is *empty*. The no-mind or no-soul doctrine involves the dissolution of the self. In the Western tradition doctrinal theologians stress the type of experiencing associated with the Beatific Vision which permits of interpretation in terms of a separately existing soul. Western mystical writings, on the other hand, express the sense of Unity—the God–Soul Identity State—as the fundamental mode of experiencing the Divine. This latter form of experience is much more similar to the experience of *sunyata* or Nameless Tao than is that of the Beatific Vision.

It seems quite plausible that the doctrines of Buddhism and Taoism encourage mystical experience in a way that those of Judeo-Christianity do not. Northrop's famous distinction between Eastern and Western modes of thinking—the former employing "concepts by intuition," the latter "concepts by postulation"—suggests a distinction that is relevant here. Mystical modes of knowing are more properly accomplished in cultures which promote the importance of aesthetic and religious sensibilities as autonomous modes of insight. One might expect that Anglo European cultures with their stress upon scientific and moral interests would be somewhat less able to capture the essential features of mystical experiencing. We are certainly not, as a rule, disinclined to accept the superiority of Western science over that of the Orient and we are even more likely to criticize the emphasis of spiritual "otherwordly" concerns of the East when they militate against the production of ethical systems of value.[8]

We surely ought to open our eyes to the possibility that there are cultural reasons why we find it difficult to appreciate the direct expression of mystical intuitions. If we accept this view as hypothetically viable, we can test it by reading our indigenous mystics less in terms of doctrinal principles and more in terms of the phenomenology of religious experiencing. We might even be so bold as to criticize the impurity and inadequacy of certain expressions of our mystics on the grounds that they have been betrayed by the language and conceptual habits of their culture. China had its Newtons and its Galileos, but they did not have a cultural context within which most adequately to express their insights. Likewise, we have had our mystical geniuses, but, almost without exception, they were forced to concern themselves overmuch with the guidelines of doctrinal orthodoxy and theological system.

The motivation toward theoria and the understanding of the order of things in aesthetic rather than logical or rational terms derives from the need to resolve contraries of context experienced at the theoretical level. Of the conceivable forms such resolution might take, two are worth noting. The most obvious form of resolution is instanced by certain forms of neurotic behavior involving the cultivation of a blindness or insensitivity to contrariety in experience. This results when one attempts to substitute cruder for more refined categories as a means of reintegrating former discriminations. Such a short-circuiting of the movement toward theoria can be seen among ideologues and "true believers" the intensity of whose commitment signals the fundamental insecurity they experience in the face of ambiguities and conceptual conflict.

Besides the strategy leading to the collapse of theoretical alternatives, it is possible to move toward a world "in which personal identity merges into all the processes of relationship in some vast ecology or aesthetics of cosmic interaction."[9] This strategy involves the acceptance of contraries in their articulated form. The Taoist sensibility which promotes the recognition of cosmological structures describable in terms of polar tensions among contraries is a primary illustration of such a strategy. At its most general level such a technique merges with that of the Ch'an or Zen Buddhist who celebrates the ultimately aesthetic character of the tensions involved in logical contradiction and paradox.

These two strategies of response to the contrarieties experienced at the theoretical level have always existed as alternative expressions of the so-called mystical experience. The "unitive consciousness" of the mystic may either be described as a nondifferentiated nothingness which constitutes the apparent cancellation of discrete experiencing ("the night wherein all cows are black") or it can be experienced as the fully articulated being of things requiring a continually shifting locus of experiencing of things in their insistent particularity. These do not constitute two experiences, but two distinct ways of describing a single experience: one which looks to theorial experiencing from the theoretical perspective, the latter which attempts to articulate the experience in the aesthetic and mystical terms relevant to it.

Since the theorial vision is not wholly rationalizable it cannot be said to satisfy the fundamental theoretical requirements of even the most speculative of philosophies in the Anglo-European tradition. The aesthetic vision presupposes neither a *scientia universalis* nor an *ontologia generalis*. Thus the vision of experience as fundamentally aesthetic is generalizable neither in terms of a consistent set of principles nor in terms of a single ontological structure.

The theorial vision is an-archistic; it is wholly "without principles" in the classical sense of *external determining sources of order*. According to this view each isolatable event is self-creative. It is, therefore, its own *archē*, and the *archē* of no other event. The specific character of the process of self-creativity precludes events from serving either as causes or consequences of anything outside themselves. The idiosyncratic norms of self-creative events render impossible the construction of a system of principles as required by the aim at *scientia universalis*.

The construction of a general ontology as the basis for theorial understandings is likewise impossible. The aesthetic vision denies what is essential to the development of any traditional ontology—namely, the unitary character of the actual world. From the perspective of theoria, there are as many actualizable worlds as there are events in the process of becoming. The sum of these ordered worlds cannot possess any identifiable order. Thus what is normally conceived as the Cosmos is seen to be Chaos, understood as Becoming-Itself.

Notions of Being and Non-Being in classical Western philosophy are but abstractions from Becoming-Itself construed as Chaos. In its generic sense, "Being" is any single order abstracted from the sum of all orders. Conceptions of Being per se which assume a single world-order, authored or sustained by a single Absolute Agent, defined by a single set of natural laws, or developing in relation to a single end or logically coherent set of ends, are acceptable to the aesthetic vision only as limited abstractions.

If Being is defined in terms of a single abstracted order, Non-Being must be seen as the potential for all other orders, or aspects of other orders, whose otherness is construed relative to that order presupposed as Being. Thus Becoming-Itself is a mixture of Being and Non-Being. This is Chaos. The intuition of Chaos, in its indifference to any particular order, is perhaps best described as the experience of emptiness.

The principal dogma grounding theoretical understandings, as well as the notion of a single-ordered world which they presuppose, is the concept of the substantial self. Thus the fundamental character of the relations in this world is that of Self and Other. The otherness experienced in the modes of knowledge, action, and passion provokes the construal of that which is other in terms of tensions, conflicts, and interactions qualified by the category of power. Otherness is met by strategies of control, manipulation, and domination. Obviously, the style of communication enjoined by theorial contexts would be quite different from the theoretical variety. In place of the aim at persuasion which seeks to establish rational consensus, there would be the aim of aesthetic harmony based upon the articulation of differences and the correlation of these differences in polar relationships which balance opposites without recourse to positivist reduction or dialectical sublation.

Though it may seem initially tempting to find in the contrast between Oriental and Anglo-European philosophies a simple contrast between theorial and theoretical impulses, such would be altogether too heavy-handed. The situation is much more complex. All prominent perspectives on the world are predominantly theoretical. To be sure, most of the extant theorial visions are to be found within the Eastern traditions. Taoism, Ch'an and Hwa Yen Buddhism are perhaps the best examples. But these are hardly "mainstream" views in any cultural complex. If we are to understand the challenge of communication among the traditions of Anglo-European and Oriental philosophers, for example, it is necessary for us to understand the manner in which the criteria of aesthetic and rational orders are to be understood one in relation to the other.

The criteria of theoretical and theorial understandings apply to the contrasting visions of Oriental and Western philosophies in the following manner: whereas Anglo-European philosophers are putatively rational in their approach to theory, Oriental philosophers are most often at least putatively aesthetic. That is to say, the immanent principles which define the aesthetic aims of much of Oriental thought, on the one hand, and the rational aims of almost all of Anglo-European thought, on the other, are ideal with respect to each vision. Neither is wholly successful in achieving what it sets out to realize.

By describing Anglo-European thinkers as most often only putatively rational I mean to call attention to the pervasive problem of self-referential inconsistency which plagues both speculative and empirical perspectives in the West. In the first instance, speculative thought has never been able to remain content with wholly rational ontologies. Classical and contemporary metaphysicians have not been able to remain "within the limits of reason alone." It has always been necessary, implicitly or explicitly, to employ nonrational appeals as a means of indicating either the ground or goal of speculation. Whether this appeal is made at the beginning of metaphysical speculation, as in the case of the later Heidegger, or whether, as in the case of a philosopher like Whitehead following the Platonic tradition, the appeal to a "likely story" is made as a last resort, the nonrational element in speculative philosophy has never wholly dropped from sight. Moreover, if that appeal beyond system is to have any justification at all, it must be found by recourse to a context more general or more inclusive than the rational.

This suggests that speculative systems may ultimately have, as their context of justification, Chaos, the aesthetic sum of all orders within which any single vision of the world finds its most general locus.

Empirical philosophies fare no better in their attempts to realize total rationality. Empiricist methodologies exclude evidential sources in ways that are continually demonstrated to be arbitrary and tendentious. Positivisms which find, for example, the evidences of art, ethics, and religious experience to be meaningless are so narrow and provincial in their selection of evidences that they soon find themselves unable to account for data essential to the understanding of the width of civilized experience. Moreover, as the embarrassing career of the verificationist principle of logical positivism so well illustrates, the grounding of presumptive empiricisms is never itself rational, even when judged by internal theoretical criteria.

By claiming that most Oriental visions are only putatively aesthetic I mean to say that most Eastern philosophers have not remained content with the evocation of aesthetic sensibility, but have sought to establish an orthodoxy, whether it be Confucian, Buddhist, or Vedantic. Neo-Confucian uses of Taoist notions are a case in point. The cosmological and ethical interest of many Confucian philosophers promoted a disciplining of "the Way" in accordance with systematic principles which compare favorably with the best of classical Western metaphysical systems. But even with these qualifications it remains true that the guiding genius of classical Chinese philosophy and culture, for example, has been aesthetic sensibility. On the other hand, the immanent rationale of Western culture has been science as the rational understanding of nature.

The simple fact that aesthetic systems cannot assume the preeminence of logical order without rendering senseless many of their most significant insights, and rational systems cannot accept the dominance of aesthetic over logical harmony without dissolving into untoward forms of vagueness and ambiguity, indicates the seemingly insurmountable difficulty of communication between these two types of vision. It is the case, however, that if there is to be any real attempt at such communication it could be conceivable only on the presuppositions of the aesthetic context since it includes the concept of logical harmony as a special case of aesthetic contrast. Consistent with the notion that we are in fact dealing with levels of communication, it is necessary to require that the more general level take precedence in some sense over the more specific.

Among putatively rational philosophies there are two principal strategies of communication: the reductive and the teleological. The strategy of the positivists represents the extreme case relevant to this discussion. The attempt to reduce all meaningful propositions to those subject to a logical or stipulatively empirical principle of verification or falsification constitutes the extreme of reductionism. In contrast to the reductive critique, the aesthetic critique accepts the varieties of theoretical vision as approximations of an aesthetic order the ontological character of which transcends language. The reductive critique, grounded in the presumption of the preeminence of logical order, dismisses whole enterprises of human cultural experience as meaningless. The aesthetic critique does not so dismiss rational or logical systems, but incorporates them and harmonizes them in accordance with the criteria of intensity and contrast. Granted that from the point of view of the reductionist such incorporation would be unacceptable, nonetheless, from the perspective of general cultural experience, preference might be given to the aesthetic critique simply because a richer world results from the aesthetic vision of communication than from the reductive.

The claim that a richer world is preferable to a logically coherent one is of course an aesthetic claim and cannot be accepted as an argument in favor of the aesthetic vision per se. Though the sort of communication that takes place between theoretical and theorial contexts would not be acceptable on rational or logical grounds, there is, nonetheless, *some* viable means of carrying on communication between these levels. No such manner exists if the reductive critique is allowed. The regressive impulse exemplified by theoretical forms of reduction is counterproductive from a communicational perspective.

There is evidence that after many years of dominance by the reductive mentality Anglo-European philosophy is turning again to the teleological mode of philosophic communication. A dramatic illustration of this turning is the renewed interest in Hegel's thought. The employment of Hegelian dialectic as a means promoting intertheoretical communication is one way of avoiding pernicious forms of philosophic reduction since dialectic must be employed within the context of a broad speculative system if it is to serve more than the ends of sophistic debate. The insight concerning the relation of dialectic and system originated perhaps with Plato who used dialectical argumentation as a systematic and normative tool. Plato did not, of course, have a system in the sense of a finally articulated metaphysics and cosmology replete with categorial scheme. He did, however, explicitly require of the dialectician the presupposition of a system as the *telos* of his argumentation.

The choice of Hegelian philosophy as a medium for the mutual articulations of alternative philosophic schools is in large measure attributable to the fact that the principal modalities of contemporary Anglo-European philosophy—existentialism and phenomenology, Marxian thought, pragmatism, and linguistic analysis—owe much of their character to their origins in reactions against Hegel, or against positions commensurate with Hegelian views. As Richard Bernstein, one of the more interested observers of the Hegelian renaissance, has so clearly shown, the development of most contemporary philosophies, particularly the empirical and linguistic varieties, parallels the dialectical transitions in Hegel's *Phenomenology of Mind* from Sense Certainty through Understanding to Reason.[10] The recognition of this fact accounts for the increased desire among contemporary philosophers for a greater philosophic generality and a metaphysical ground. The return to Hegel in part, then, involves an attempt to understand something about the immanent development of contemporary thought and to discover suggestions for future articulations.

Any use of dialectic detached from the notion of a common system only impedes progress in philosophic articulation by indicating partialities, inconsistencies, and incoherences not as a means of directing a particular vision toward immanent improvements, but only in order to demand a shifting of philosophic allegiances from the vision criticized to its dialectical opposite. For if the participants in a philosophic debate do not see themselves in dialectical relation within a common world, a system, they are actually in disagreement concerning the character of the world itself. Without the assumption of a shared system there can be no wholly rational communication grounded in parity or mutual viability. A common system provides a context within which conflicting claims among philosophers can be articulated and sublated rather than simply ignored, refuted, or dismissed.

The teleological strategy for promoting philosophic communication is obviously superior to the reductive, but it suffers from the same defect as all theoretical understandings—namely, it lacks sufficient breadth. This is particularly so with the Hegelian system since it was articulated in such detail by its creator. Doubtless a better choice for the construction of teleological models of intertheoretical communication would be the Platonic sensibility since the governing norm of Plato's philosophy is not a completely articulated system which establishes the facticity of its propositions. The guiding principle of Platonic thought is the *value* of rational harmony. Platonic eros, the *appetitus naturalis* of medieval and Renaissance philosophers, names the most general characteristic of the activity of philosophy. Dialectical thinking presupposes a system but nonetheless requires the transcendence of any given system.

The construction of a theoretical vision establishes an implicit or explicit metaphysical and cosmological understanding requiring the world to take on a certain specific set of characteristics which exclude alternative possible worlds. The coexistence of alternative theories with conflicting cosmological implicates is hardly the result of mere caprice on the part of the system builders. This phenomenon is caused by the persistence of inconsistencies, incoherences, and paradoxes within any given system. The irrefragable problem of the One and the Many in Anglo-European philosophy, or the conflict between the claims of sense and the claims of reason celebrated in Zeno's paradoxes, are persisting difficulties which advertise the inadequacy of any given systematic philosophy.

No single philosophic system is adequate to interpret the total matrix of experiencing since the delimiting functions of systematic theory must always lead to the exclusion of at least some pertinent data. This would suggest that the *appetitus naturalis* which aims at the perfection of understanding must ultimately involve the transcendence of rational system and the acceptance of the preeminence of aesthetic over rational harmony as characteristic of the true natures of things. If this is so, then the dialectical mode of communication merges at its highest levels with the aesthetic mode of theorial understandings.

Stripped bare of the subtleties of nuance essential to the detailed treatment of such a large theme as intertheoretical communication, my constructive proposals amount to this: the *telos* of intertheoretical communication involving empiricist and speculative systems must be seen as a progressive movement away from the narrowness of factual understandings which presume the existence of isolated data in the direction of theoretical understandings promoting dialectical interchange within the presumption of system. The recognition of the theory-dependence of all facts requires that theoretical communication be carried on in as general and as inclusive a system as is possible. The dialectical search for extreme generality demands the transcendence of merely rational forms of communication in favor of the realization of an aesthetic harmony of orders or contexts existing at the level of theoria.

The motivation in all acts of communication worthy of the name is eros. This natural desire is, however, best expressed in aesthetic rather than rational or moral terms. The final goal of communication is the realization of completeness. Such a goal requires the transcendence of rationality since reason rests upon notions of systematic consistency and coherence which determine orders less general than that characterizable solely by recourse to intensity and contrast. Thus in the act of communication the aim cannot be to resolve conflict through reduction, persuasion, or dialectical sublation. Tensions must be articulated and celebrated to the degree that they enhance the multifariousness of one's experience of the world. Moreover, communication of the profoundest sort ultimately involves the dissolution of selfhood since the self depends upon the viability of a specific context or order sustaining coherent patterns of decision and action.

The ground of all communication is a sense of otherness. But that otherness is truly realized only insofar as one can appreciate the intrinsic excellence of each insistently particular item in the Totality. Such appreciation involves insight into the absolute uniqueness of each item. An individual is unique if it is seen *sub specie aeternitatis*. Only then is it seen to be solely itself in its just-so-ness. Then it is *truly* other. But such otherness is precisely what constitutes true emptiness. For to possess the character of "own-being" a thing must be determinate. To be determinate means to be in relation to *some* others. The absolute otherness (i.e., emptiness) presupposed by the aesthetic ontology envisioned here involves indetermination.

We can expect only the continuation of fruitless conflict and frustration if intertheoretical communications are predicated upon notions of empirical contexts of justification or rational system. For these require the adjudication of differences in such a way as to cancel significant contrasts and intensities. Since intensity and contrast name the most general characteristics of the Totality, the controlling dynamic of real communication cannot be that of consensus, but must be the vision of intersubjectivity in which changing patterns of polar contrast, construed aesthetically and mystically, permit continually deeper and more profound access to the complexities of Chaos as the sum of all orders.

I have been stressing the role of the aesthetic sensibility in philosophic communication. We should now look somewhat more closely at the peculiar character of the mystical experience in this context. To the skeptic, of course, the most unsatisfactory aspect of the mystic's claims regarding his experience is his assertion that he has gained some kind of certain knowledge or true understanding of things. From the rational point of view *certainty* takes the form of demonstrability, and this the mystic clearly cannot claim. The nondemonstrability of the knowledge claims made by the mystic is attributable, of course, to the presumed ineffable character of the experience.

The mystic's claim that he cannot express what he has experienced does not mean that he cannot successfully *allude* to it. And though this must mean that some of the characteristics of the experience cannot be communicated, its essential nature is communicated to the degree that the essence is construed in terms of subjective form of feeling rather than objective content. That the certainty felt in relation to the experience cannot be propositionally communicated may constitute a major failure of language vis-à-vis the mystical phenomenon. But if it is somewhat controversial to say "I know, but I cannot say," it is much less controversial to claim "I feel, but I can't express the feeling." Even in the most common-sense of understandings we allow feelings to transcend language to some degree. For this reason we allow our poets to employ language more as an evocative tool than as an instrument of direct communication.

The ineffability of mystical experience is more closely associated than is sometimes realized with the fact that in mystical experience, to a degree even greater than that recognized in the evocations of most poetic creations, the subjective form of feeling is the principal content of the experience. In mystical experience the noetic quality merges with the affective quality, so that to say "I know" means, "I feel." Indeed, at the level of mystical experience at which visions and voices are experienced, it is more correct to understand the experience of a vision of Christ or of the Virgin Mary as a feeling-kind-of-seeing; likewise voices are entertained through a feeling-kind-of-hearing. Failure to recognize that the principal content of the mystical experience is the subjective form of feeling, and not that which is propositionally translatable, has led some empiricist philosophers (who shall remain mercifully unnamed) into asking such ridiculous questions as, "How do you know your vision was of Jesus, having never seen him before?"

The separation of knowing and feeling in paradigm instances of perception and knowledge has accustomed us to the belief that noetic claims which are primarily feeling-oriented are highly suspect or downright meaningless. But when Whitehead, for example, asserts, "In Spring we feel the grass greenly," he is making a claim presumedly relevant to all acts of knowledge.[11] Conscious perception and reflective forms of knowledge are sophisticated developments from more fundamental ways of experiencing the world. It is the concrete data of the immediate past which comprise the most relevant resource for each noetic experience, and the initial data of experience include a form of feeling the world. The attempt to separate the affective tone of an act of perception or knowledge from the content of the act flies in the face of the realities of the phenomenon of experiencing itself.

The mystic's description of his experience as ineffable, but nonetheless noetic, is in part an expression of the intrinsic limitations of propositional communication per se. It is also partly based upon contingent limitations placed upon the act of communication within our Anglo-European cultural context. Certain of the Eastern cultures provide a more amenable context for the communication of mystical experience. Ch'an and Zen Buddhist pedagogic techniques illustrate how one might proceed in the attempt to communicate the facticity of mystical experiencing at its highest level. In Anglo-European cultures we have been much less committed to the development of a pedagogy of mysticism. As a consequence, mystical phenomena have never held an important place in our culture.

The noetic component of mystical experience is distinct from that involved both in what we call knowledge of facts and theoretical understandings. Facts may contradict one another, to be sure. When they do it may well be possible to show that each fact entails commitment, however implicit, to a particular theoretical vision. We may be able to account for contradictory facts by articulating the contrast between the differing theories entailed. Judgments concerning the viability of one fact or another then would involve judgments as to the viability of the relevant theories.

Likewise, if we begin at the level of theories we may find that two theories are in greater or lesser conflict with one another. The situation is slightly more complex here. If we wish to judge the relative superiority of one theory over another we could have resort to such criteria as consistency, adequacy, explanatory power, elegance, and so on. But if we wish to assess the facticity of the theories in question in terms of their relative grounding in experienced certainty, we must have recourse to the categorial assumptions on which the theories are grounded. But, as we have argued, these assumptions transcend the theories in question and cannot be adequately tested by recourse to the theories which they ground. We may only have recourse to the intuitive certainty of the contrasting categorial assumptions. Here the claims of the mystic become important.

As facts find the justification of their facticity within the context of theories, theories find their justification within a context housing contrasting intuitions of the way of things. This cannot simply be a metatheory, since metatheory is employed in order to entertain contrasting facts. What is required is a vision which promotes the entertainment of the contrasting categorial intuitions of rival metaphysicians. Now the only sensible claim that a metaphysician can make with regard to his primary intuition is that it is essentially one with the intuitions of his rivals. (Otherwise he falls victim to the Fallacy of Private Rationality.) And this is but to say, what the mystic insists upon, that there is indeed a *philosophia perennis* which, though present in an intuitive realm shared by all who responsibly seek completeness of understanding, is not demonstrably present, at least as regards the employment of distinctively different propositional language in the articulation of the metaphysical visions.

I need not necessarily be construed as maintaining that the only candidate for intuition is that which is characterizable as a categorial assumption of a speculative theory. It is certainly possible to have an intuition of the facticity of an item of experience which is not (at least not at present) open to theoretical justification. But it is an interesting and very perplexing question whether or not one may in truth have the intuition of a finite fact that is not in principle open to theoretical justification within some stipulated context. It will be a consequence of the vision that I am adumbrating here that if such a prima facie intuition were possible it would turn out to be a surrogate for a categorial notion of highest generality. An implication of this belief is that the intuition of the suchness, the just-so-ness, of an item is the ground of any coherent vision. This makes the ontological experience of suchness the prerequisite for any viable cosmological understanding. Ontology grounds cosmology in every case.

When "facts" and "theories" conflict with one another, they do so on logically assessable grounds. It makes sense to say that some propositions are prima facie contradictory; it likewise makes sense to say that some propositions, as implications of theories, are in conflict. This conflict requires the existence of certain logical criteria in order to assess incompatibility or contradiction among theories. One may discover the relevant criteria by recourse to the categorial intuitions which ground the theory since these intuitions doubtless receive some propositional articulation within the context of the theory. Thus it is possible to assess any logical incompatibility among the propositional expressions of these intuitions. But if we seek the ultimate justification of these notions the appeal can be neither to the theory which they ground nor to some metatheory. If we make the former appeal we are involved in the most pernicious form of question begging. If we appeal to a metatheoretical context, we must take a stance external to both theories which leads us to mischaracterize the issue altogether by offering a substitute theory as a candidate for belief for each of the theorists. If we were to seek a consensus, we would have no need of justifying either set of categorial intuitions, but would rather have to attempt to falsify these intuitions and substitute another category or categories.

The strategy of the mystic in confronting conflicting visions bears some similarity to the above. But the mystic does not offer an explicit alternative to a categorial intuition; rather he suggests a theorial context which, though it is not open to propositional articulation in any final form, nonetheless promotes an enjoyment of the contrast of alternate philosophic visions without the necessity either to reduce one vision to the other or to sublate both by recourse to a vision of presumably greater logical coherence or generality.

The conflict between theistic and nontheistic mysticisms, usually addressed in discussions of the contrast between Oriental and Western forms of mystical experience, is focused precisely here. If we seek a *philosophia perennis* which takes seriously mystical experience as a primary datum, apparently we shall find it in what has been termed nontheistic varieties of mystical experience. From nontheistic mystical perspectives, concepts of God are interpretations of a primary experience. It is certainly unnecessary to claim that the experienced certainty of the mystic must be tested in propositional form. The immediacy of the experience contains *as actual content* the experience of its own veracity. Propositional significances given to the mystic's experience are secondary to this experienced truth. A vision of Jesus Christ is simply that. How would one know that it was Jesus? One knows because the experienced truth of the presence of Jesus is the content of the experience. The vision is not meaningfully tested by asking, "How tall was he?" or "What was he wearing?" The seeing of Jesus, the hearing of his words, is not a seeing or a hearing in the ordinary sense of the terms, but, in fact, a congeries of causal feelings which cannot be interpreted by a comparison of the phenomenal appearance with some presumed ontic reality.

An implication of this discussion is that the experience of the facticity of a theoretical vision involves an appeal to an intuition the content of which transcends the theory in question. And though the stipulative meaning of the categorial intuition is given within the context of the theory, the facticity of the categorial intuition is not to be justified in any way by the theory. The experienced certainty of the categorial intuition involves the same dynamics as that of the mystical experience outlined above. Thus the aim of the speculative theorist is the same as that of the mystic—completeness of understanding. If we ask after the origin of this motivation toward completeness of understanding we may reasonably respond that it comes from a vague intuition of the Totality. Obviously this intuition has never received adequate articulation, else the history of speculative theory would have come to an end. But it did not end with Plato, or with Aristotle, or with Saint Thomas, or with Descartes, or with Kant, or with Hegel, or with Whitehead. Nor will it end with any subsequent speculative thinker. The immanent goal of speculative thought is not the articulation of a final system of propositions. The ultimate aim of the speculative philosopher is the celebration of the continued efficacy of the intuition of the Totality, the quest for the completeness of understanding which grounds all responsible thinking. And this aim is a distinctly mystical one.

All propositional knowledge depends upon theories. These theories are not just the specific, specialized, or ad hoc theories of a particular discipline but are, primarily, cosmological theories which give an account of the way of things. The motivation leading to the development of these theories is the drive toward a completeness of understanding itself grounded in an intuition of the Totality of experiencing. Thus knowledge of any kind has as its ultimate justification a context which can only be called mystical in the sense that it involves a noetic experience of the Totality ultimately inexpressible in propositional form.

The fundamental question with regard to mysticism is whether or not one can have an unmediated or uninterpreted experience. If one holds that unmediated experience is impossible, then one cannot hope to find a universal core in mystical experiences any more than in any other type of expressions. The claim that pure experience, unalloyed by linguistic or other types of cultural interpretations, is in fact possible would lead one to believe that precisely such an extralinguistic experience is the sole viable candidate for a nonrelative type of experience. There is, of course, no way to settle this issue with dialectical procedures or deductive arguments, since what is at issue is a question as fundamental as the character of experiencing per se.

A successful argument supporting the autonomy of mystical experience would involve the claim that there is a viable distinction between cosmological and ontological considerations which answers to a distinction at the experiential level. Those who claim that there can be no universal core in mystical experiencing deny the possibility of an ontological experience. On the other hand, those who promote the claim that mystical experiences are expressions of a *philosophia perennis* do so because they explicitly or implicitly recognize the viability of such ontological experiencing.

We cannot be certain of the precise relationship between the objective content of experience and its subjective form. But this much seems clear: what we are accustomed to calling intuition or intuitive certainty is the characteristic means whereby we seek to justify the facticity of the content. When Aristotle sought to save the unity and integrity of scientific knowledge by appealing to the necessity of intuition he understood that incorrigible knowledge could be maintained only if the means whereby one comes to know the first principles of the sciences could lay claim to greater certainty than that which was known through the employment of these principles. He understood, as well, that any claim to knowledge implicitly entails a claim to the certainty of some principle or principles.

It is impossible to remain humble in the quest for knowledge since arrogance is expressed at the very beginnings of the quest when one lays claim to that minimal insight permitting the formulation of even the most tentative or fallibilist of claims. If, for example, Karl Popper's confession of faith in reason is in fact a concession to irrationalism as he himself claims,[12] then his entire project is questionable, for if one concedes to a philosopher an initial irrationality in the form of a first premise, then a whole host of consequent irrationalities in the form of tainted inferences will inevitably follow. It is embarrassingly obvious that one cannot responsibly claim that what follows from one's premises is more rational than the premises themselves. Yet this is continually done.

Knowledge must involve claims to the authoritativeness of either those principles which ground the inferences in question, or those principles which establish the meaningfulness of the concepts and linguistic conventions employed in the construction of the arguments. This authoritativeness ultimately derives from an experience of intuitive certitude. Asked to justify our first principles, beliefs, convictions, we will initially point to evidence: the consistency of the formulation of our view, its coherence, its compatibility with this or that selection of data, the moral cosequences of so believing, its practical results, its efficacy in clarifying other items of experience, and so on. But what truly counts as evidence for or against a belief is already decided upon within the context of the belief itself.

The principle of sufficient reason can be justified by showing that in important cases there are indeed explanations for events, and that in no significant case is an explanation of an event not discoverable. But this belief may be challenged on both asserted grounds: first, by showing that some rational explanations provided for events are in fact construals of an arbitrary form which, though they may save appearances, do not adequately characterize the events in question. Second, one may point to those phenomena that have not in fact received rational explanations. The reply of the defender of the principle of sufficient reason will, in the first instance, be to present additional arguments for his explanation. In the second case, he will claim that it is only a matter of time until an explanation is discovered. The first situation is exemplified by conflicts over such issues as "freedom" and "creativity"; some thinkers claim that no rational explanations of these phenomena are possible, others show to the contrary that they are explicable in terms of physiology, psychology, and so on. The second instance resolves itself into a waiting game, one in which rationalist attempts to characterize apparently nonrational phenomena, such as many of the events in the microphysical world, are continually assaulted by the irrationalist as being ad hoc rationalizations. Nothing is ever finally settled in this manner. The value of the dispute (if there be any value) is likely to be found in the interstices between the *sic* and *non*.

In rehearsing the distinction between the objective content of experience and the subjective form of feeling, we have found that with regard to what may be termed the first principles, or basic assumptions, there is a more intimate relationship between the objective content and the subjective form than might otherwise be the case. Each of us has some knowledge which he holds in a relatively neutral way, depending on the context. "I have a nickel in my pocket" may be expressed with a minimum of interest, or with increased emotional form if that nickel is essential to one's immediate well-being. But the degree of subjective involvement is relative to context. Other propositions are not so relative. "I know my Redeemer lives" would likely involve a subjective form of feeling of joy and gratitude. (If, that is to say, the proposition is uttered in its traditional significance and not merely mouthed as the refrain in Handel's *Messiah*.) The question is, of course, whether there are any sorts of propositional statements which evince experiencing of the type in which the subjective form of feeling wholly dominates the experience. Logical propositions of the type "A is A" may be expressed with a minimum of subjective associations, of course, though it is likely that Aristotle and Leibniz, for slightly different reasons, were profoundly moved when they first uttered this proposition. But the sort of propositions we seek are of a type such that the subjective form of feeling all but exhausts the experience being interpreted or described.

If I were to claim the following: "An Angel of the Lord came to me in a vision and spoke, saying, 'The Truth is not to be found through philosophic reflection, all that is necessary is that you believe the Word of God as it is contained in the Holy Scriptures,' " one might respond, "How did you know it was an 'Angel of the Lord'?" I might reply that "I just know." What would be suggested by the apparent fact that I had

not myself questioned the veridical nature of the event is that the certainty
of the revelation being from God was carried in the revelation itself.
How could this be so? Obviously it could not be that I was assured by the
fact that the angel had wings and was surrounded by a halo of light.
Something about the experience carried its own authoritativeness. Now if
we grant that the truth-value of such an experience can be tested only at
the propositional level, we must concede that only judgments about an
experience, not the experience itself, can be asserted to be true or false.
In that case it is clear that I have judged the experience to be true apart
from ordinary tests for veridicality which might be employed. The experience was extraordinary, not publicly verifiable in any direct sense,
and not repeatable in any controlled manner. Nonetheless, I say I know
it to be true. Apparently I experienced the judgment of its truth along
with the experience itself. The sense of certitude dominated the experience. This is but to say that "the feeling of the certainty of" was part
of the content of the experience.

Such experiences are not at all uncommon at the level of dreams. Most
of us are quite accustomed to having dreams about certain events or persons the empirical correlates of which do not match the events or personages in any direct sense. For example, I once dreamed I was in the
Yucatán, looking for a place to get native cuisine, but only finding
American fast-food restaurants with American waiters and clientele.
During my entire "visit" to the Yucatán I saw not one Mexican citizen,
not one Mayan or Aztec ruin, not one example of traditional Mexican
architecture; I could more likely have been dreaming of New York City,
or of Houston, Texas—but I wasn't. I was dreaming of the Yucatán.
How did I know? I just knew. The visual and auditory correlates were
not associable with the Yucatán; the feeling correlates, however, were.
My seeing and hearing were dominated by the subjective form of feelings
associated with my real-life waking experiences of the Yucatán Peninsula.
In the dream the causal feelings associated with that familiar area of
Mexico dominated my other modes of experiencing.

Thus must it be in mystical visions in which it is claimed that "The
Lord came to me in a dream"; or "The Virgin Mary appeared at
Guadalupe in the form of an Aztec maiden." The causal feelings constitute the primary aspect of the experience; the subjective form of feeling *is* the essential content of the experience.

Such an interpretation may, of course, account for the feeling of certitude accompanying a mystical experience without in any sense defending the veridicality of the experience itself. What such an interpretaion
would defend, however, is the plausibility of a relatively nonmediated ex-

perience. One could easily see how the description of a vision could lead one to the use of propositions which completely short-circuit the enquiry. Someone might ask me to describe my dream of visiting the Yucatán. "Well," I would say, "first I went into a McDonald's restaurant, then into a Kentucky Fried Chicken place, then to a hot-dog stand." The closest I could come to defending the view that I was dreaming of the Yucatán is to tell of my feelings of frustration at not being able to find native cuisine. But this says nothing of the Yucatán, only of my sense of certainty that I was there!

Of course, my sense of being in the Yucatán requires that I know something of what I mean by "Yucatán." Thus I must have visited there or read of the place, or otherwise have formed an opinion of its character and ambience. But there is, nonetheless, an unmediated aspect to the dream. This is the sense of certitude, apart from ordinary evidences. What is immediate is "a sense of the presence of." The same holds true in mystical visions. There can be a sense of the presence of Jesus or an Angel of the Lord, or whomever. This is precisely the character of revelation which confounds scientific or empirical analyses. Such a revelation involves the experience of truth prior to the grasp of meaning. The particular meanings of an event of revelation may not be immediately clear. Nonetheless, revelations involve a profound sense of meaningfulness which is, as often as not, experienced as Truth. The equation of truth with meaningfulness is a characteristic of mystical experiencing which often eludes its rational investigators, since it is all too easy to confuse the conventional associations of propositional expressions with the sense of meaning underlying them.

More individuals have had quasimystical experiences through the medium of dreams or of drug-induced states than otherwise. A characteristic of extremely profound dream experiences or psychedelic highs is the relative frustration one feels attempting to convey the meaning of the experience. The nearest we can come is to say something like, "Words cannot convey . . . ," for when we say this we signal to the other person that we have had a profound experience and he then can register the feelings associated with similar experiences of his own. This highly indirect mode of communication can be assured of conveying a common experience only if all ineffable experiences are of the same type, or are, in some meaningful sense, the same experience.

Experiences with psychotropic drugs are often thought to be extremely profound not primarily because of the perceptual distortions involved but because of the experience of *thisness* or *suchness* qualifying these episodes. The sheer banality of the verbal descriptions of hallucinogenic experiences contrasts dramatically with the profound sense of meaningfulness almost always claimed for them. I once heard a tape recording of such an experience which contained the phrase, "This pen . . . this . . . ," uttered with such excruciating intensity as to suggest that the individual in the drugged state was moved to the point of ecstasy. Propositionally, there is no more direct characterization of the experience of the pen than, "This pen . . . this . . . ," but it was obviously not the proposition itself which conveyed the experience. The experience was an ontological one. It was an experience of the be-ing of the pen. Nothing mysterious, really. A pen, like anything else, is what it is. "A is A." Hardly an occult doctrine. The meaningfulness of this experience is that it contrasts with our ordinary experience of things in cosmological terms. We normally experience things in terms of their utility or functionality with respect to ourselves or other things. The determinateness of an item is the result of its being determined by other things. To experience something in itself is to see it neither as an outcome, nor as a productive agent of any other thing, but as just itself. It is no longer an instance of a type, or a member of a class. It is present solely in its insistent particularity.

In ordinary senses of true and false it makes little sense to ask whether such experiences are *true*. They simply *are*. Are they meaningful? They are certainly meaningful to those who experience them as such. But do they have propositionally expressible *meanings*? That question would likely be answered as follows: the propositions one might employ to characterize such experiences might all refer to a single experience of meaningfulness. The ontological perception of a table, or a pen, or a flower, or a fly has as its meaning the insistent particularity each item possesses by virtue of being just what it is. The ontological characterization of a thing in terms of its just-so-ness should not be confused with the cosmological description in terms of its character determined by other things. Ultimately, of course, the cosmological and ontological aspects of things merge in the world of the mystic, since a thing is what it is by both determining all other things, and being determined by them, within the most general of aesthetic orders.

Cosmological perceptions concern the notion of a single-ordered cosmos in which the essential character of individual items is determined in relation to laws or rules or patterns of meaningfulness that include some possibilities and exclude others. Chaos, the Implicate Order, the hologrammatic pluriverse we have discussed heretofore, is a context within which many orders obtain. The unity of these orders is, obviously, not propositionally expressible but is nonetheless experienceable at the level of mystical intuition.

The conclusion of this extended discussion is precisely *not* that we ought to eschew propositional systems and concentrate wholly on developing means of achieving mystical insight. We need not abandon the attempt to adjudicate among factual claims simply because that cannot be done in a final and once-for-all-time manner. Nor am I arguing that the presumed relativity of knowledge claims advertised by the fact of the conflicting claims of theoretical systems may serve only as a stimulus toward the transcendence of the mundane world in obedience to a soteriological aim. Though the primary form and function of responsible knowing is mystical, mystical experience is hardly irrelevant to more mundane forms of knowledge. One of the responsibilities of the mystic is to advertise the relevance of that vision which grounds his thinking to the concrete welter of circumstance forming his actual ambience. This responsibility is realized through the return of eros to the world of praxis.

CHAPTER SEVEN
EROS DESCENDING

The chastening poignance of our culture's noblest maxim—"All men by nature desire to know"—is a consequence of the fact that the tensions and contradictions accompanying the articulation of our principal cultural values seem inevitably to challenge any claim we might wish to make to finality of understanding. This failing affects not merely the understanding of disinterested truth, but equally concerns our knowledge of the good as the basis for action, of the beautiful which yields refinement of aesthetic sensibility, as well as of the holy which serves as the ultimate ground for the erotic drive toward the intuition of the totality. Even those somewhat more modest philosophic understandings which seek an articulation of the various species of cultural importance seem to lead, finally, to contradiction and paradox.

If the desire to know forces us into either provincial dogmatisms which lay unjustified claims to certainty, or skeptical indifference which cancels commitment to the search for completeness of understanding, we cannot but see that we have failed in the fundamental project in terms of which we have heretofore defined the meaning of responsible human existence. If, that is to say, we find ourselves victims, alternately, of both the quest for certainty and the flight from it, we are nothing more than living parodies of that which our tradition tells us we must be.

In this work I have attempted to highlight the pernicious irrelevance of the desire for consensus as a means of grounding our cultural enterprise. In so doing I have hoped to mitigate the impact of the continued failure of such a search upon our cultural psyche. The transcendence of both skepticism and dogmatism is possible only if we move beyond the relatively narrow bounds set by our almost exclusive concern with rational and moral interests. Retuning our cultural sensorium in order to give aesthetic and mystical values their proper due can lead to a revisioning of the very character of intellectual culture and of philosophy's role within it.

Those indulgent readers who have stayed with me to this point might feel, with no little justification, that I will have failed to execute even the rather modest task I set for myself in the beginning were I to conclude my argument with the somewhat nebulous musings of the last chapter. In order to make good both my constructive and prolusory aims it will be necessary in these concluding pages to articulate at least some of the important consequences of the return of eros from the realm of theoria to the sphere of concrete praxis. Considering the subject of the descent of eros requires us to confront somewhat more directly a topic we have touched upon in various contexts throughout this essay—I refer to the notion of *irony*.

It is doubtless an indication of the depressed interest in the subject of philosophic irony that we must look to a literary critic for the most profound of recent discussions of the subject. In *The Well Wrought Urn*, Cleanth Brooks celebrates the ironic sensibility in these terms: "Irony," he says, "is the most general term we have for the kind of qualification which the various elements in a context receive from the context."[1] Philosophic irony, then is determined by the fact that the context of philosophic understanding is that ellipse formed by the mutual operations of the drive toward completeness of understanding and the demand for systematic unity; the desire for adequacy of philosophic insight and the necessity of logical consistency; the wish for continued openness at the level of enquiry and the requirement of closure in the face of the needs of practical application or implementation.

The fundamental irony emergent from this circumstance is, of course, the irony of self-reference. The fact that to be aware of anything else we must have an accompanying awareness of ourselves means that thought is something which necessarily turns back upon itself. Thus the statement "I know that four and three are seven" says at least as much about the process of knowing as about the character of numbers and their relations.

One of the more fascinating things about the notion of self-reference is that it leads inevitably to paradox: some kinds of self-referential knowledge are characterized by logical inconsistency. Thus the self-referential statement "This very sentence is false" must, we believe, be either true or false. But on examination we see that if it is true, then it must be false. Only if it is false can it be true. There is more involved here than merely a pernicious trick of our language which may be avoided by a judicious application of the theory of types.

The theorem of Kurt Gödel, mentioned earlier, involves the discovery that, in any systematic theory which lays claim to the complete explication of its subject matter, there are systematically undecidable propositions. That is, there are statements such that the theoretical system which contains them provides no means for deciding their truth or falsity. In Gödel's idiom, the paradoxical statement "This very sentence is false" is transformed into "This systematic proposition has no proof." So what? Who, other than a few logicians and mathematicians, would care about such things? At one level or another, of course, we *all* care about such things. That the incessant struggle to achieve completeness of understanding involves continual self-criticism and the acknowledgment of limitations is a truth that cannot but interest us.

The irony of understanding is that we are, willy-nilly, self-contained beings whose thoughts must be placed in systems, theories, visions, and doctrines which, by enclosing a world, allow us to understand only what is so enclosed. Without the self-contained structure of a painting, or a musical composition, or an axiomatic system, nothing would be knowable. But all that can be known is what the system allows us to know. Apparently, there is much more beyond.

There is certainly nothing new in the recognition of the irony of self-reference. It is constitutive of the theories of our very first thinkers. Socrates was claimed to be the wisest man in Athens because he knew that he did not know. The fundamental irony celebrated by Socrates is found in his recognition of the limits of that knowledge which one may accrue through open enquiry and dialectical interchange, through, that is to say, concentrating upon *questions* as guides for eros. Platonic irony derives principally from the recognition of the limits of knowledge which are entailed in the employment of system and principles as the ends of eros. Together Plato and Socrates illustrate that twin-focused ellipse which forms the context of philosophic knowledge. The desire to maintain open enquiry is self-contradictory, since one must presuppose principles which, if articulated, constitute a system. The stipulation of systematic unity is self-contradictory, since any system in fact is (and in principle must remain) incomplete. The eros which drives us toward completeness of understanding leads us to seek both to include all knowledge there is to include and to include it in a meaningful whole. Neither of the two foci may exist without the other, of course, and the elliptic character of all philosophic understanding derives from the eccentricity of its twin foci.

The foundation of the more complex ironies associated with thinking per se is to be found in the almost simplistic discovery of Socrates concerning the intrinsic connections of knowledge and ignorance. The Socratic dilemma is one of the stocks in trade of all philosophers, and we drag it out on ceremonial occasions for the mild amusement of our students. "Consider this," we say. "If I claim real knowledge, I but advertise my ignorance; if I confess my ignorance, I demonstrate at least minimal knowledge. Only if I assent to the fact that my most authentic knowledge is found precisely in my lack of knowledge can I make any sense, for then I advertise my understanding of the limitations placed upon my claims both to know and not to know. So, you see, that the proud should be brought low and the humble raised up is built into the very nature of things." At this point we usually glance about to see if our students are suitably impressed.

The slightly comical ring that such a philosophic exercise has about it should not be surprising, of course, since the principal source of Plato's characterization of the Socratic dilemma is Greek comedy. The *eiron* (ειρων), whose mock-humility masked his ambition and cunning, always gained the upper hand at the expense of the *alazon* (αλαζων)—a haughty, pretentious, pseudosophisticate, whose unjustified sense of self-importance made his fall a source of delight for Greek audiences. Plato, however, seems to have taken this seemingly comic situation with some seriousness, transforming it into a characterization of the ironies of life beyond the realm of the theater. For in the performance the *alazon* only pretends to be more than he really is and the *eiron* less. Those who live in the real world, however, have no choice. We are determined to appear to be either more or less than we truly are. If we take a proud stance, our pride advertises its true character. No less is this the case if ours is a humble posture.

Irony is the saving consequence of the fact that neither the sphere of theory nor of human praxis is finally coherent. Neither can be finally named, or encapsulated in univocal concepts, or rendered systematic. On the other hand, they cannot be approached without the presumption of system and coherence. Our world must appear to be either more or less than it truly is. The philosopher Platocrates recognized the dilemma and sought through his slightly schizoid stances to celebrate both openness and system, both the confession of ignorance and the claim to know. He accomplished the task about as well as any two philosophers could ever expect to. But the tensions, the contradictions, remain.

The irony of our understanding of Plato is an irony Plato explicitly advertised. The critical tension in his thinking that establishes the contrast between the systematic, dogmatic thinker and the open-ended, open-minded enquirer is one that Plato consciously built into his thought. And it is a tension that is not to be easily resolved. We ought not, as is so often done, read Plato as the *alazon* and Socrates as the *eiron*, and resolve the contradictions in Socratic thought at the expense of the author of the (presumed) comedy. Nor ought we read Plato from our vantage point at the end of our tradition of philosophic thinking and find that his desire for systematic completeness has met with tragic failure. Properly understood, Plato's philosophy is as immune to the tragic as to the comic interpretation. His thought is beyond both tragedy and comedy, having realized the apex of philosophic irony.

The sense of irony emergent from the recognition of the limits placed upon the elements of philosophic endeavor by the context of thought itself, however much it may hover in the background of all our speculative activities, certainly cannot be said in any sense to dominate our cultural self-consciousness. In place of the saving irony that was to be the gift of our first philosophers to their intellectual heirs, there is a damning sensibility which, recalling (somewhat obliquely) the writings of Matthew Arnold, we might term *moral seriousness*. Our primary sense of the world is that it is, indeed, *a serious affair*. The classical scientific search for univocal meanings on which to ground our understandings of the nature of things, and the dogmatic attitude expressed by moralists who wish to articulate and promulgate true ethical principles as a means of structuring the realm of human praxis, are fundamental forms in which this seriousness has been expressed.

In its most general character, our seriousness is a response to the perception of existence as radically contingent. A principal source of this perception of contingency is to be found in the notion of *creatio ex nihilo*. According to the belief derived primarily from our Hebraic heritage, our world is the consequence of an arbitrary act of a Divine Agent. As creatures, our existence is to be explained in terms of that initial cosmogonic act. Our Hellenic forebears, likewise, contributed to our sense of the contingent character of existence. Among the Greeks the experience of contingency was institutionalized through gods of Fate and Chance, and celebrated in both oral and written traditions until it was subjected to a full-scale counteroffensive in the dogmatic strain of Plato's philosophy which demanded unity and intelligibility of both the cosmological and political spheres. No less significant, of course, was Aristotle's vision of science as a way of knowing free from natural and social contingencies.

It is easy to understand how these conceptions gave rise to a sense of moral seriousness. The only viable response to commands made by the noncontingent Author of the Universe is *obedience*. Likewise, the only proper response to the understanding of the world in terms of philosophic principles which organize and order its noncontingent aspects is to act in accordance with those principles. The convergence of the Greek and Hebraic sensibilities through the development of Judaic-Christian culture ramified the seriousness of our fundamental *Weltanschauung*.

Our mood of moral seriousness had its most significant origins in the presumption of a Supreme *Archē* as the author of our existence. This *Archē* may be either the Absolute Will celebrated in Genesis, or a Divine Mind patterned by the Eternal Ideas of Plato, or some other functional equivalent to be found in the family of philosophic principles comprising our cultural resource. A direct consequence of this presumption is the emergence of a serious commitment to the maintenance of a single-ordered world established in accordance with a principle, or system of principles, to which we are rationally and morally bound.

Perhaps the most significant insight concerning the character of our cultural self-consciousness is that it is somewhat schizoid because of the presence of elements which seem totally irreconcilable—namely, seriousness and irony. This condition is complicated by the fact that we find it impossible to claim that either the sense of irony or of seriousness has a single ideological source. Certainly no one would consider the philosophy of Aristotle to be anything but a morally serious enterprise. And irony is clearly present, even if primarily in its indirect, dramatic sense, in Hebraic culture. For there we see that God chooses a ragtag collection of professional refugees for his very own people, and, in a variation of the theme, appears as a lowly carpenter, only to end by becoming a victim of the tools of his trade. But it must be said that the overriding message is that of such moral solemnity that we seldom have occasion to appreciate these ironies. Only rarely do we experience the delicious thrill of the ironic tension lurking in the apothegmatic phrases of the theologians—*Credo quia absurdum est . . . Fides quarens intelligam . . . Cur Deus homo*?

What does it mean to say that we have been formed in accordance with such apparently conflicting elements as a sense of seriousness and an ironic vision? Viewing the world from the giddy perspective of the ironic moralist is not an easy task. We always seem constrained to allow one of the two elements to dominate. For the greater part of our tradition, particularly since the period of the theological synthesis of Hebraic and Hellenic sensibilities in the early centuries of the Christian epoch, it has been the rational and moral senses that have laid the heaviest claims upon us. We have sought to establish ourselves and our culture through obedience to forms of thought and praxis grounded in literal truths and firm convictions. If, in accordance with the aim of the present essay, we approach the question of the proper balance of irony and moralism in our natures, we shall find that we must invert the priorities and discover in the distinctly ironic vision the means whereby to confront our cultural ambience. The moral individual dominated by a sense of irony sees the world patterned by contradiction and paradox. For every significant claim about the nature of things an equally viable counterclaim may be made. For every "Yes," a "No." The ironic sensibility celebrates the inexorably incoherent, even contradictory, status of all claims to knowledge. It finds the consequence of the search for truth to be a plethora of conflicting truths, and uncovers in the many claimants to systematic completeness a chaos of woefully inadequate visions of the way things are. In our Anglo-European tradition there are two classic strategies which we have sought to substitute for the extremely difficult style of encounter demanded of the ironist. Each of these surrogate strategies attempts to narrow the vision of things to a single modality of entertainment. And each excludes the other from the boundaries of its perspective. These strategies aimed at canceling the tensions associated with the ironic vision are, of course, the tragic and the comic perspectives.

At the close of the *Symposium*, the sober Socrates is engaged in persuading some half-sleeping inebriates of the thesis that the true poet could be a writer of both comedies and tragedies. This should come as no surprise to those who grasp the essence of the Platonic vision, for it is Plato who most readily understands that the tension between Appearance and Reality which grounds the ironic sensibility is essential to both comedy and tragedy. And it is the form of the dialogue, the master of which is Plato himself, that constitutes the ironic genre. The dialectical mode of enquiry maintains the irreconcilable tensions that so clearly reflect the character of mundane existence and that both the tragic and the comic senses attempt to avoid.

The essence of tragedy is the intuition of loss. Loss is inevitable because of the inherently limited character of the experience of value. The often paralyzing recognition of the finitude of individual attainments is familiar to all. Insult is added to injury, however, when we are forced to recognize that the limited values we do in fact realize cannot be our permanent acquisitions. Either our values fade, leaving us with a sense of despair, or we ourselves fade, leaving our attainments behind without the assurance of continued celebration. The sense of tragedy is the sense of loss in these two dimensions. Its primary therapeutic value is that it leads us to the assumption of a permanent source of value beyond this mundane world, in which experiencing does not entail loss. Even if the faith in a transcendent realm is abandoned, we nonetheless may develop stoic principles which will allow us to meet "the menace of the years" fearlessly, even if only as Camus's Sisyphus encountered the menacing absurdities of his existence. The tragic sense is one means of masking ourselves so as to survive the seriousness of the world we live in.

The comedic mask functions in the same manner. The comic attitude, like the tragic, is motivated by the need to reduce or to cancel the unavoidable tensions of life. Laughter functions to reduce psychological tensions having their ultimate grounding in the irreconcilable contradictions confronted in the realm of praxis. Byron's revealing line, "and if I laugh at any mortal thing, 'tis that I may not weep," suggests that the comic sense is parasitical upon the tragic. In order to avoid our tragic encounters with the transitoriness of passing fact, the fading of beauty, the destructive consequences of moral evil, alienation from the primary source of value, we *make* fun. The making of fun where no real occasion for fun exists is essentially what comedy is about. Tragedy and comedy are, indeed, but two masks worn by the same character alternately, depending upon the exigencies of the moment; that is, depending upon which mask best represents him in such a way as successfully to reduce the unacceptable tensions of his ambience. Thus the obvious truth of Socrates' argument at the end of the *Symposium*. Both tragedy and comedy are but one-sided expressions of the ironic sensibility.

Both tragedy and comedy serve to reinforce the mood of high moral seriousness. The ironic sensibility requires one to confront the way of things more honestly and more directly, without resort to therapeutic strategems. The recognition that neither joy nor sorrow has a final claim upon existence cannot, of course, lead the ironist to seek some cosmic Tertium Quid which resolves the paradoxical tensions of lived circumstance. Rather, he sees with a clarity born of the honest acceptance of the way of things that, beyond the strategems which promote an "either-or" (or "neither-nor") attitude, there is the truth of "both-and."

This recognition in no way cancels the element of moral seriousness. The ironist sees, however, that the claims of the moralist must be made indirectly if they are to be efficacious. An implication of this view is that the cause of moral seriousness is better served by a contemplation of the

subtle ironies of Socratic wisdom than by the most dedicated commitment to construction of Plato's Ideal State.

Recall the scene at the trial of Socrates on the charges of impiety and
corrupting the youth of Athens. Plato recounts in detail Socrates' speech
in his own defense. It is the final sentences of those remarks which ought
concern us here. Socrates has been condemned to die. He has accepted
the sentence, gently blaming his accusers for wishing him no good. He
addresses his final words to the men of Athens by asking a favor of the
sympathetic among his audience.

> When my sons are grown up, I would ask you, Oh my friends, to
> punish them; and I would have you trouble them, as I have troubled
> you, if they seem to care about riches, or anything, more than about
> virtue; or if they pretend to be something when they are really
> nothing,—then reprove them, as I have reproved you, for not car-
> ing about that for which they ought to care, and thinking that they
> are something when they are really nothing. And if you do this both
> I and my sons will have received justice at your hands.[2]

Here Socrates is saying, "If, men of Athens, you will but do that for
which I have been condemned, then justice will have been done to me
and to my sons." A strange statement, to be sure. The sentence of the
court was unjust, and it was based on unjust accusations. The results of
the trial could hardly seem to have been less likely to have any just consequences. But, as a matter of fact, Socrates' hope for justice to be realized
in the future was not at all a vain hope. The subsequent history of our intellectual culture stands as testimony to the contributions we have con-
sistently made to the "Justice for Socrates Fund."

Socrates is no ordinary martyr. In his role as social critic, as self-
proclaimed gadfly of Athens, he was one who chastised, ridiculed, and in
so doing, celebrated the profound ironies consequent upon human
pretensions. In this way Socrates provided the model and inspiration of
the moral activity of the philosopher. The tone of moral seriousness is
never finally present in his utterances. Irony reigns to the very end. Consider Socrates' dying words:

> Crito, I owe a cock to Aesclepius. Would you pay the debt?

Hardly the kind of words one would wish to carve on a monument. At
one level this is the utterance of a man who wishes to leave this life owing

no one, not even the gods. At another level, we see, perhaps, the desire for purification by appropriate sacrifice. But who can escape the itchy suspicion that Socrates, who has been condemned for atheism, and is dying of a slow-working poison, is taking one last opportunity to tweak the noses of his accusers by giving sacrifice (thus refuting the charge of atheism in the most dramatic way) to a god (the god of health and long life) whose efficacy is being directly challenged by the fact of Socrates' death?

Irony? The "facts" are clear. Whatever else may be said of the matter, Socrates was actually accused, was actually tried, drank hemlock, and dutifully died. But what are the significances of these facts? What have been the moral consequences of Socrates' life and thought? Certainly those consequences would have been different if it had not been for his creative use of the ironic sensibility. For irony has moral effects, indirect as they are, superior to those deriving from attempts to promote the aims of justice by giving a dogmatic definition of the term, or by enforcing a mode of behavior held de facto to be just—as if we could cure a disease by pronouncing the name of the medicine. The moral influence of the philosopher, and of those who would use the philosopher as model, derives from his ironic sensibility. Socrates demonstrated this fact when he showed that Justice is the Justice of Injustice.

But this is only one half of the story. If we find that there are morally serious consequences associated with the ironic sensibility, we as surely discover that there is a lurking irony in the moral seriousness of our character. Certainly if we take the tradition at its face value we are not immediately overwhelmed by the presence of irony. The religious sensibility of Judeo-Christianity, whatever its greatness in other respects, is as close to humorless as a religion could be. Occasionally one sees ironies of the spirit peeking through such lines as, "Render unto Caesar . . . ," or "Resist not evil," or "My God, My God, Why hast Thou forsaken me?" But the sayings of Jesus are so distorted by the undue importance we have given to the rantings of a pharisaical tentmaker as to have lost much of their subtlety. And perhaps all of their irony.

Though we recognize that our inheritance from Hebraic culture has been predominantly that of moral seriousness we also recognize that irony exists, at least potentially, in Hebraic literature. Numerous suggestions of irony could be instanced from the Old Testament prophets, and particularly from the wisdom literature. But with the possible exception of some of the statements of Kohheleth in Ecclesiastes, or of the dramatic conclusion of the Book of Job, none of these statements points to the kind of tensions, contradictions, or incongruities at the very heart of things as do the examples from Greek philosophy. One cannot but agree with A. R. Thompson when he says that "whenever an ironist acquires a genuine faith and a genuine desire to establish it, he stops being an ironist and preaches."[3] If there is always a transcendent truth to be proclaimed, a lesson to be learned, true irony cannot survive. There is irony of the specifically dramatic kind in the Old Testament, of course, but the irony of self-reference is almost by definition impossible. The Book of Job without the Prologue, or the book of Ecclesiastes without some of its theologically orthodox glosses, doubtless would present fine ironies, but it is the case that they do not exist without those emendations precisely because there was a faith to defend, a set of truths to uphold, a right to proclaim, and wrongs to oppose. The morally serious tone of the Old Testament message is such as to override any suggestion of irony and to preclude its uncensored expression.[4]

The New Testament is even less inclined to the ironic. The morally strict message of Saint Paul obfuscates, if not obliterates, the wisdom of Jesus. There is a severe contradiction between the teachings of Saint Paul and those of Jesus—between the "by their fruits shall ye know them" gospel and the "salvation by faith alone" doctrines. The Sermon on the Mount and the Letter to the Church at Rome express such a disparity of spiritual understanding as can only astound the unbiased reader. Yet the contradictions are not felt in the manner of irony; rather, they are resolved almost exclusively by accepting the tentmaker's glosses on the sayings of his master. The structure of the New Testament parodies Greek comedy. Jesus unwittingly serves as the *eiron* and Saint Paul the *alazon*. However, it is the *alazon* who is raised up and the *eiron* who suffers humiliation. No irony here. Simply very bad comedy.

By taking altogether too seriously the consequences of the "fallen nature" of human beings, and thus concentrating upon concepts of sinfulness as expressed through ethically identifiable behaviors, the Judeo-Christian tradition has obscured the very essence of the religious sensibility. Just as the philosopher can lose his way if he approaches the unavoidable contradictions and relativities involved in the search for truth as if they were the whole point of the enterprise, so the religious person can lose his way if he conceives the moral import of the religious sensibility to exhaust the meaning of religion.

As I have argued before, the function of the philosopher is the articulation of importances, not the certification of truths. In religion the value of holiness transcends in importance that of morality, and defines, therefore, the character of religious experience. Claiming that "holiness" is a value distinct from, and more fundamental than, "goodness" will likely seem suspect to those within traditional religious communities. But it is a claim that is easily defended.

The paradox encountered in spiritual insight is that only when one transcends finite contexts, letting the dead bury the dead, can one be truly spiritual. But this transcendence of finitude continually threatens to lead one into amoral, if not actually immoral, actions. God's test of Abraham's faith involved highly questionable demands which, judged by any normal set of moral criteria, would be found reprehensible. If we place God beyond ordinary senses of good and evil, then, by implication, we place the servants of God beyond them as well. Thus neither God nor Abraham is found to be immoral by virtue of their conspiracy against Isaac. Nor do we find Jesus reprehensible because he demonstrated what from anyone else would be extreme insensitivity toward the sufferings of the poor. "The poor you shall always have with you," indeed! As a class, perhaps. But certainly not those particular poor who suffered because they were denied the proceeds from the costly ointment misspent on Jesus' feet and hair. We do, on the other hand, wish to find Judas culpable for his betrayal of Jesus. But surely this is unsound. The *felix culpa* was an essential ingredient in the story of salvation. No Judas, no crucifixion; no crucifixion, no atonement; no atonement, no salvation. "For God so loved the world, He sent a betrayor . . . " We look in vain for that verse in Scripture. Unless we look between the lines.

Precisely what do these actions of God, of Jesus, of Judas have in common? Just this: they were holy deeds. They were not, however, in any meaningful sense moral. The irony is clear. There is, finally, no room for the claims of morality in religious experience. There are in fact no ethical consequences to consider once we extend our frame of reference beyond the loyalties we feel to self, family, society, nation, the planet Earth, this particular galaxy, and so on. The moral seriousness which, in our culture, has most often grounded the religious impulse, ends by rendering morality irrelevant.

The poor will always be with us. The world will continue to be woven in a pattern of justice over injustice, in a knit-one-purl-two march to the end of history. To be religious is to be in, but not of, the world. If, therefore, our moral seriousness is *serious enough*, it will cease to be moral. The irony of spiritual insight is that it serves as a goal which, once attained, cancels the apparent reason for the quest. Just as the detachment of the ironic sensibility has moral consequences of an indirect but nonetheless important character, so the moral commitment initiating religious activity has ironic consequences equally important, and equally indirect.

Ours is a strange world, indeed. In the philosophic spirit we find a means of approaching our experiences in the ironic mood and thereby of coming to recognize that the moral consequence of the ironic sensibility involves the bringing of justice out of injustice. If we fail to maintain that ironic sense, if we allow our moral impulse to cancel the sensitivity to the inconsistencies of experience by arbitrary appeals to truth and dogmatic certainty, then we find that these claims are always unjust. Thus do we bring *in*justice out of the search for justice; falsity out of the search for truth.

Beginning with a foundation in moral seriousness we find ourselves moving beyond this or that finite loyalty in an increasing desire for the experience of the Holy, seeking the unchanging Ground which alone can justify any moral stance. Once discovered, lo! we find morality irrelevant. We experience the irony of the infinite, the irony born of the recognition that infinity is pointless, useless, and, given solely logical or moral criteria, without meaning.

True as it may be to say that we are best able to understand ourselves as deriving from the contradictory sensibilities associated with irony, on the one hand, and seriousness on the other, it is equally true that we have accepted the serious stance as the dominant aspect of our character. What requires us to reevaluate the balance between irony and seriousness in our cultural psyche is that the contradictions associated with our rational and moral perspectives can no longer be ignored. If we refuse the saving graces of the ironic sense, we shall have no means of recognizing the fundamental limits placed upon our understanding in the realm of praxis. We shall all then serve as haughty *alazons* waiting to be brought low by the increasing self-consciousness of intellectual culture.

One purpose of this essay has been to focus upon the ironic tension between knowledge and ignorance, primarily as that tension is illustrated in philosophic activity. By continuing that thread of argumentation I may be able to demonstrate how in fact the ironic sensibility might be resurrected. For it is precisely the dialectic of dogmatism and skepticism that suggests the context for the most efficacious appeal to the ironic sense. This will become clear if we return once again to the ironic relations of knowledge and ignorance as they are specified in terms of a conflict first highlighted by Plato—namely, the quarrel between the poets and the philosophers.

Among countless other ironies, Plato willed to Anglo-European culture the quarrel between poetry and philosophy, between metaphors and principles, which has patterned our intellectual life ever since it was first so insistently celebrated. Plato's resort to unmatched eloquence to argue for the serious conflict between the poet and the philosopher set the example that all honest thinkers were to follow. That any great philosopher must ultimately have recourse to metaphors which extend

sensibility beyond literal sense, thus opening himself to the charge of
poetizing, is one of the ironies with which we are, willy-nilly, forced to
live.

The poet recognizes the tensions and contradictions contained within
any worthwhile metaphor. In "saying what something is by saying what
it is not," what, indeed, do we say? The irony of metaphor is immediate
and direct. We use a word which is foreign to the literal significance of an
item in order to deepen our understanding of it. Through the use of
metaphor we increase the depth and breadth of our understanding by
challenging the univocality of terms. We thus stretch language and increase its connotative content. Describing the functions of metaphors in
this fashion says no more than that metaphors are used as *principles* of
communication and thereby serve philosophic ends. But principles per se
are also metaphorical. As we have noted before, the fundamental principles of a philosophic system cannot be literal or univocal terms. The
Principle of the Good, Creativity, and so on are metaphorical expressions which seek to extend our understandings of a philosophic sort.
Metaphor is intrinsically ironic in the sense that appearance and reality
are in tension in every metaphorical expression. Principles are just as
ironic, and for the same reason. What appears to be the case in the use of
principles turns out to be false if taken literally. The principle dissolves
into a metaphor. Contrariwise, if we place too much importance upon a
metaphor it begins to function as a principle.

The poet is a philosopher and the philosopher a poet. This irony was
not lost upon Plato. Doubtless he had some fun excluding the poets from
his ideal state in a language that is without peer among dramatic writers.
That Plato may not have been welcome in his own *Republic* is, if one
reflects but for a bit, one of the expected ironies in the thinking of
Platocrates.

According to Plato, real knowledge consists in the grasp of principles
as the beginning points of thought and action. The Form of the Good is the
Principle of Principles the grasp of which would allow one to understand
the relationship of all the principles of understanding. But the Principle
of the Good is only a principle if it is *grasped*. Until such time, that principle is in fact a metaphor which suggests, evokes, lures one to further efforts at understanding. The tension between poetry and philosophy in
Plato's work is a tension between contrasting functions of language as a
tool of philosophic understanding.

The antinomies of existence recognized at the level of praxis may be articulated in terms of the distinctive functions of language. "Time," says
Plato, "is the moving image of eternity." In this enigmatic phrase we

may uncover an insight into the meanings of both time and eternity. From the perspective of the realm of praxis, eternity is to be understood in terms of the experience of passing time. Time as "moving image" is a metaphor for eternity; and eternity is the principle in accordance with which time could be understood. From the perspective of realized eros, however, the functions of the language alter; eternity becomes a metaphor for time, and time the principle of eternity. Thus, in the metaphorical expression celebrated by every professor of sophomore literature—namely, "the road was a ribbon of moonlight"—we can learn something about both roads *and* moonlight if we but allow the relations of tenor and vehicle to shift.

Michael Polanyi has elaborated a theory of the functions of language which approximates the analysis here.[5] Polanyi applies the distinction of focal and subsidiary awareness from gestalt theory to paradigm instances of perception. For example, if we were to consider the manner by which a blind man becomes aware of his environment through the use of a cane we should recognize that focal awareness is achieved by the tip of the cane while the more direct feelings associated with the sense of the cane in the palm of the hand are subsidiary. This illustration of the complexity of our relations to our ambience is quite helpful in considering the interrelationships of metaphorical and literal language.

In the act of knowing, claims to factual knowledge involve awareness of the facts as focal, but also must involve subsidiary awareness (however inchoate) of theories as the contexts establishing the facticity of the facts. If we shift our focal attention from facts to the theoretical context, we can now say that we are subsidiarily aware of the facts as implicates of the theory. But another sphere of subsidiary awareness is significant in this instance, for we are also subsidiarily aware of the grounding of the theory in a nonrational ultimate category or categories the focal awareness of which would involve the aesthetic intuition I have discussed as theorial understanding. Intellectual activity proceeds from knowledge of facts to the understanding of their theoretical contexts, and finally to the theorial context of theories which is the Chaos of aesthetic and mystical intuitions.

The necessary shift of linguistic functioning associated with the movement backward and forward among theorial, theoretical, and factual understandings entails the fact that the quarrel between poetry and philosophy is irresolvable at the level of discursive knowledge. And that is but to say that the tension in the language entailed by this conflict must exist as long as language is a tool of praxis. From the limited perspective of embodied existence, the acceptance of which is the grounding of practical wisdom in the ironic sensibility, language has no greater utility.

Plato and Aristotle each acknowledged that true wisdom is possessed by both the *philomythos* and the *philosophos*. This recognition involves the celebration of language as the source both of principles and of metaphors. Myths are most often etiologic stories telling of the "beginnings" which serve as the poet's principles. Principles are the articulated beginnings of rational thought and action which, as categorial conditions of speculative thought, may exist solely as metaphorical deliverances. The union of the *philosophos* and *philomythos* is discoverable in both poetic and philosophic creativity. That in our tradition this fact has been celebrated by poets and philosophers as well provides all those who seek to grasp meaning at its highest reaches with the comforts of both eros and irony.

If this discussion of the ironic relations of principles and metaphors illustrated by the tension between the *philosophos* and *philomythos* appears somewhat overdrawn, it can be balanced somewhat if I illustrate the tension between poetic and philosophic language from the side of the poet. A number of individuals could serve as examples of poetic ironists, of course. Among twentieth-century candidates, Yeats, Mann, Joyce, Shaw, Beckett come immediately to mind. The best example of the ironic poet, however, is an individual who has not achieved nearly the fame of those just named. I refer to the Argentine, Jorge Luis Borges. However posterity shall assess his literary endeavors, there can be little question that he expresses the tension between the poetic and the philosophic in the most consummate of manners. For this reason, Borges's work is a marvelous repository of the ironic sensibility.

There are doubtless very subtle reasons why we might expect literary figures to celebrate the tension between principles and metaphors during the culminating phase of our cultural epoch in a manner not unlike the way a philospher advertised it at the beginning. Whatever these are, it cannot but be instructive to compare the philosophic and poetic approaches to the irreconcilable tension which forms the dynamic of each activity.

What follows is merely an extended gloss on two sentences of the poet, Borges: the first, a poignant confession of a personal failing which, writ large, is the failure of art itself; the second, a gnomic manifesto aimed at the justification (one might even say, vindication) of the aesthetic enterprise and, thereby, of Borges himself. That the confession is inefficacious since the priestly public to whom Borges bares his soul must count his sin a supererogatory virtue, and that his vindication of art must be thought by the most influential of our philocalists to be an insidious betrayal of art, only serves to advertise the exceedingly depressed condition of the aesthetic enterprise in contemporary culture.

In the prologue to his *A Personal Anthology*,[6] Borges cites Benedetto Croce's view that "art is expression." Attempts to conform to this definition of art have, he says, yielded "the worst literature of our time." After noting how very difficult it is to achieve expression since it requires the precise reproduction of a mental process, and after stating how very few are the true illustrations of the expressive act in literature, Borges offers the following insight into his literary activity: "Sometimes," he confesses, "I, too, sought expression. I know now that my gods grant me no more than allusion or mention."[7]

It is extremely important that we recognize this feigned self-abnegation for what it is: a transparent mask covering those opaque, ironic features which (though they, too, possess a masklike quality) constitute the true face of the poet. The true poet knows, and he wishes us to believe, that what the gods have granted him in lieu of expression is by far the greater gift. He knows, and he would have us share this wisdom, that the desire for aesthetic expression is the original sin of the poet. He who would seek the gift of expression must leave the poet's labyrinthine garden, must travel somewhere east of Eden, in search of another utopia where philosophers hold sway. For the power of expression belongs to the philosopher whose intellectual respectability poets are so often tempted to covet. The talent for expression can be nurtured by the poet only if he is willing to abandon his role as *maker* and strive to become a *thinker*. And thinking requires that one so organize his perceptions and so direct his enquiries as to promote the possibility of representation, reproduction, and translation, prerequisites of the expressive activity. The use of metaphor, the means of extending sensibility beyond sense, is the *via constructiva* of the poet. It may be a *via dolorosa* for the philosopher.

The philosopher's claim that there is a tension, even a contradiction, between the activities of the *philosophos*, the lover of causes and principles, and the *philomythos*, the lover of myth and sensuous metaphor, certainly has not settled the case. When John Keats assures us that all we know on earth (and all we need to know) is that "Beauty is Truth; Truth Beauty," many are so warmed by the friction fires of that poet's ambiguity as to forget just how much of what we need to know while on this earth requires us to confront the ugly, the tawdry, and the banal.

The insistence of some poets and philosophers to the contrary notwithstanding, the quarrel between poetry and philosophy is a very real, and perhaps irrevocable, fact about the nature of intellectual culture. This is what every true poet, every authentic philosopher, knows. This is a truth which poets cannot express but to which their writings infinitely allude. Almost alone among his contemporaries, Borges has recognized the extreme cost of such understanding. By remaining true to the realization of that experience of intensity and contrast the harmony of which is Beauty, Borges proves himself a poet. But by attempting to remain a poet while yet uncovering ontological truths, he has knowingly, willingly, sacrificed that consistency and coherence which comprise the twin hobgoblins of lesser poets.

A most peculiar characteristic of Borgesian prose is that it does not form a corpus. Borges's writings are mutually inconsistent and, taken as a whole, self-contradictory. He has presented us with a shifting mosaic, a free-hand model of Indra's net, a glimpse inside Fa Tsang's Hall of Mirrors. Though not without honor in his world, he would doubtless have won far greater fame on the planet Tlön, his spiritual home, of which he writes:

> Their books are also different. Works of fiction contain a single plot with all its imaginable permutations. Those of a philosophical nature invariably include both the thesis and the antithesis, the rigorous pro and con of a doctrine. A book which does not contain its counterbook is considered incomplete.[8]

Borges's writing is grounded in the purest of aesthetic intuitions which allows him to recognize that the realm of human praxis is not a reflection of a single-ordered Cosmos, but of all possible orders. The ontology of Borges's fictional world includes, of course, that of the world of putative reality. There are just enough actual facts mixed in with his fictional accounts that the line between reality and fantasy is irrevocably blurred. Distinctly different worlds, each with its own laws and regularities, overlap and insinuate themselves into our consensual realm. The finite act of poetic creation is the paradigm of creativity itself, and the worlds resulting from the creative act of the poet are as real and as true as is the world of common experience sketched by the frozen metaphors of previous acts of artistic creativity.

The conception of creativity as reducible to a transitory episode of aesthetic construal detaches each significant moment of experience from every other. The world of ordinary experience is no longer contrasted with a supramundane world of Eternal Verities. Time is no longer the moving image of eternity, but the Eternal exists at every moment as a fragmented reflection of the process of becoming. In one of his justly famous essays, "A New Refutation of Time," Borges seeks refuge from the incessant assaults of transience and decay by recourse to a philosophic argument extending Berkeleyan idealism to its logical conclusion. "Outside each perception (real or conjectural) matter does not exist; outside each mental state spirit does not exist; neither then must time exist outside each present moment."⁹

Having accepted the Berkeleyan denial of matter, and ramified it by the use of Hume's arguments against the existence of the self, Borges maintains that there is no longer any reason to affirm the existence of time. Thus he appears to refute the existence both of succession and of contemporaneity. Nothing occurs before or after any other thing. Succession and contemporaneity denied, there is no longer any cosmological foundation for the present. Time dissolves, and each event is self-contained and complete. Time is fragmented and in each fragment one can see a whole universe, self-sufficient and complete. No single fragment has any relations with anything outside itself.

But Borges is not convinced that his argument asserts the only truth about the nature of time. The final paragraph of his essay on the refutation of the time seems to reject his entire project:

> *And yet, and yet* . . . To deny temporal succession, to deny the astronomical universe, are measures of apparent despair and of secret consolation. Our destiny . . . is not frightful because it is unreal; it is frightful because it is irreversible and iron-bound. Time is the substance of which I am made. Time is a river which sweeps me along, but I am the river; it is a tiger which mangles me, but I am the tiger; it is a fire which consumes me, but I am the fire; The world, unfortunately, is real; I, unfortunately, am Borges.¹⁰

In this philosophic refutation, and the poetic counterclaim, we discover the basis for Borgesian irony and, perhaps, of irony per se. Intellectual historians may see lurking behind the expression of this classic dilemma two of the most problematic individuals Western culture has yet produced—Zeno of Elea and Siger of Brabant. The fact that these individuals lived sixteen centuries apart, and Borges yet another seven hundred years after the latter (if, that is, we accept the reality of time), adds a certain poignance to the dilemma which each confronted so masterfully: the contradiction of reason and experience.

Zeno encountered this contradiction by reflecting upon the question of the reality of change. Arguing in support of Parmenides' claim that "Only being is; not-being is not," Zeno's paradoxical arguments were grounded upon the insight that the notion of change and becoming entails the fact that a thing both is and is-not. An arrow must be in a place and not in that place at one and the same time if we are to make sense of its apparent motion. For if it is in a place at each moment of time, then it is never in transition from one place to another. But it always *is* in a place at each moment of time. Thus it never moves. We must conclude that one cannot rationally defend the notion of change and becoming. *Only being is*. It is certainly possible to make certain ad hoc assumptions about the meaning of the divisibility of space and time which allow a mathematical resolution of the Zenonian paradoxes. But this may only be accomplished by divorcing mathematical theory from any relevant experiential context, and thus by ignoring the existential significance of the paradoxes.

The vast majority of subsequent reflections on the conflict between reason and experience were predicated upon the rejection of the ultimacy of becoming. Of course, one could as easily draw the conclusion that reason is to be held suspect since it requires us to believe facts so contrary to our experience of the world. Regardless of the option taken, however, the conflict between the claims of reason and experience remains. Both claims certainly cannot be true. Or can they?

Enter Siger of Brabant. The thirteenth century was patterned by attempts to adjust orthodox theologies to the rediscovered works of Aristotle. The brilliant synthesis of Aristotelian thought and orthodox Christian doctrine achieved by Saint Thomas was not the only important illustration of that adjustment. A less compromising approach was taken by the theologian Siger. When Aristotle's theories conflicted with Christian doctrine, Siger claimed authority for both.

Generations of theologians and philosohers have either ridiculed Siger's irrationalism or else have so watered down his bold strategem as to render it a kind of harmless, indecorous expediency. We may see in Siger, as in Zeno before him, a spiritual forebear of the ironic poet. Zeno had opted for an uncompromising consistency and had thereby reduced to absurdity the timid, qualified rationality that serves to secure us in the world but does not permit us to understand it. Siger had sought an uncompromising adequacy to experience and in so doing had demonstrated how little coherence is to be found in the complex of beliefs and understandings that form our cultural consciousness. Together, Siger and Zeno provide bold support for the ironist's assault upon the merely rational meaningfulness of the world.

The predominant image in all Borgesian prose is that of the labyrinth. Reality is a confusing, bewildering, vertiginous state of affairs. Just as in a labyrinth we find no way to get there from here, so in our experience we are ultimately reduced to immobility when we try to discover a way out. The route of the senses leads into a cul-de-sac. The alternative path of reason leads again to an impassable barrier. A trust in the reality of passing time provides a starting point. Ultimately, however, if we are to proceed it is necessary to deny the reality of time altogether. But how do we proceed at all in a timeless world?

The labyrinthine character of existence is not best illustrated by the apparently most complicated states of affairs. The extreme poignance of our existence in this world is to be discovered, instead, in the insight of Zeno that the most frustrating and impassable of labyrinths initially seems the simplest of barriers. For Borges, as for Zeno, the ultimate labyrinth is symbolized by the straight line. Before we may proceed from A to B, it is necessary to traverse half the distance from A to B. And before that half has been traversed we must go half again the distance, and so on through an infinity of passing time.

The two points defining the untraversable path may indifferently be called reason and experience; time and eternity; being and becoming; faith and understanding; freedom and determination; mind and nature; God and the World; knowledge and ignorance. These antinomies are irresolvable because they form the termini of a deceptively simple straight-line labyrinth which lures even the most modest among us to solve its mystery, but then mocks each and every such attempt. Only if we cease trying to get from A to B and recognize that whatever significance we can hope to discover in this life is in the journeying, not in the arriving, shall we stop trying to escape from the labyrinth and begin to enjoy our endless passage through it.

The fundamental problem for Borges, as for Socrates, lies in the paradoxical relations between knowledge and ignorance. Borges's concern with the antinomy of knowledge and ignorance has the dimensions of a full-scale obsession. If Borges is to know, he cannot be satisfied with knowing only some things. He must know *everything*.

Ignorance, in the form of forgetting, omitting details, obscuring differences, is constitutive of all acts of knowledge. This is one of the profoundest of ironies. That Borges and Plato celebrate precisely the opposite consequences of that irony is much less significant than that both so keenly recognize the ironic relation between knowledge and ignorance. Plato finds the fundamental act of knowing in the intuition of the Form of Forms, the absolute principle of all knowledge and praxis. Borges, on the other hand, celebrates the detailed character of omniscience. He writes of the library of Babel which contains in its volumes all the possible permutations of twenty-five orthographic symbols and is, thus, a repository of almost infinite nonsense admixtured by a relatively scant sum of meaningful statements.[11] He tells us of the *Aleph*, "the place where, without any possible confusion, all the places in the world are found, seen from every angle."[12] This is the source of an infinite, simultaneous intuition of the whole, not as a single principle of coherence, but as a myriad of discrete perceptual events that can be characterized solely by enumeration. In these and other such symbols, Borges ironizes omniscience by an insistence upon a numerably finite complexity, unrelieved by system and coherence.

Whereas Plato approaches knowledge philosophically and encounters the ironic relation of knowledge and ignorance in terms of the transcendence of principles, Borges appreciates knowledge from the perspective of the poet and encounters that same irony by virtue of the infinity of sensuous perceptions. If Plato had but grasped the Form of the Good in a final act of philosophic intuition he would have realized the completeness of understanding *in principle*. This is the aim of eros. If Borges had but "world enough and time" to complete, by recourse to fragments of metaphorical allusion, the infinite mosaic which is the Totality he would have expereinced the final irony which is the meaninglessness of enumerated, en-listed reality.

The difference between Plato and Borges illustrates the difference between the *philosophos* and the *philomythos*. And though that difference is itself irreconcilable, the poetic philosopher and the philosophic poet share a common vision. The fact that this vision is one of paradox and contradiction advertises the burden both of the philosopher and the poet. And if the philosopher finally yields to the siren call of permanence and form luring him beyond the flux of passing fact, whereas the poet surrenders to the experience of time as perpetual perishing, this cannot gainsay the honesty and clarity with which each peers into the Chaos that grounds his truth.

Philosophic truth is captured by dialectically articulated system. It is the truth born of obedience to rational principles. Poetic truth is spawned by the fragmented and allusory character of lived experience, grounded in the acceptance of solely metaphorical connections among events. For the poet irony is the ultimate fact and poetic creativity must find its primary reward in its celebrations of the realm of praxis. For the philosopher the principal dynamic is that of eros driving beyond praxis, and irony is a consequence of the return of eros to the practical sphere. That the final word is to be given to the ironic sensibility ensures that the sensitive individual, be he philosopher or poet, must confront the peculiar condition of ontological embarrassment. The ontological embarrassment encountered in the realm of praxis is only to be overcome by recourse to the ironic sense. It is irony alone which can transform doubt to wonder and thereby, in Kierkegaard's phrase, "master the moment."

Eros leads to theorial understandings of the world expressed in terms of the transcendence of rational system. Irony finds its proper home at the level of praxis below the theorial level. Irony is the return to praxis after the realization of eros. Eros is experienced at all levels of perception and understanding as the motivation toward completeness. True irony presupposes the sense of completeness and depends, therefore, upon the highest of erotic understandings. Thus the presence of the ironic sensibility is evidence of a profound mystical accomplishment.

Aesthetic and mystical intuitions of the Totality patterned by the most general form of harmony are experienced erotically on their own terms, but ironically as they are seen to be relevant to the realm of praxis. Claims to certain knowledge, or belief in the incorrigibility of facts or theories, are fundamental impediments to the attainment of the primary intuitions. Claims to certainty constitute the embarrassment of irony. We are continually embarrassed by the individual excellences of the various items of our experience to the extent that we cannot accommodate them within our consistent understandings of the world. As long as we discipline our understandings by appeal to the claims of logical consistency and rational system we shall not achieve the spiritual insight that can wholly justify any claim to knowledge. We shall thus be barred from the experience of the ironic return of eros to the realm of praxis.

One of the reasons we have so much difficulty calling upon the beneficent contributions of the ironic sense is that we consider mystical understandings solely with respect to the realm of theoria. If we attempt to translate mysticism into praxially relevant terms we have resort to that most weaselly of weasel-words, "ineffability." Implicit within the claim of ineffability is a vision not only of the way things are, but also of the way language functions in the characterization of that which is. The simplest way to express the mystic's attitude toward language is that it functions at one and the same time both as a signpost and as a barrier.

The mystical character of language can be directly illustrated by reflection upon one of the purest strains of mystical philosophy—that of classical Taoism.

The way that can be told of is not an Unvarying Way
The names that can be named are not unvarying names.[13]

Thus begins Lao Tzu's telling of the Way. Without a refined sense of irony, and no little patience with paradox, one would be ill equipped to read further in the *Tao Te Ching*. For to the logical, and literal, mind Lao Tzu's apparent insistence upon telling that which he claims cannot be told seems just silly. The criticisms borne by this and other Taoist classics demonstrate how difficult it is for some to enter sympathetically into the Taoist sensibility. The T'ang poet P'o Chu-I playfully expressed the puzzlement so many critics of Taoism have experienced:

> Those who speak do not know;
> Those who know do not speak.
> This is what we are told by Lao Tzu.
>   . . . .
> How then could it be that he wrote
>   no less than five thousand words?

An eleventh-century Taoist made at least the beginning of a cogent response: "I make an embroidery of drakes and let you examine and admire them. As for the golden needle I cannot pass it on to you."[14] This response, however, is directed not only to the critics of Taoism, it is equally aimed at those who have gone overboard in their sympathies for Taoist irrationalism and seek to wallow in that seething, unarticulated silence which the more sophomoric of our mystics have celebrated as Truth. A donkey cannot achieve silence simply by refusing to bray. Nor is there true silence after his braying has ceased. Real silence, and the truth it contains, is not so easily won. We who must relate to our world through consciousness and intellect know that meaningful silence is the articulated quietude surrounded by words, propositions, and arguments which, while serving as vessels of rational meaning, nonetheless mutely confirm the mystical remark of Ludwig Wittgenstein cited earlier—"The unutterable is (unutterably) present in what is uttered." Thus mere silence (the auditory equivalent of the night wherein all cows are black) is by no means enjoined by the mysterious allusiveness of mystical language.

Once there was a traveler on his way to the Ch'ing Liang Monastery. As he rounded a bend in the winding road he encountered a sign directly in the middle of his path. The sign read:

YOU ARE NOW APPROACHING CH'ING LIANG

Strangely, the sign completely blocked the path, preventing further passage. The traveler was pleased to know that his destination was near.

But he was, of course, frustrated by the fact that the very means whereby he knew this served to deny him direct access.

Not only the words of the mystic, but, equally, those of the chemist and the carpenter, psychiatrist and saint, function both as signposts and as barriers. Paradoxically, words serve us best when they simultaneously point beyond and prevent penetration into that beyond. Thus mystical experiences are not strictly ineffable. It is broadly incorrect to say that language functions only negatively in its description of mystical experience, for there is a meaningful sense in which language promotes an understanding of its own limitations at the same time as it evokes a sense of the reality of that which is (inadequately) described. Just how successful one might be in exploiting these twin potentialities of language as a means of communicating something of the character of the mystical experience depends upon just how sensitive we may be to the possibilities of the ironic sensibility.

If we grant that mystical experience is ineffable it is difficult to account for the fact that we have mountains of articulated accounts of that experience. Such accounts must be understood ironically if we ourselves are reflecting on their relevance to the realm of praxis, and erotically if we are relating to them as a means of attaining mystical experience. Irony is the proper mood in terms of which one may initially confront "ineffable" experience. Simply by virtue of our character as experiencing beings we possess, however vaguely, an insight into the realm of theoria. Our receptivity to the deepest and most profound levels of aesthetic and mystical understandings requires the ironic sense, for irony is the only means of holding on to such experience at the mundane realm of praxis. If we are troubled by the conflicts, paradoxes, and contradictions encountered in the attempt to understand the world in factual and theoretical terms, we shall be impeded from recognizing the manner in which that conflict points beyond to the harmony of theoria. So embarrassed, we shall retreat to the reductive mode of thinking which attempts to discover certainty in univocal understandings. Thus we shall perpetuate the conflict of dogmatism and skepticism.

Traditionally, neither irony nor eros has provided the fundamental perspective upon mystical experience. Such experience has functioned primarily as evidence for dogmatic theological statements. These dogmas form the basis for institutionalized forms of religious understanding and activity. Institutionalized religion is a result of spiritual embarrassment precluding the sense of irony necessitated by our existence in a world of partialities, contradictions, and paradoxes. This is not said in order to dismiss the whole of Western forms of mystical literature. In the statements of most mystics, even those polluted by dogmatic theological interpretations, the sense of eros and the vision of irony are still dimly present. The erotic intuition may be but *putative*, and the ironic vision may be experienced only dramatically, since the mystic in his state of moral seriousness may have only the dimmest of recognitions of the ironic consequences of his experience at the level of praxis, but eros and irony are nonetheless in evidence.

The principal implication of this argument with respect to the philosophic tradition is that the accomplished philosopher is, like the true mystic, a bodhisattva who, having tasted enlightenment, returns to the practical world to serve his fellow beings. Plato himself made this proposal for philosophers, of course, in his *Republic*. Once the intuition of the Good was achieved, philosophers should return to the mundane world to serve as enlightened rulers. At its best, speculative philosophy, which, in its theorial dimension attempts to mirror the Totality, is an activity of the bodhisattva, who, as ironic moralist, is careful never to let his moral impulses lead him into a state of ontological embarrassment.

That philosophy begins in wonder (θαυμα) means that the erotic drive is formed by the theorial acceptance of the world on its own terms. But, in obedience to the moralistic component in our character, the same philosophy which begins in wonder often ends in embarrassment. And we have sought to rid ourselves of the pains of embarrassment either by dogmatic certainty or skeptical doubt. But the initial wonder of the speculative philosopher promises two kinds of fruition: the level of theoria grounds the intuition of the Totality; at the level of praxis, the benign consequence of this erotic realization is the ironic sensibility. Irony is, of course, the final fact. It exists both beneath and beyond the realm of theoria and the sense of fulfilled eros: *beneath* in the sense that it involves this actual world as a specification of Chaos; *beyond* in the sense that the erotic intuition is presupposed by the ironic sensibility.

The tension between the philosophic spirit and the moral impulse ingrained in each of us as Anglo-Europeans can only be survived if we boldly accept the irrevocability of the conflict. The gateway to the proper appreciation of the character of our existence is to be found in the invisible areas of openness in our character where moral seriousness and the sense of irony continually converge, but never fully meet.

The tension between the ironic and the moral sense, as I have outlined it, is specifiable in terms of two other tensions already considered—namely, those between utopian and utilitarian modes of speculation, and first- and second-problematic thinking. The contrast of utopian and utilitarian thought is celebrated in the relations of horizontal and vertical transcendence. Utilitarian thought recognizes the application of theoretical principles to the sphere of human praxis; utopian speculation has continual reference to the realm of theoria housing the insistent particularities unconditioned by system and principles. Likewise, second-problematic thinking requires resort to principles as determining sources of order which in their most general functions provide grounds for believing in a single-ordered Cosmos. First-problematic thinking, on the other hand, accepts the more primitive intuition of "many worlds" as a fundamental fact. The irrevocable tensions between rational and moral stances which demand resort to principles, and aesthetic and mystical visions which require the transcendence of principles, lead to a revisioning of the means of encountering our experienced ambience. For to our predominantly theoretical type of knowing we must add the sort of knowledge which is essentially unprincipled.

Mystical and aesthetic visions, as sources of the ironic sensibility, are expressions of this sort of knowing. The senses of one-in-many and many-in-one which comprise the mystical and aesthetic senses are instances of unprincipled knowing. In the mystical intuition, the sense of unity is not determinate and therefore cannot be described in terms of character or function. It is not transcendent and cannot, therefore, serve as a ground of principled order. Its enjoyment is a consequence of the dissolution of the center of experiencing and thus cannot be a relationship in any ordinary sense. It is an experience without content, expressed as a subjective form of feeling referable to neither self, nor other, but to that mutuality which is the ground of experiencing itself.

The aesthetic experience, on the other hand, is the experience of infinite allusiveness which both permits the enjoyment of a thing in itself and simultaneously suggests an infinitely complex world created by the object enjoyed. In the strict sense the object of aesthetic enjoyment is the focus of an experience of ecstasy, and the world entertained from the perspective of the object is created by that object. The act of ecstasy is a deferential act. Deference characterizes those situations in which "principles" qualify acts of self-creativity rather than serve as determining sources of order. Ecstasy is a free act. If ecstasy is forced, alienation is the consequence. It is such a sense of alienation that is always threatened by the application of moral principles.

Ecstasy is accompanied by the en-stasy occasioned by the experiencing of oneself as the locus of excellence. The ultimate conditioning experience is that of (forgive the barbarism) "constasy"—the sense of all things standing together in a multivalent complex of spontaneous orders. The constatic sense is the mystical vision which serves as the background for the twofold forms of aesthetic experiencing associated with ecstasy and enstasy. The fundamental forms of experiencing associated with the ironic vision bring one into contact with individuals and particulars, whether the terminus of the experience be the self or the world. The implications of this type of experiencing for our understanding of the significance of principles per se should be clear.

In our classical traditions knowing involves insight into the principles of order which characterize the Totality as a Universe, and the application of these principles to particular instances of that orderedness. Thus to claim that we have knowledge of an object is to say that we understand it in terms of its determining principles. These may be expressed as abstract universals, as laws of organic functioning construed in terms of purposes or aims, as outcomes of material and causal interactions, or simply as conventional linguistic concepts. We "know" an object in terms of something other than the object, something which transcends it. We know it by virtue of principles as determining sources of order.

In the ironic mode, knowledge involves knowing the intrinsic excellence of an object or event. One knows an object through a grasp of its idiosyncratic and unique significance. This noninstrumental knowledge is the consequence of an intuitive grasp of an item as "self-so," as a spontaneous and self-creating event. No principles as external determining sources of order obtain. Everything has its own principle, and Nature is just a name for the totality of things or events understood each on its own terms. Such knowledge is noninstrumental in the sense that it does not involve a construal of objects or events in terms of anything other than the events or objects themselves. No unified hierarchy of aims or goals, no causal laws, no unqualified anthropocentricity, may be involved in such understandings. Acting and feeling in accordance with such noninstrumental knowledge promotes a radically transformed sphere of social praxis in which each item of one's encountered ambience is intuited as self-defining, as both *causa sui* and *sui generis*.

The crucial fact about this combination of aesthetic and mystical experiencing is that it yields no sense of an ontologically privileged order. The sense of ontological parity undergirding these types of experiencing is fundamental. Each and every object of experience is self-creative. The variant excellences extant within a particular cosmological context are those resulting from the interrelationships of *kosmoi*, the overlapping of orders. The viability of these overlapping orders is guaranteed by deferential relationships involving ecstasy in the act of deference, and enstasy in its reception. In the ontological sense there are no *differential* excellences. Each thing has its insistent particularity and as such is a potential object of ecstasy.

In the cosmological context, patterned by the conventions of causal laws and principles, there are differential excellences insofar as there are preferred actions, understandings, or desires. In this realm of human decision and action our concept of the world and our place within it is conditioned by our construal of types of relationships. There are, from this perspective, *possible*, *plausible*, and *necessary* relations among things. Possible relations are those imaginative associations serving to enforce the enrichment of experience for its own sake. Plausible relations are those among the possible relations which can function as the interpretive and constructive hypotheses from which theories and strategems of practical relevance may be fashioned. Necessary relations are of two kinds: putatively metaphysical connections without which there could be no coherent thought or being, and pragmatic connections unequivocally essential to the immediate task at hand.

The criterion which forms the general strategic principle in deciding upon relational priorities is reflected from the ontological realm. The criterion is this: so act as to promote the experience of the insistent particularity of the events and objects constituting your ambience. I have put this principle in the form of an imperative in order to highlight its obvious irony. This imperative can hardly be a principle in the ordinary sense. In the first place, it is impossible to obey this imperative, for the paradox of every spiritual commandment resides within it: a principle or rule freely obeyed ceases to be heteronomous and becomes one's own.

One of the great difficulties in the spiritual life is that in spelling out guidelines for conduct one is likely to understand these as instrumental rules for the achievement of something spiritual. It is characteristic of principles as external determining sources of order that they have an instrumental efficacy in some sense detached from the subjective form of feeling with which they are entertained. This, of course, cannot be so with spiritual principles wherein the subjective form of feeling is the sole content. One cannot accept spiritual principles as external determinants; unless internal they are meaningless.

If one would learn of the Tao, the first thing one learns is that the Way that can be spoken of is not the true Way. If the kingdom is sought as one would seek a goal, it is lost, for the Kingdom of God is within you. *Brahman* and *atman* are one. Nirvana is already realized. The sort of actions one must perform in order to reach the spiritual dimension are not actions at all. They are noninstrumental, spontaneous, creative activities having no aim except that residing within the action itself.

Thus the ontological criterion cited above is not a principle in the pejorative sense. It is a self-destructive rule. If followed it becomes unnecessary. Its reference is to the ontological realm in which there is a

parity of orders and of items of experiencing. The rule then suggests that
we act in such a way as to cancel contexts within which theoretical and
practical priorities exist. It is a rule which suggests that we seek the emptiness of all things. The realization of emptiness is the realization of
Chaos as the sum of all orders.

If one understands that the nature of things is such that the ultimate
terminus of any true act of understanding is Chaos, one has achieved the
beginnings of noninstrumental understanding. Perfecting this kind of
understanding depends upon the ability to recognize the insistent particularity of each item encountered in experience. At the level of
cosmological existence that particularity is grasped in the act of knowing
which involves a recognition of the ontological parity of all things. Except one be a bodhisattva and the wisest of all philosophers, one cannot
be expected to see the just-so-ness of each thing. But even in the basically
instrumental type of relations with one's ambience, there is the possibility
of recognizing in some dim way the ontological value of encountered
items.

My discussions of the various relations of theoria, theory, and praxis
throughout this essay have intended to alter the traditional understanding of theory and practice. The realm of praxis, as I am construing it, includes both the praxis of thinking as well as the praxis of technical,
political, and social actions. The realm of theoria patterned by the
realization of the end of eros is fundamentally a realm of mystical insight. The realm of praxis, as relevant to the theorial realm, is the sphere
within which one can entertain Chaos as the sum of all orders through
the medium of the ironic vision.

Theoria names the intuitive mode in accordance with which one
receives the welter of experience unconditioned by the desire for consistent, coherent, systematic engagement with the world. Theory is a consequence of systematic construal in accordance with principles which promote consistency and coherence. Theory belongs to the realm of praxis in
the sense that theoretical understandings are the consequences of practical motivations obedient to the aim of the control of the processes of
experience. Theory is grounded in instrumental understandings of the
world; theorial understandings are aesthetic and mystical appreciations
which would let things be as they are. Theoretical knowledge has logical
criteria as disciplining principles. Theorial visions transcend strictly
logical criteria, finding in logical consistency a special mode of the more
general notion of aesthetic harmony.

Praxis may be differentially contrasted to both theoria and theory. In
its more traditional senses praxis is both occasion and consequence of
theoretical activity. And theories are, of course, both interpretations of

praxis and potential guides for it. With regard to theoria, however, both theory and practice are modes of praxis. Contrasted specifically with theoria, practical activity is enlightened praxis. Enlightened praxis is illustrated by the activity of the individual who returns to the mundane realm of human affairs after a contemplation of the emptiness of the theorial sphere. This form of praxis can itself be both the occasion and the consequence of theoria. As the return of eros, enlightened praxis is expressed in the ironic sensibility. But such irony may as well serve as a stimulus to its own transcendence by disposing one to the lure of eros.

These reflections provide the basis for an interpretation of praxis, in its fundamental sense, not as political action or economic production, nor even as theoretical construction, but as *aisthesis*, creativity. What is missing from our traditional Anglo-European understandings of praxis is the notion of enjoyment as a mode of practical engagement of the world. Aesthetic activity has most often been understood in terms of the expressive rather than the experiential mode. Creativity, on such a view, involves the creation of something external to oneself. Creation in this sense involves *otherness*. If, however, we understand creativity at the experiential level as characterized by a mode of enjoyment, we shall see that there can be no real otherness in any act of creation. Creativity is reflexive; self-creativity is the only true mode of the creative act.

As I have noted before, three principal accounts of creation are given in the traditional mythical sources of Anglo-European speculation. The first is exemplified by the myth of Genesis. Whether one interprets the Genesis account as *creatio ex nihilo* or as the construal of order from out of the primal confusion and disorder of Chaos, the act of creativity is by fiat. Creation is a direct expression of power through an act of the will. Plato's *Timaeus* renders creativity in terms of a victory of the persuasive activity of a rational Demiurge over the resistant forces of primal necessity. Here creation is seen as a rational, as opposed to a volitional, activity. Hesiod's *Theogony* tells of the gaping void of Chaos that emerged with the separation of Earth and Heaven. The dynamism of cosmological creativity is the attractive power of *Eros* drawing Heaven and Earth into a fecund relationship. Creation is here associated with the passion of *love*. Drawing upon these traditional sources, Anglo-European thinkers have understood the notion of creativity in its ontological, cosmological, and existential senses as either a volitional, rational, or passional notion. The subsequent importance of these three visions of creativity in our cultural tradition is unquestioned. One has but to note the manner they became incorporated in Plato's philosophy to understand how these visions have served to determine our understandings of creativity.

The philosophic principles Plato sought in his general social theory were principles of functional specialization permitting the harmonious interrelations of distinct psychic and social modalities, and principles of education meant to exploit the potentialities of these specialized functions. These principles were Universals; they were Eternal Forms as norms for thought, action, and passion. The Principle of the Good, the ground of all principles of normative measure, was at once the presupposition of the dialectical enquiry constituting the structure of Platonic pedagogy and the final goal of that enquiry. The principles of specialization were grounded in the analogical relations between the functions of the psyche (thinking, acting, and feeling) and the classes of the model society (the philosophic rulers, the guardians, and the craftsmen, or technical class). The primary virtues (wisdom, courage, and temperance), the realized harmony of which promoted the quality of justice in the soul and in the state, were the means and the end of the successful application of the principles of functional specialization.

Plato did not invent these principles, nor did the *physiologoi* who preceded him. They existed in embryonic form in Homer who characterized the human personality in terms of *psyche*, *noos*, and *thymos* construed as organs of "life, perception, and of (e)motion."[15] We have already encountered these notions in even more primitive form in the cosmogonic myths that ground our cultural sensibility. These principles, which Plato "writ large" in his ideal society, have a long history in the philosophic development of Western thought. They are reflected in Aristotle's organization of the cultural disciplines into theoretical, practical, and productive enterprises; in the Alexandrian and Augustinian contributions to the development of the concept of the Christian Trinity as an organization of Logos, Will, and Spirit; in the speculations concerning the importance of justice, power, and love (themselves reflections of the Trinitarian elements) as principles of social and interpersonal relations, and in countless other forms and fashions throughout the history of our intellectual culture.

The analogy between the psyche and the polis has been determinative of much of our classical social and political understandings. Reason, will, emotion may be shown to be instances of conventional constural and represent, therefore, not reflections of cosmic order but agents for the creation of taxonomic structures. Order, as we come to know of it in our Anglo-European political tradition, is not cosmos but *taxis*, that is, not the natural and spontaneous order of nature per se but the artificial order born of instrumental acts of construal. And if, as our dominant cosmogonic myths suggest, each of the psychic dynamisms is an agency of construal then there is no recourse beyond the principle of power as long as we remain within our classical heritage. The critique of governmental power always involves a critique of the psyche which, writ large, forms the model for society and the state. But a critique of the psyche is a critique of the cosmological principles involved in the very meaning of cosmos per se. As long as theorists stop short of a metaphysical or cosmological analysis, we can expect that there will be no philosophic vision relevant to the interpretation of the realm of praxis which does not employ the same family of assumptions that have occasioned the defects of theory per se.

The vision I have been developing in these pages does not presuppose the meanings of reason, appetite, and will associated with the traditional interpretations of psychic functioning. The sort of theory I am discussing begins with a metaphysical and cosmological analysis grounded in first-problematic thinking. This provides the basis for a critique of the sphere of praxis which takes into account the possibility of forms of social order grounded in a novel concept of psychic order which is in turn based upon novel understandings of the meaning of order from the ontological and cosmological perspectives.

The failure of Anglo-European theorists to develop a realistic alternative to classical social theory results from the appeal to rational principles as external determining sources of order. We cannot purify the will or the emotions any more than the reason. The difficulty is not to be found in the misuse of these psychic functions but in the manner in which they operate in the construction of theories. These principles of personality structure, as well as the pedagogic principles which were meant to educate the individual into a condition of psychic and social harmony, are cosmetic expedients which establish relationships to the world, not as it is, but as it has been construed.

The challenge to utopian speculation in our tradition should now be clear. Thinking, acting, and feeling, as means whereby we come to recognize our humanness and the humanness of our world, are instruments for the overcoming of Chaos. The almost universal acceptance of reasonings and moral praxis as means of establishing social order is, thus, tantamount to the affirmation of the primacy of disorder, of negative Chaos. The suspicion of utopian speculation, like the suspicion of any overly idealistic theory, is grounded in the intuition of the origins of the world in the agonal relation to Chaos. It is this Chaos which sets the limits to the possibilities of human nature as the model for social order and harmony.

The problem with every principled attempt to establish a model for cosmological or social order is that it is, purely and simply stated, *ar-*

bitrary. Though we have a general consensus in our culture that "in the beginning was Chaos," we certainly lack any agreement as to the proper principles which we ought employ to bring order out of our chaotic beginnings. If there is any doubt about this fact a brief reflection upon the relativity of theory and praxis in contemporary culture would most certainly allay it. There are simply no truly authoritative principles. And without a sense of authoritativeness we find it necessary to resort to persuasion to enforce our sense of the correctness of principles. Failing that, it is necessary to impose these principles by recourse to the irrationalities of power. Utopists cannot resort to the arbitrary use of power without falling into some unacceptable form of determinism. And the argument for principles involves educative activities which cannot but seem arbitrary to the extent that the principles are not intuitively shared. Such intuitive sharing of principles has never been possible in our culture heretofore. What we share is the sense of primordial Chaos, not the sense of principled order.

To the extent utopian speculation shares the same theoretical problematic as classical theory it cannot be radical enough to perform the necessary critique of traditional forms of philosophic understanding. For the acceptance of this fundamental cultural problematic entails the acceptance of the fragility of reasonings and the moral sense and the artificiality of principles as determining sources of order. Laid bare our philosophic visions are so many desperate attempts to build dams against the dark, formless waters of primal Chaos. Sanguine philosophers continue to apply, layer upon layer, an ever thicker veneer over the complexities and incongruities to which, as Children of Chaos, we are held subject.

As long as philosophic speculation assumes the priority of negative Chaos it cannot function as a radically positive lure toward true understanding. We must employ an alternative problematic for philosophic theory if we are to provide the kind of models for individual existence which one might call "utopian" in the best sense. If it is to provide a real alternative to classical theory, utopian thinking must deny altogether the necessity of principles as external determining sources of order. That is to say, utopian speculation must be radically an-archic. The key to the necessary philosophic revisioning is to be found in a radical interpretation of the notion of creativity.

Our distinctive rendering of creativity requires that we move beyond the rational understanding of the concept as well as beyond the presumption that volitional and affective modes of creativity are in any sense fundamental. The semantic contexts upon which Anglo-European philosophic understandings depend make it extremely difficult, if not impossible, to develop a notion of creativity which does not require articulation in terms of acts of construal patterned by otherness, dependence, and extrinsic relations. Another way of saying this is that traditional resources of philosophic reflection in so-called Western culture challenge the metaphysical ultimacy of the notion of creativity, leading to its interpretation in terms of the power of volitional action, the power of rationality, or the power of appetition.

Part of the genius of A. N. Whitehead is expressed in his challenge to the ultimacy of the volitional characterizations of creativity in Anglo-European metaphysics. By grounding novelty and harmony in a hierarchical ordering of atemporal forms, Whitehead provided an alternative to the conception of the world as dependent upon a unilateral exercise of volition. In so doing he traveled far toward the notion of creativity as *reflexive*. In this way he provided the beginnings of a defense of the metaphysical ultimacy of self-creativity. This aspect of Whitehead's thinking constitutes a lasting contribution to the articulation of the concept of creation. However, a coherent and consistent rendering of the meaning of creativity as fundamentally reflexive demands a step beyond Whitehead.

By promoting the notion of "God" as the preeminent source of the lure toward novelty, order, and harmony, as well as the preeminent source of their realization, even Whitehead challenges the metaphysical ultimacy of creativity in the sense that rationality and intelligibility are given systematic priority through the affirmation of a primordial order of atemporal forms of definiteness. A realm of preexistent forms of definiteness, housed in a preeminent source of order, harmony, and novelty, quite obviously challenges the parity of creative actions.

The theorial intuition, upon which the most direct understanding of creativity may be based, is the sense of a primordial harmony illustrating the self-creative activities of each item of the totality in accordance with its insistent particularity. This intuition inverts the priorities of traditional metaphysics and cosmology. On this view the primary mystery is not how things hang together in an ordered fashion, but rather why things sometimes fall apart. This vision does not hold the problematic which occasions philosophic speculations to be the question of the source of order, as is the case with almost all thinkers grounded in Hebraic and Hellenic concepts of Chaos and Creativity. The problem is the source(s) of *dis*order! There is no necessity for recourse to an initial or primary instance of creativity functioning as Cosmic Coordinator since the intuition of Chaos is an intuition of a primal harmony which is both spontaneous and ordered. That this is diametrically opposed to the intuitions of Chaos as "dark, formless Void," or "yawning gap," or "confusion and disorder," goes a long way toward explaining the contrast between first- and second-problematic philosophies.

For novelty to be protected within a philosophic vision, something like *creatio ex nihilo* is required. Appeal to preexistent forms as grounds for novelty clearly challenges any meaningful sense of novelty. The sources of novelty in the natural world are the self-creative centers of experiencing which are the final real things. Each center emerges *ex nihilo*. There can be no ultimate metaphysical separation of the active and passive dimensions of creativity. The fact that they have been experientially and epistemologically separated in all too many instances provides one basis for a meaningful account of the acknowledged disharmonies in experiencing.

Order and harmony in this actual world at a given moment, in contrast with the givenness of the harmony of Becoming-Itself, is the result of deferential acts grounded in the reciprocal interfusion of finite centers of experience. The metaphysical determinateness of each item is a consequence of this deferential activity. Novelty is to be understood in terms of the uniquely centered character of each item of experience with respect to this actual world and to Chaos. One ought not feel the need to appeal to a Creator God in order to articulate further one's sense of the order and harmony of the world, for to do so would be to lose the meaningfulness of creativity. One is forced to choose between the primacy of creativity or the primacy of rules of systematic order.

The concept of "power" characterizes the intuition of the primacy of system and principles of order. *Creatio ex nihilo* in its classical meaning is, thus, the fundamental ground of power relations. This may easily be seen by reflecting upon the source of our understandings of *creatio ex nihilo* in the Genesis myth. Creation by fiat is a consequence of an act of Primordial Will. If there is to be a sound defense of the ultimacy of creativity in contradistinction from the notion of power, it is necessary that we find some means of clarifying the relations of these two notions. We discover that means in the distinction, already rehearsed, between "otherness" and "emptiness." That distinction, as it is relevant to our present concerns, is characterizable as that between *dualism* and *polarity*.

The notion of power, expressed in its most uncompromising form, connotes *determination*. To say that something is determinate is to state that its fundamental character is to be construed in terms of something other. A is determinate with respect to B if the essential meaning of A requires reference to B. To the extent that such reference is required, it must be said that B determines A. The paradigm case of determination is found in *ex nihilo* doctrines which claim that in the creative act God determines the character of the World while remaining metaphysically indeterminate with respect to his creation.[16] On this view God may be said to be determinate only with respect to himself.

I believe that we find in this understanding of determination the bases for the contrast of the concepts of power and creativity. Beginning with the notion of determination entails beginning with power as metaphysically ultimate. If one employs the notion of creativity, then, in the instance of the relations of God to the World cited above, one may say that only God creates. Ontic forms of creativity are dependent upon God as the primordial instance of creativity. If one wishes to extend the notion of determinateness to God Himself, one may say that God, as self-determinate, is self-creative. If, however, one begins with the notion of creativity as fundamental, it is necessary to find that the concept of self-creativity is not to be limited to a single instance or set of instances. It is essential that the things of the world be essentially self-determinate. Ubiquity of self-determination ensures both that the notion of Creativity is metaphysically ultimate and that the world is real in more than a Pickwickian sense.

Belief in the ubiquity of self-determination entails acceptance of relations of polarity as more fundamental than dualistic relations. What this means is that reflexive creativity always involves a parity of determination. The means whereby one may make sense of this parity is to say that each item in the universe both determines and is determined by every other item. The Buddhist philosophies express such mutual determinations in terms of the notion of codependent origination. Each item in the totality of things is self-determinate and, therefore, self-creative.

Taoist philosophy characterizes this notion of self-creativity in a slightly different manner. Taoist forms of naturalism have led less to a concern for the explication of the meaning and consequence of the emptiness of the theorial realm and more toward the (ironic, to be sure) characterization of the nameable realm of praxis. At this level, each item of experience is claimed to be self-creative in accordance with the balanced polarities of yin and yang. Yin, the creative source, and yang, the creative action, are mutually conditioned. Whatever may be named, that is, whatever is subject to articulation, must be considered to possess both yin and yang components. Yin is not a power which determines yang, nor does yang determine yin. Yang is always yang-proceeding-toward-yin, and yin is yin-proceeding-toward-yang. Light is becoming-darkness and darkness is becoming-light.

The demand for metaphysical and epistemological complementarity in Taoist and Buddhist philosophies is a rigorous demand. Anglo-European metaphysics, with its greater concern for rational articulation, has been led from the epistemological dualism expressed in its articulations of the creative act into the presumption of a metaphysical dualism which has served as both cause and consequence of the undue emphasis placed upon the notion of power as determination.

The proponents of *creatio ex nihilo* as a singular act in terms of which all things were brought into being find it extremely difficult to distinguish the concept of creativity from that of power. In traditional *creatio ex nihilo* doctrines it seems clear that the creative act is the paradigm instance of the exercise of power since it results in the unilateral determination of the created order. It is not, in principle, necessary to distinguish between power and creativity at the cosmological level, and the fact that the proponent of *creatio ex nihilo* may find it impossible to do so would not in itself count against his vision of things. However, if on the other grounds it is necessary to distinguish between power and creativity, or to construe the meaning of power in terms of that of creativity, then the traditional understanding of *creatio ex nihilo* is rendered less plausible.

Obviously, the great difficulty for the radical view of creativity is to account for the apparent interconnectedness of things given the fact that each event is self-creative. It is the polar character of each event that establishes the ground for such an explanation. For the notion of creativity to make any sense at all it must be understood as self-creativity in the sense of a passive-active polarity. But in order meaningfully to assert the possibility of an indefinite number of self-creative events, self-creativity must be interpreted as cocreativity. This may be done only if the polar character of each event is seen as the paradigm instance of the relations among events. To claim that events may be cocreative is but to say that the primary basis of relationships among entities is that of deference.

To the extent that we seek to be rational and moral beings we do so because the beings we seem to be wish to maintain those orders which sustain us. The larger issue, of course, is whether we are fundamentally the sort of beings we seem to be. The universe is a vast complication; were it not so it would be meaningless, and there would, of course, be no complicated beings such as we humans are to know this to be so. The (vain)glorious science of metaphysics is possible because the cosmological determinations of our being so constitute us as to permit our manageably finite perspective to provide us relative access to the character of things. We, of course, have little by way of access to the world which is not directly and immediately determined by the type of envisionment of it disciplined by the sort of beings we presume ourselves to be. But we are not, most fundamentally, *sorts* of beings; we are insistently particular beings. We are not real because we approximate norms or ideals, but solely by virtue of being the beings we in fact are.

The moral and rational world conditioned by the desire to maintain the *sort* of beings we are is implicated in the experiences of aesthetic and mystical enjoyments which significantly qualify the ease with which we assent to the fundamental character of ideals and norms. The artist Max Beckmann painted on flat, framed canvas in order, he said, to defend himself against the infinity of space. May we not suspect that as rational beings we think in categories, framed by the demands of consistency and coherence, in order to escape nightmares occasioned by what for us are even more dread infinities?

The contrast between principled and unprincipled sensibilities is fundamentally a contrast between two intuitions of the character of things. The one is based upon creativity, the other upon power. The one construes the notion of power in terms of the more fundamental notion of creativity, the other does the reverse. Whereas the intuition of power explains how things become determinate by virtue of the actions of something transcendent, creativity explains determinate being always by appeal to the notion of self-determination. Power is a dualistic concept requiring something over against which one can exercise influence. Creativity is always reflexive and polar. It is essentially, self-creativity. Power relations are characterized by otherness, dependence, and extrinsic relationships. Creativity is expressed through mutuality, deference, and intrinsic relationships. Power is expressed through rational, volitional, or passional acts of construal; creativity is expressed through acts of deference grounded in the spontaneous recognition of the possibilities promoting mutual harmony. Creativity requires something like ontological parity if it is to function as a criterion of description and explanation; power requires a hierarchy of ruler and ruled, conditioner and conditioned, creator and created, being and nonbeing.

The presumption that creativity is a kind of power and that power qualifies the character of the interrelations of things leads to the understanding of social relations in terms of agency and passivity. There are *doers* and those *done to*. Human interactions, then, are acts of construing and being construed. But the view that human beings may serve as efficient causes, or the effects of such causes is "ruled out" by unprincipled forms of social interaction. Unprincipled knowing, nonassertive action, and objectless desire form an ironically inverted psyche which permits the noninstrumental entertainment of nature and society. The knowledge of the insistent particularity of things does not allow the imposition of forms of organization as the basis of understanding. True understanding presupposes deference to the intrinsic excellence of the "object" of one's knowledge. This knowledge is the ground and goal of actions performed in accordance with the particularities comprising one's ambience. Such action does not itself lead to the imposition of a form of behavior, but is based upon cooperation with that behavior emergent from the self-creative activity of others. Objectless desire, the unprincipled form of appetition, permits enjoyment without attachment, that kind of feeling in and through another which does not depend upon objectification and need not occasion the desire to manipulate, dominate, or control. Such detached emotion is the ground of deference and mutuality which, when combined with unprincipled knowledge and action, maximizes the possibility of harmonious relationships.

* * *

We have, at last, come full circle. At the beginning of this essay we attempted to demonstrate the pernicious consequences of the narrow dependence upon rational and moral understandings in the construction of a philosophic vision. We close by celebrating the perhaps disquieting consequences of the unmediated recourse to aesthetic and mystical forms of experience. In so doing we have encountered a speculative context ultimately beyond the reach of rational and moral injunctions. But that the realm of ontological particulars transcends the strictures of reason and the moral sense does not preclude the fact that the world of praxis is "enjoined" by the ontological sphere. There is a peculiar kind of relevance associated with the ontological vision of the ironist. Were we to look at the sphere of public praxis through ironic eyes we would not be forced to see our societies as fragmented parodies of some normative system of aims and values defining the way the world *ought* to be. Our contemporary social realms may best be seen (no pun intended!) as "mosaic" societies in which the fragments of existence each make essential contributions to the social world. Experienced as a positive chaos, such a world is necessarily fragmented and allusory, each item in it reflecting and giving meaning to every other, with no single point of view providing an ultimate focus of significance. So envisioned, the realm of social praxis is primarily an individualized, privatized sphere in which each individual possesses an intrinsic, inalienable excellence.

If we could see our world in these terms, there would be no need to take it seriously. Since there is no Supreme *Archē* as source of meaning and value, there is no need to set the world right. There is no "far-off Divine event toward which all creation moves." Unlike the attitude of moral seriousness, the sensibility which the ironist proposes we substitute for it is such as to maintain and to ramify the tensions and contradictions that exist at the very heart of our experience of the world.

Unless we can free ourselves from the bias that forces us to conceive the Cosmos as a single-ordered world which it is our responsibility to recreate in social and political dimensions, we shall surely not escape the temptation to exploit the instrumental power born of our narrow and perverse anthropocentrism for totalitarian ends. Taking the world too seriously will lead us to despair of the relativity of action, thought, and circumstance which gives our present societies such a disordered cast. If we do despair we shall be seduced into believing that *any* order is better than negative Chaos, the only alternative to posited order the serious-minded can envision.

It is doubtless true, as the poet proclaims, that

> Life, like a dome of many-colored glass
> Stains the white radiance of eternity.

But it is among the many things that we perforce must dwell. And though we participate in the staining of eternity simply by virtue of our finitude, it is the variety of colors appreciated through our fragmented awareness, the gift of the infinite to the finite beings we are, that enriches us and justifies our humanness. The truth that philosophy finally contains is of the many-colored vision that prevents us from falsely claiming easy access to the white radiance of eternity.

In a rare ironic mood, Alfred North Whitehead warned against narrowness in the selection of philosophic evidences. "Philosophy," he said, "may not neglect the multifariousness of the world—the fairies dance, and Christ is nailed to the cross."[17] Were we finally to realize a vision so wide as to permit us to revel with the fairies at the foot of the cross, what, we may wonder, would its rational and moral consequences be?

NOTES

Prelude: What Anarchy Isn't

1. See *Metaphysics*, Book V, ch. I.

Chapter One: The Cultural Sensorium

1. *Art as Experience* (New York: Capricorn Books, 1958), p. 22. In his somewhat cranky set of philosophic *retractiones*, published with Arthur F. Bentley under the title *Knowing and the Known* (Boston: Beacon Press, 1944), Dewey insisted upon the term "transaction," denoting "the knowing-known taken as one process," in place of the term "interaction" he had employed earlier. In so doing he was trying to avoid confusion between the concepts of knowing processes which allow for certain independence of knower and known and those which do not. But as may be easily seen from the definition of experience just cited, Dewey was already quite clear with regard to that distinction before he altered his terminology. For interaction "carried to the full" becomes participation and communication and is thus expressive of mutuality rather than mere "in-betweenness." Mutuality prevails when, as we have said, the environment of a sophisticated organism is itself equally sophisticated. Human societies are therefore transactional, and the unit of social analysis is not the isolated individual but the transactional system patterned by the most sophisticated forms of mutuality. In their simpler forms transactional systems may be designated primarily in terms of personal interactions; at the most complex level we may most conveniently understand the notion of the transactional system to approximate our more traditional understanding of "culture."
2. Ibid.
3. I have discussed the philosophic basis for this theory of cultural interests in much greater detail in my *The Civilization of Experience* (New York: Fordham University Press, 1973), pp. 112–135.
4. A more complete understanding of the role of history in a general theory of

culture may be gleaned from my *The Uncertain Phoenix* (New York: Fordham University Press, 1982). My use of historical evidences is similar to that contained in works such as Barbara Tuchman's *A Distant Mirror: The Calamitous Fourteenth Century* (New York: Alfred A. Knopf, 1978) and Carl Schorske's *Fin-De-Siècle Vienna: Politics and Culture* (New York: Alfred A. Knopf, 1980). In each of these works there is an attempt to highlight the relevance for our contemporary cultural self-understanding of certain periods of cultural crisis in the past. History as a repository of models of cultural experience is a distinctly synchronic enterprise, and the use of history as a means of providing that sort of aesthetic distance permitting a more objective appraisal of one's own experience by reflection upon analogous experience is certainly a legitimate practice of the philosopher of culture.

5. The quotation is from Heraclitus. See Philip Wheelwright, ed., *The Presocratics* (New York: Odyssey Press, 1966), Fragment 315, p. 70.

6. G. M. A. Grube, trans., *Plato's Republic* (Indianapolis: Hackett, 1974), 572b–c, p. 220.

7. Ibid., 576b, p. 224.

8. *Parts of Animals: On the Memory*, ch. 1, 449a–450b.

9. See Norman Kemp Smith, trans., *Immanuel Kant's Critique of Pure Reason* (New York: St. Martin's Press, 1961), A124, p. 146.

10. Trans. Reginald Snell (New York: Frederick Ungar, 1965).

11. See S. T. Coleridge, *Biographia Literaria* (New York: E. P. Dutton, 1965), ch. 13, esp. p. 167.

12. See Whitehead's *Process and Reality* (New York: Macmillan, 1929), pp. 395–428.

13. *The Psychology of the Imagination*, trans. Bernard Frechtman (Secaucus, N.Y.: Citadel Press, 1972), p. 273.

14. The term is, of course, A. O. Lovejoy's. See *The Great Chain of Being* (New York: Harper & Row, 1960), passim.

15. *The Philosophy of Modern Art* (New York: World Library, 1967), p. 63.

16. Ibid., p. 64.

17. Recently, a philosopher friend and I had occasion to visit New York's Museum of Modern Art. Because of a pressing schedule, we were forced to limit our tour to about half an hour. What does one do with thirty minutes at the Museum of Modern Art? The rule that comes to mind is, "Run, don't walk, to the nearest *objet d'art*." In following that rule we had little time to discuss the paintings or sculpture or to compare one with the other, or to note the technical innovations of this or that avant artist. We only had time to enjoy the art. Frenetic bees, skating fast, we deferred to encountered excellences. For a brief period after the visit my perceptions altered. Outside the museum I was struck by the world in the just-so-ness of its details. Things not only in themselves but for themselves, challenged old, inertial, perceptual patterns, offered themselves to me in their differential excellences, invited my ecstasy. It didn't last. It never does. But the insight remaining after that and similar experiences is obvious: if my experience is at all generalizable to that of others, the strictly aesthetic experience of art may be the exception rather than the rule. We may in fact be so accustomed to applying extraneous thematic or technical criteria to our experiences of art that it takes an unusual situation such as being forced to race through a museum to shake us from our dogmatic stupor.

18. "Supplementary Essay" (*Poems, 1815*), in W. M. Merchant, ed., *Words-*

worth: Poetry and Prose (Cambridge: Harvard University Press, 1970), p. 277.

19. *Science and the Modern World* (New York: Free Press, 1967), p. 94.

20. This is Becker's postulate. Its status in modal logic depends, of course, upon the specific semantic system employed.

21. See Charles Hartshorne, *The Logic of Perfection* (Lasalle, Ill.: Open Court, 1962) for a complete explication of this form of the ontological argument.

22. See William Rowe's account of this argument in his *Philosophy of Religion* (Encino, Calif.: Dickinson, 1978), pp. 16–29.

23. Claiming that mystical religion constitutes the "purest strain of religious sensibility" cannot but disconcert many who would wish to insist upon the viability of non-mystical religions. But from the standpoint of this work, non-mystical religions must be interpreted as consequences of permitting strictly moral and rational interests to influence unduly the religious sensibility. Of course, I do not mean to settle the issue simply by fiat. In Chapter Six I have provided what I believe to be a plausible defense of the priority of mystical religion.

Chapter Two: Utopia and Utility

1. See Owen Barfield's *Saving the Appearances: A Study in Idolatry* (New York: Harcourt, Brace & World, n.d.). See also, Colin Turbayne, *The Myth of Metaphor* (Columbia: University of South Carolina Press, 1971) for an extremely insightful discussion of the tension between what I am calling the theoretical and theorial approaches to understanding. This is best illustrated in Turbayne's consideration of the career of Descartes's mechanistic interpretation of nature, pp. 34–40.

2. Barfield, pp. 50–51.

3. See my discussion of David Bohm's cosmology in Chapter 4. Bohm has provided the basis of a participative theory of the micro- and macrocosms.

4. The most important conclusions relative to this revisioning are to be found in the final chapter of this essay, "Eros Descending."

5. See Plato's *Seventh Letter*, trans. L. A. Post, in Edith Hamilton and Huntington Cairns, eds., *The Collected Dialogues of Plato* (Princeton: Princeton University Press, 1961), 341d, p. 1589. I am aware that there are still those few who would deny the authenticity of this letter. But such denials are almost always based upon a prior philosophical interpretation of Platonic thought which holds any mystical inclinations highly suspect. As my understanding of Plato leads me to be quite sympathetic toward such inclinations, I find the *Seventh Letter* eminently Platonic.

6. Ibid., 343a.

7. Ibid., 344b.

8. Ibid., trans. Hugh Treddennick, 99b–d, p. 80.

9. Ibid., trans. R. Hackforth, 28d–e, p. 1106.

10. *Timaeus*, ibid., trans. Benjamin Jowett, 31b, p. 1163.

11. See Gregory Vlastos, *Plato's Universe* (Seattle: University of Washington Press, 1975), pp. 23–25.

12. See Chapter 4.

13. For example, in *The Collected Dialogues*, see *Symposium*, 177d, p. 532, and *Lysis*, 204c, p. 146.

14. See Emerson's essay, "Plato" in Lewis Mumford, ed., *Ralph Waldo*

Emerson: *Essays and Journals* (Garden City, N.Y.: International Collectors Library, 1968), p. 589.

15. In *The Collected Dialogues*, see *The Republic*, Book VI, 499c–d, p. 735.

16. It is significant that Sören Kierkegaard, in his pseudonymic works, provides the best illustrations since Plato of the use of such a "supplemental conscience." For it is Kierkegaard who possessed perhaps the profoundest understanding of Socratic and Platonic irony.

17. *The Open Society and Its Enemies*, vol. 1, *The Spell of Plato* (New York: Harper & Row, 1962), pp. 164–165.

18. Ibid., vol. 2, *The High Tide of Prophecy: Hegel, Marx, and the Aftermath*, p. 245.

19. See ibid., pp. 231f.

20. In *The Collected Dialogues*, see *Laws*, 685a, p. 1280, and *Timaeus*, 59c–d, pp. 1184–1185. In this connection see Paul Friedländer's discussion of Plato's attitudes toward written philosophy in *Plato: An Introduction* (New York: Harper & Row, 1958), pp.108–125.

21. Cf. ibid., pp. 77–84.

Chapter Three: The Myth of Consensus

1. See Charles Norris Cochrane, *Christianity and Classical Culture* (New York: Oxford University Press, 1957), p. 113, note 1.

2. Norman Kemp Smith, trans., *Immanuel Kant's Critique of Pure Reason* (New York: St. Martin's Press, 1961), A852, B880.

3. Ibid., A856, B884.

4. Ibid., A838, B866.

5. Ibid., A839, B867.

6. Michael Murray, ed., *Heidegger and Modern Philosophy* (New Haven: Yale University Press, 1978), p. 80.

7. From "Lecture on Ethics," p. 5. See ibid.

8. *Tractatus Logico-Philosophicus* (New York: Humanities Press, 1961), 6.44, p. 148.

9. *Philosophical Investigations* (New York: Macmillan, 1953), Part I, Paragraphs 36–47 (pp. 18–23) and passim.

10. *A Companion to Wittgenstein's "Philosophical Investigations"* (Ithaca, N.Y.: Cornell University Press, 1977), p. 24.

11. Quoted in ibid., p. 25.

12. Ibid., p. 26.

13. Ibid., p. 427.

14. *Tractatus*, 7, p. 150.

15. *An Introduction to Metaphysics* (New York: Doubleday, 1961), pp. 31, 42.

16. Hannah Arendt, *Heidegger and Modern Philosophy*, p. 303.

17. Ibid., p. 306

18. *Introduction to Metaphysics*, p. 31.

19. Heidegger's analysis was hardly unique or esoteric. José Ortega y Gasset anticipated Heidegger's discussion of the problem of political hegemony. In his justly famous *Revolt of the Masses*, published in Spain in 1930 (five years before *Introduction to Metaphysics*), Ortega provided an analysis of which Heidegger's is the reflection.

20. Hannah Arendt, *Heidegger and Modern Philosophy*, p. 303.

21. Though Heidegger has obviously the greater philosophic prestige, the French pessimist par excellence, Jacques Ellul, has provided the most widely read and influential work on technology, namely, *The Technological Society*, trans. John Wilkinson (New York: Alfred A. Knopf, 1964).

22. In *Heidegger and Modern Philosophy*, pp. 304–328.

23. "The Age of the World Picture," in *The Question Concerning Technology and Other Essays*, trans. William Lovitt (New York: Harper & Row, 1977), p. 153.

24. *The Revolt of the Masses* (New York: W. W. Norton, 1932), ch. 20.

25. *Religious Affections*, ed. John Smith (New Haven: Yale University Press, 1959), p. 273.

26. *The Collected Works of Charles Saunders Peirce*, vol. 1, ed. Charles Hartshorne and Paul Weiss (Cambridge: Harvard University Press, 1965), 1.611, p. 273.

27. Vol. 2 (New York: Dover 1950), p. 672.

28. Ibid.

29. *Art as Experience* (New York: Capricorn Books, 1958), pp. 38, 39.

30. *The Quest for Certainty* (New York: Capricorn Books, 1960), p. 312.

31. Ibid., p. 313.

32. See *Experience and Nature* (New York: Dover, 1958), pp. 106–108.

33. *Adventures of Ideas* (New York: Macmillan, 1933), p. 367.

34. *Process and Reality* (New York: Macmillan, 1929), p. 13.

35. Ibid., pp. 395–396.

36. *Modes of Thought* (New York: Capricorn Books, 1938), p. 11.

37. *Philosophy and the Mirror of Nature* (Princeton: Princeton University Press, 1979), p. 370.

38. Ibid., p. 367.

39. Ibid., pp. 369–370.

40. Ibid., p. 377.

41. For Rorty's principal assessment of Whitehead's philosophic significance, see his "The Subjectivist Principle and the Linguistic Turn," in *Alfred North Whitehead: Essays on His Philosophy*, ed. George Kline (Englewood Cliffs, N.J.: Prentice-Hall, 1963).

42. See p. 313.

43. See *The Philosophy of Alfred North Whitehead*, ed. Paul Schilpp (New York: Tudor, 1941), p. 664.

Chapter Four: The Ambiguity of Order

1. For a discussion of the many-worlds vision as found in classical Taoism and Buddhism, see my *The Uncertain Phoenix* (New York: Fordham University Press, 1982), ch. 5, "The Way Beyond 'Ways.' "

2. Philip Wheelwright, ed., *The Presocratics* (New York: Odyssey Press, 1966), p. 182.

3. Ibid.

4. See *On The Heavens*, Book III, chs. 4–6.

5. See *Opticks*, Book III, Part I (London: G. Bell & Sons, 1931), p. 403.

6. *The Essays*, trans. Charles Cotton, Book II, 12. The Great Books of the Western World, vol. 25 (Chicago: Encyclopaedia Britannica, 1954), p. 252.

7. Montaigne's irony, coupled with his benign misanthropy, makes of him a

spiritual member of that band of Taoist sages living almost two millennia before him. The sense of existential parity afforded all things by the early Taoists is a paradigm instance of first-problematic thinking. The immanental naturalism of Chuang-tzu, for example, led him to deny the existence of a single-ordered world and to affirm Chaos (*hun-tun*) as the nonintegral source of a plurality of orders.

8. A. O. Lovejoy, *The Great Chain of Being* (New York: Harper & Row, 1960), p. 52.

9. The term "acosmism" is somewhat ambiguous. I should make clear that by the concept I mean simply the denial that there is a single-ordered world.

10. See Lovejoy, p. 141. The quote is from *Allgemeine Naturgeschicte un theorie des Himmels* (1755).

11. Ibid., pp. 320f.

12. Ibid., p. 332.

13. D. W. Sciama, "Evolutionary Process in Cosmology," in Milton K. Munitz, ed., *Theories of the Universe: From Babylonian Myth to Modern Science* (New York: Free Press, 1957), pp. 413–418.

14. See C. S. Peire, "Uniformity," in Justus Buchler, ed., *Philosophical Writings of Peirce* (New York: Dover, 1955), pp. 218–227 for a discussion of this notion.

15. Ibid., p. 226.

16. Ibid., p. 227.

17. Ibid.

18. "Funes the Memorious," in *A Personal Anthology* (New York: Grove Press, 1967), p. 43.

19. Ibid, p. 41.

20. For a discussion of the relations of selective and formal abstraction, see my *The Civilization of Experience* (New York: Fordham University Press, 1973), pp. 118–119.

21. H. E. Huntly, *The Divine Proportion* (New York: Dover, 1970), p. 70.

22. A. N. Whitehead, *Modes of Thought* (New York: Capricorn Books, 1938), p. 82.

23. This argument underlies Whitehead's discussions of the relevance of the Second Law to the understanding of natural processes in *The Function of Reason* (Boston: Beacon Press, 1958) (q.v.), and is most intelligently elaborated (independently of Whitehead) in Rudolph Arnheim's *Entropy and Art: An Essay on Order and Disorder* (Berkeley: University of California Press, 1971). A consequence of this argument is that if we attempt to maintain a univocal concept of order it is essential that the notion of entropy must, according to context, be contrasted sometimes with order, sometimes with disorder.

My discussion of the "logical" and "aesthetic' interpretations of order is similar to the type of analysis given in Whitehead's *Modes of Thought*, ch. 3, "Understanding." However, Whitehead's general metaphysical vision requires him to stress the significance of the logical pole of orderedness in a manner that I have not found necessary, or congenial.

24. See *Process and Reality* (New York: Macmillan, 1929), passim.

25. See Karl Popper and John Eccles, *The Self and Its Brain* (New York: Springer International, 1977), passim.

26. *Adventures of Ideas* (New York: Macmillan, 1933), p. 293.

27. *Wholeness and the Implicate Order* (London: Routledge & Kegan Paul, 1980), p. 149.

28. See *Languages of the Brain* (New York: Brooks/Cole, 1977). For a popular account of Pribram's researches in this area, see "Holographic Memory" in *Psychology Today*, February 1979, pp. 71–84.

29. *Wholeness*, p. 151.

30. *The Journal of Philosophy*, November 1972, pp. 649–650.

31. "The One and the Many," in *Pragmatism* (New York: World, 1955), p. 105.

32. Ibid.

33. "The World Well Lost," p. 663.

34. "Two Dogmas of Empiricism," in *From a Logical Point of View* (New York: Harper & Row, 1963), p. 46.

35. Ibid., p. 42.

36. Ibid., p. 43.

37. See, for example, M. J. Cresswell's essay, "Can Epistemology Be Naturalized?" in Robert Shahan and Chris Swoyer, eds., *Essays on the Philosophy of W. V. Quine* (Norman: University of Oklahoma Press, 1979), esp. pp. 113–14.

38. "Philosophy and the Scientific Image of Man," in *Science, Perception and Reality* (New York: Humanities Press, 1963), p. 40. For a discussion of the various forms of "the myth of the given," see "Empiricism and the Philosophy of Mind," in ibid., pp. 127–196. Sellars need not be interpreted as eschewing givenness in all its forms. He is primarily opposed to the presumption that there is a *finally* given. See "Scientific Realism or Irenic Instrumentalism," in *Philosophical Perspectives* (Springfield, Ill.: Charles C. Thomas, 1967), p. 353.

39. "Philosophy and the Scientific Image of Man," p. 1.

40. See William James, *The Will to Believe* (New York: Dover, 1956), p. 118.

41. See *The Principles of Psychology*, vol. 2 (New York: Dover, 1950), pp. 283–324.

42. *Ways of Worldmaking* (Indianapolis: Hackett, 1978), p. 4.

43. Ibid., p. 6.

44. *Languages of Art* (Indianapolis: Bobbs Merrill, 1968), p. 6, note 4.

45. *Worldmaking*, p. 5.

Chapter Five: The Metaphoric Muse

1. *The Tragic Sense of Life*, trans. J. E. Crawford Flitch (New York: Dover, 1954), p. 17.

2. I have myself provided such a critique in *The Uncertain Phoenix* (New York: Fordham University Press, 1982).

3. See *World Hypotheses* (Berkeley: University of California Press, 1966).

4. "The Root Metaphor Theory of Metaphysics" in Warren Shibles, ed., *Essays on Metaphor* (Whitewater, Wisc.: Language Press, 1972), p. 15.

5. Ibid., p. 24.

6. Ibid.

7. See *Atomic Theory and the Description of Nature* (Cambridge: Cambridge University Press, 1934, p. 96.

8. See Ian Barbour, *Myths, Models and Paradigms: A Comparative Study in Science and Religion* (New York: Harper & Row, 1974), pp. 77–78.

9. W. V. Quine, *From a Logical Point of View* (New York: Harper & Row, 1963), p. 41.

10. The term is W. V. Quine's.

11. Bohm has attempted to develop such a view in *Wholeness and the Implicate Order* (London: Routledge & Kegan Paul, 1980). Paradoxically, of course, his theory of implicate and explicate orders is, in effect, a theoretical defense of metaphysical complementarity.

12. The phrase belongs, I believe, to Jorge Luis Borges.

13. This distinction is employed by Philip Wheelwright in his *The Burning Fountain: Studies in the Language of Symbolism* (Bloomington: Indiana University Press, 1954), passim. I am using the terms "mystical" and "mysterious" with slightly different meanings than Wheelwright, though I believe my understanding is not incompatible with his on this issue.

14. See David Tracy's "Metaphor and Religion: The Test Case of Christian Texts," in Sheldon Sacks, ed., *On Metaphor* (Chicago: University of Chicago Press, 1979), pp. 89–104 for a discussion of the instrumental function of religious metaphor.

15. *The Complete Writings of Chuang Tzu*, trans. Burton Watson (New York: Columbia University Press, 1968), p. 39.

16. Ibid., p. 40.

17. Ibid.

18. Ibid.

19. See Joseph Rychlak, *A Philosophy of Science for Personality Theory* (Boston: Houghton Mifflin, 1968) for a cogent discussion of the functions of theory.

Chapter Six: From Otherness to Emptiness

1. Edward Albee dramatizes this phenomenon in both a literal and an allegorical fashion in his play *Who's Afraid of Virginia Woolf?*

2. See "Logical Categories of Learning and Communication," in *Steps to an Ecology of Mind* (New York: Ballantine Books, 1972), pp. 279–308. The word "logical" in the title of the article was, perhaps, not used advisedly by Bateson, as we shall have occasion to see in the following discussion.

3. Ibid., p. 293.

4. Much has been written as to whether or not one might justifiably claim that Eastern and Western forms of mysticism are of the same character. The difficulty involved in trying to settle this issue is that it is almost impossible to find mystical writings in the West which have not been interpreted theologically (i.e., dogmatically) either by the mystic in the act of expression or by a father confessor concerned with maintaining orthodoxy, or by systematic theologians concerned with co-ordinating mystical experience with other forms of ecclesiastical experience and expression. In those relatively few cases in which the Western mystic remains true to the fundamental character of his experience, it does appear that there is a rapprochement between Oriental and Western mysticism. See the various writings which compare Meister Eckhart with the Zen sensibility, for example.

5. "Logical Categories," p. 304.

6. Steven Katz, ed., *Mysticism and Philosophical Analysis* (New York: Oxford University Press, 1978), p. 62.

7. Ibid., p. 63.

8. See Arthur Danto, *Mysticism and Morality* (New York: Harper & Row, 1972) for a critique of some of the ethical consequences of Oriental mysticism.

9. Bateson, "Logical Categories," p. 306.

10. See *Praxis and Action* (Philadelphia: University of Pennsylvania Press, 1971), passim. Also see Bernstein's article, "Why Hegel Now?" in *The Review of Metaphysics* 30 (March 1977).

11. See *Process and Reality* (New York: Macmillan, 1929), pp. 225–279 for a succinct discussion of Whitehead's epistemology.

12. See *The Open Society and Its Enemies*, vol. 2 (New York: Harper & Row, 1962), p. 231.

Chapter Seven: Eros Descending

1. Cleanth Brooks, *The Well Wrought Urn* (New York: Harcourt, Brace & World, 1975), p. 209.

2. *The Apology*, trans. Benjamin Jowett (New York: Random House, 1937), 41–42, p. 423.

3. *The Dry Mock: A Study of Irony in Drama* (Berkeley: University of California Press, 1948), p. 257.

4. For an argument in defense of the presence of "irony" in Hebraic literature see Edwin Good, *Irony in the Old Testament* (Philadelphia: Westminster Press, 1965). Good's argument depends upon a definition of irony considerably at odds with that I am defending.

5. See Polanyi's work, written with Harry Prosch, *Meaning* (Chicago: University of Chicago Press, 1975), pp. 66–81.

6. *A Personal Anthology* (New York: Grove Press, 1967).

7. Ibid., pp. ix–x.

8. "Tlön, Uqbar, Orbis Tertius," in *Labyrinths*, eds. Donald Yates and James Irby (New York: New Directions), p. 13.

9. "A New Refutation of Time," in *A Personal Anthology*, p. 60.

10. Ibid., p. 64.

11. "The Library of Babel," in *Labyrinths, pp. 51–58.*

12. "The Aleph," in *A Personal Anthology*, pp. 147–155.

13. *Tao Te Ching*, trans. Arthur Waley (New York: Random House, 1958), p. 141.

14. This quotation and the poem of P'o Chu-I are cited from Chang Chung-yuan, *Creativity and Taoism* (New York: Harper & Row, 1963), p. 30.

15. Bruno Snell, *The Discovery of the Mind*, trans. T. C. Rosenmeyer (New York: Harper & Row, 1960), p. 15.

16. For an extremely subtle discussion of the notion of determinateness in relation to the concept of creativity, see Robert Neville's *God the Creator* (Chicago: University of Chicago Press, 1968), passim.

17. *Process and Reality* (New York: Macmillan, 1929), p. 513.

INDEX